C09

# WESTMINSTER
# BABYLON

# WESTMINSTER BABYLON

Alan Doig

ALLISON & BUSBY

An Allison & Busby book
Published in 1990 by
W. H. Allen & Co. Plc
Sekforde House
175/9 St John Street
London EC1V 4LL


Copyright © 1990 by Alan Doig

Printed in Great Britain by
Biddles ltd, Guildford & Kings Lynn


ISBN   0 85031 966 8 HB
       0 7490 0047 3 PB

Sir – I am disgusted with the scheme for a register of the business connections of MPs and councillors and people like that. It is simply a whitewashing job, to deprive the decent, disgusted British people of their right to know.

What we want is a register of their connections with call-girls, and full details, please! How often have people in high places employed these girls, was it one or more at a time, and what were they up to?

We need to know exactly what is disgusting us. Very likely things are going on that would make us even more disgusted than we are now. If there are films and tapes, we want to see and hear them. A television inquiry using this evidence would draw the largest viewing figures of all time. The whole nation would be watching in utter disgust.

The French say 'To know all is to forgive all', but how can we forgive if we don't know? For their own sake, these people must 'come clean', even if it means coming disgustingly dirty. We must cleanse the Aegean Stables, even if it reveals that these pinnacles of public life have feet of clay. We have been kept in the dark too long. It is time to drag the red herrings from under the carpet.

Yours,

'DISGUSTED'

Dagenham.
*(A Choice of Peter Simple; 1973–1975).*

'We know no spectacle so ridiculous as the British public in one of its periodical fits of morality. In general, elopements, divorces and family quarrels pass with little notice. We read the scandal, talk about it for a day, and forget it. But once in six or seven years our virtue becomes outrageous. We cannot suffer the laws of religion and decency to be violated. We must make a stand against vice. We must teach libertines that the English people appreciate the importance of domestic ties. Accordingly some unfortunate man, in no respect more depraved than hundreds whose offences have been treated with lenity, is singled out as an expiatory sacrifice. If he has children, they are to be taken from him. If he has a profession, he is to be driven from it. He is cut by the higher orders and hissed by the lower. He is, in truth, a sort of whipping-boy, by whose vicarious agonies all the other transgressors of the same class are, it is supposed, sufficiently chastised. We reflect very complacently on our own severity, and compare with great pride the high standard of morals established in England with the Parisian laxity. At length our anger is satiated. Our victim is ruined and heart-broken. And our virtue goes quietly to sleep for seven years more.'

Lord Macaulay, 'Moore's Life of Lord Byron', *Critical and Historical Essays*, 1851

# Contents

*Acknowledgements*                                                    ix

PART ONE: THE SEARCH FOR SCANDAL                                       1

Chapter 1:  Pamella Bordes and the Nearly
            Scandal                                                    3

Chapter 2:  Reputations, Rules and Flaws                             13

PART TWO: PRIVATE STANDARDS, PUBLIC
          MORALS                                                     25

Chapter 3:  MPs and The Tradition of Essential
            Qualities                                                27

Chapter 4:  Setting The Agenda For Today's
            Scandals                                                 45

Chapter 5:  Macmillan's Members; Ian Harvey,
            Ian Horobin, Charles Fletcher-Cooke, John
            Galbraith, John Profumo and Anthony Courtney             55

Chapter 6:  Conclusion: Profumo, Scandal and
            the Media                                                95

PART THREE: BEHIND EVERY STORY LURKS A
            HEADLINE                                                 99

Chapter 7:  A Decade of Gossip, Scares and
            Scandals; Part I                                        101

Chapter 8:  A Decade of Gossip, Scares and
            Scandals; Part II                                       125

PART FOUR: SCANDALS – RESIGNATIONS AND
           TARNISHED REPUTATIONS                                    153

Chapter 9:  For Their Lordships' Pleasure: Lord
            Lambton and Earl Jellicoe                               155

Chapter 10: 'The Problem Is, Of Course, One of Money.' The Friends of Reginald Maudling. 165

Chapter 11: Not Even A Minnow; John Cordle 179

Chapter 12: The Disappearing Minister; John Stonehouse 187

Chapter 13: Slag Heaps, Kitchen Cabinets and The World of Harold Wilson 201

Chapter 14: The Trials of Jeremy Thorpe 215

Chapter 15: The 1976 Resignation Honours List and Political Croneyism 241

Chapter 16: 'Sex Please, We're British.' The Parkinson Scandal 261

Chapter 17: Keith Hampson and A Night At The Gay Theatre 275

Chapter 18: Jeffrey Archer's £500,000 – Not a Penny More, Not a Penny Less 279

Chapter 19: The Trivial Pursuits Of Harvey Proctor 291

Chapter 20: BT Shares and The Many Names of Keith Best 295

PART FIVE: PUBLIC STANDARDS, PRIVATE MORALS 301

Chapter 21: Conclusion: The Private Lives of Politicians 303

*References* 321
*Additional bibliography* 333
*Index* 337

# Acknowledgments

Which Liberal MP could be described as an unscrupulous and dishonest adventurer, devoid of integrity and decency, who married his first wife for her money, bankrupted her and drove her mad (she died a pauper in a lunatic asylum), departed for America to find a rich widow, then returned to England with her and her money to secure a safe Parliamentary seat?

His name was Alexander Lyle-Samuel, Liberal MP for Eye in Suffolk until 1923. Mr Lyle-Samuel has long since left the Party and Parliament and is no doubt enjoying his just reward elsewhere. Nevertheless he has left one enduring legacy. In 1919 he took the *National News* to court to uncover the sources of this unflattering description but, to his horror, lost. The wise Lord Justice Scrutton stated that the private life of an MP may be relevant to whether that MP is fit to hold public office: 'His private life may be such as to show that he is wholly unfit . . . to occupy any public office.'

There has, however, been increasing concern that any aspect of the private lives of politicians, and those around them, is now fair game in the media's search for scandal or, as one tabloid editor put it, for a story 'more dramatic and sensational than the last'. **Westminster Babylon** is about this search: what are the media looking for, and why? What type of stories most interest them and which hit the headlines? Why do politicians attract the attention?

One may agree with the statement of another judge, some seventy years later, who said that it was not enough just to say in his court that someone was a former MP: 'it is questionable in my view whether that averment taken by itself provides any indication of a person's standing in public life'. It could be argued that attention given to the private lives of politicians is, as one newspaper said of the Archer case, a traditional dance involving sex, politicians and tabloids 'whose movements and gestures have been lovingly handed down from generation to generation. . .but whose symbolic meaning has been lost'. The media and politicians would both appear to believe politicians are very important people. Where they differ is about what they think is important – the person or the politics – but who is right and who is wrong? Is there a link between the two and, if there is, is the balance right?

In trying to answer these and many other questions I have fortunately had the assiduous presence of Mr Jeffrey Archer at my side. Not, of course, in person and nor to keep an eye on the book's literary qualities but because of that extremely large payment which has sent shockwaves rippling through the publishing world: more than one publisher has chosen not to get their feet wet. The question of the private lives of Members of Parliament, the stories printed about them and the periodic scandals that punctuate the world of politics may be a matter of continuing public controversy but it is also one of ever-present danger.

This book has had, therefore, a long and difficult gestation period, but I am extremely grateful to Clive Allison for his confident and commonsense approach to publishing it and to Peter Day, Antonia McMeeking and Glyn Maxwell for their hard work in very difficult circumstances. I am also grateful to those friends and colleagues who share an interest in scandals in politics, who have helped with the book or who have, knowingly or otherwise, just helped: Alan Garrigou, Maurice Punch, Bernard Hoetjes, Graeme Moodie, Jeanette Becquart-Leclercq, Andre Frognier, Hans Blomkvist, Alan Parker, Fred Ridley, Stephen Riley, Neil Collins, Wolfgang Muller, David Morgan, John Frears, Craig Marsden, Anthony Glees, Susan Lee, David Jepson, Val Johnston, Frank McCann, Val McCann, Christopher Doig, Natalie Doig, Lorraine Fletcher, Pat Brooksbank, Ann Hipkin, Barbara Keeffe, Debbie Hughes, Ann Lockhart, the Roxby All Stars 5-a-side football team, and, with very special thanks, Jill Westhead.

Alan Doig

# PART ONE

# *THE SEARCH FOR SCANDAL*

# Chapter One

## Pamella Bordes and the Nearly Scandal

*Ambush!*

The climax of the chase began on Sunday 2 April 1989, as the pride of the British tabloid press staked out Denpasar Airport, Bali, in the early morning. As the last call was made for the 6.30 flight to Hong Kong their quarry rushed from behind some trees in the car park, her head covered by a scarf. Slowed down by immigration and passport control she was quickly surrounded by excited journalists and photographers. As she reached the bottom of the plane steps there was a scuffle as someone tried to pull off the scarf. Then, 'like Millwall fans' said one, Fleet Street's finest hurried up the steps after her and, after take-off, jostled and pushed each other in the narrow aisle as they finally cajoled her into dropping the scarf for photographs and saying a few exclusive words.

Her companion, a London solicitor, who had been discussing 'monopoly money cheque book deals' for these words a few hours before and gasped 'I can't believe what I am seeing' at the scrum around the plane steps, sat exhausted beside her.

The morning's work could have cost them £50,000, thought the tabloid press as they settled back in their seats for a breakfast of champagne and satay: 'It's a dirty job but somebody has to do it', said a photographer later. But the job was still unfinished. The solicitor had arrived in Bali with *Daily Express* executives to discuss the sale of the woman's life story – the *Express* sympathetically reported the ordeal as a nightmare and the behaviour of the journalists as 'the baying of the pack' – and arrived in Hong Kong still talking. As the fruits of that morning's labour were emblazoned 'exclusively' across the front pages of all the tabloids while their quarry lay on a £150-a-day bed in the Hong Kong Adventist Hospital awaiting treatment for facial injuries, the bargaining continued with the waiting journalists. The *Express* pulled out and, amid talk of £400,000, the *Daily Mail* stepped in and scooped the exclusive rights. The remaining journalists, said Wayne Woodhams, the hospital Administrator, 'just went berserk. They were virtually trying to wave chequebooks in her face. We had to call the police'. At 4 am on Tuesday, against medical advice, the *Daily Mail*'s entourage carried off their prize: Ms Pamella Bordes, the woman the tabloids fervently prayed was the next Christine Keeler.

Since 12 March the tabloids had been stalking the woman who promised sex, sleaze and society or, as the *Daily Mail* put it, the woman who 'moved silkily through the London social scene at the highest level and at the same time led a sleazy secret life of sex for hire . . . her story speaks volumes about human nature and corruption in the worlds of government and big business'. Lured on by rumours of compromised Cabinet Ministers, international terrorism, breached House of Commons security, pornographers and bedded members of more than one royal family, the tabloids worked fervently at home and abroad to capture the confessions of the woman branded by the *Daily Mail* as immoral and amoral.

## Upwardly Mobile

Pamella Bordes was born in 1962 into an upper middle-class Hindu family in Northern India. A school rebel, eager to break free from the claustrophobic restraints of her society, she was attracted to Bombay, the home of the Indian film industry, where she worked as a beautician and model while developing a lively social life. In 1982 she won the Miss India title and, via the Miss Universe finals in Peru, headed for New York. There she lived with a Nepalese diplomat and met Chandraswami, an Indian holy man with a penchant for unholy business deals, who added her to his entourage as decoration and occasional

4

sexual gift. When some of the deals went wrong, they decamped to France and, in Paris, Pamella was taken to one of Adnan Khashoggi's cocktail parties. With great care she charmed Khashoggi into adding her to his entourage (and his bed), thus admitting her to the international jet-set lifestyle she apparently craved and which she claimed she would do anything to join. The 'anything' in this case was indulging the sexual appetites of Khashoggi's clients, from Saudi princes to Libyan arms dealers, one of whom was Gaddafi's cousin, whom she met regularly over the next few years.

In 1984 she was married, albeit briefly, to a Frenchman and, with her new EC passport, moved to London with a minor-league arms dealer, but continued to work on the Khashoggi circuit and with her own social contacts. One of these was a lawyer with a taste for London high society; he let her stay in his house, took her to the best parties and helped her rent (on a short lease) that expensive flat near the House of Commons. Another was Marc Burca, another man-about-town with political ambitions, and an owner of various lucrative glossy magazines. At the last General Election, he had been a canvasser, personal assistant and friend to David Shaw, Tory MP and director of over a dozen companies.

In the meantime, Pamella met Andrew Neil, editor of the *Sunday Times*, at the London nightclub Tramp. Bordes, keen to find a lasting liaison or marriage with a famous and wealthy man and get out of the Khashoggi network, charmed and flattered Neil, beginning a tempestuous six-month affair in April 1988. Unfortunately it terminated in acrimony, partly over Bordes' jealousy (despite two covert trips of her own abroad) and partly over her friendship with Donald Trelford, editor of the *Observer*. A solicitor's letter warned her to keep away from Neil because of her behaviour – slicing up some £2000 worth of Neil's wardrobe, throwing bricks through his window and posting dogshit through his letter box.

Despite this setback, her friendship with Burca led to a dinner party with David Shaw. Burca told her she 'possessed the perfect CV to become a personal assistant to an

MP'. Some weeks later she contacted Shaw and asked for a job as an unpaid researcher. After a lunch with Shaw in the Commons where he 'questioned her thoroughly, did everything to put her off, testing the degree of her interest', she got one. Believing her 'intelligent and capable of low-level research work', satisfied with her reference from Burca and the fact that she was known to one reputable newspaper editor, he decided to give her a job as researcher working on his proposed bill to abolish the Net Book Agreement.

## The Pursuit of Gainful Employment

The rules governing the employment of research assistants were at that time under review. Since the *News of the World* revelation in 1987 that a Labour MP had obtained a temporary research assistant pass for a former Maze prisoner (his conviction for attempted murder had been quashed after thirteen months inside) rules for issuing passes had been tightened. MPs now had to provide 'reasonable details' on the background of appointees, allow time for applications to be checked out and drop any applications where there was any security concern. The checking-out was carried out by the police on the basis of UK information. No checks were carried out abroad.

Secondly, the increasing concern over professional lobbyists posing as research assistants for compliant MPs to secure privileged access to the House of Commons, its computer, facilities and publications, had led the House to require all research assistants to register 'any gainful occupation which they may pursue other than that for which the pass is issued'. Finally, the number of staff entitled to passes was accelerating; in 1988 some 10,000 pass-holders were putting increasing pressure on Westminster's limited facilities. One group, MPs' personal staff, was of particular concern. Ranging from seasoned secretaries to temporary US interns, these 1344 individuals were rapidly filling up available office space, overloading the library (and the photocopiers) and, in some cases, running businesses from the House. Although this figure represented a notional two per MP, there were marked divergences in the numbers actually employed. Accordingly, the Commons Select Committee dealing with Commons services decided to limit the number of staff for each MP, with the proviso that the allocation was non-transferable and each allocation could only be exceeded in 'exceptional circumstances'.

In anticipation of this limit, Shaw asked a colleague, Tory MP Henry Bellingham, to put Bordes on his allocation. Bellingham, lifelong friend of the Princess of Wales and member of the Tory backbench Northern Ireland Committee, agreed. He said that he had checked her background thoroughly although, later, when his office was asked to register her interests as a research assistant, it replied that she was not employed by Bellingham. When asked if the pass had therefore been wrongly issued, it failed to reply. (Both MPs were later cleared of any transgression of House rules by the Leader of the House, Tory MP John Wakeham.)

Bordes received her pass in October, began work in December and finished towards the end of February 1989. She met Colin Moynihan, the Sports Minister, at a party at Shaw's home. Moynihan's secretary telephoned her to invite her to a dinner party, after which they went to Annabel's but 'he did not give me the impression of being very interested in me sexually'. Nevertheless she pursued her new interest in politics and, in February, after Shaw said Moynihan wanted to invite her, got him to take her to the Tory Winter Ball. Moynihan held her hand and she was much photographed on arrival. These pictures did not go unnoticed when, in March, she announced her engagement to a stockbroker.

Bordes made no secret of her desire to marry money and for a place in society. Thus, although she had been on the occasional lucrative visit abroad, she wanted to be free from such activities and was increasingly nervous that she could be exposed. Unfortunately for her, the *News of the World* was about to reveal her 'gainful occupation'.

The announcement of her engagement had apparently alerted 'a former client' to call the newspapers because 'it's horrifying that she's a Commons researcher, and that she escorted a Minister of the Crown to such an important event as the Winter Ball. I'm astonished no-one checked her out'. However the newspaper's introduction to Pamella was 'Ricky Reed', whom the newspaper alleged was a 'call-girl' who was 'unaware' of their journalists' cover as Far East businessmen as they arranged a four-some in London's Hilton Hotel. But the former TV presen-ter Erica Lee also used the name Ricky Reed: she had been in the business of 'introducing' beautiful young women to wealthy men but, ashamed of her life, decided to give it up and publicly confess. Luckily she had an agent who managed to sell the confession for a 'six-figure' sum to 'one of today's tabloids'. Sex, he thought, could make a girl a star. The tabloid was *News of the World*.

Lee had previously arranged an all-expenses trip to Vienna for Bordes (while she was working in the Com-mons) and some other women to entertain a Saudi prince's entourage. Despite her £800 a day Bordes disliked the trip and the three-in-a-bed romps, annoying her hosts by running up a large telephone bill to relieve her bore-dom and homesickness. On her return Bordes continued occasional sex-for-hire to pay the bills while, she claimed, being pestered by 'Rikki' to meet a shy Hong Kong film producer. The producer to whom she offered sex with a condom for £500 was, according to Bordes, the *News of the World* journalist. The result was the banner headline: 'Call Girl Works in Commons'.

While the security aspects were the ostensible justifica-tion for the story, the thought of a potential Christine Keeler galvanised the rest of the tabloids. The first claims were savoured: friendships with the editor of the *Sunday Times* and the owner of the *Sunday Sport*, a £3/4 million flat with division bells, £1000-a-night sex sessions and randy Arab princes. Almost immediately, Bordes disap-peared abroad. Anonymous friends were, however, read-ily available to portray her as ambitious and cynical, with

a penchant for exaggeration and fantasy, while the tabloids appeared to have access to an extensive portfolio of
photographs. During the first week with the central figure
fled, and some explosive names being mentioned, the
story became incestuous: David Sullivan, owner of the
*Sunday Sport*, was being interviewed by *Today* about his
friendship with Bordes while his newspaper carried an
interview with her that the *Sun* was headlining the next
day.

By the weekend, however, the story was fuelled by
revelations of her relationship with Gaddafi's cousin (the
security angle), her sexual exploits (black sheets, body oil
and mirrored ceilings) and the possibility of a Cabinet
Minister (not Moynihan) trying to draw a 'smokescreen to
cover his own activities'. MPs were sounding off about
security at every possible opportunity and the hunt for a
politician, any politician, began in earnest. At the weekend Erica Lee broke cover in the *News of the World* about
the assignations she arranged for Bordes while apologising in *The People*: 'Pamella thinks I set her up . . . but she
will accept the situation. Once these things are out in the
open there is nothing you can do'.

Bordes, however, could do something. She was, said
the ubiquitous friend, preparing her story for auction
while other 'friends' continued to feed the tabloids allegations of lesbian orgies, plastic surgery and £10,000 sex
fees.

On Tuesday 29 March a *Sun* executive coincidentally
discovered Bordes in Bali, the Pacific island where she
had intended to spend her honeymoon and where a
lifelong friend lived. Within hours the tabloids ordered
every available journalist and photographer – including
two cricket writers and a photographer who had planned,
and was suitably dressed for, an evening's work in Soho
– onto Bali. In the humidity and inky darkness the
journalists began doorstepping the friend's house, enter-
taining each other with tales of mosquitoes and snakes,
filing copy about Bordes' anguish and, after a motorcycle
crash, her injuries. Inside, Bordes had been joined by a
lawyer (hired by her boyfriend) and *Daily Express* executives who had arrived on the island as frontrunners to

buy the story. Between them a plan was concocted to smuggle her off the island but, at a press conference with her lawyer, an overheard conversation alerted the rest of the journalists who rushed off to stake out the airport.

Despite the loss of the quarry to the *Daily Mail*, and Bordes' insistence that she had not slept with a British politician, the tabloids returned to England with a new titbit that the *Sunday Sport* had already hinted at before they left for Bali. Pamella had met Mark Phillips. She had attended a weekend course at Phillips' equestrian centre at the Gleneagles Hotel and spent a weekend with one of his employees at Gatcombe Park. Luckily for the story Buckingham Palace stepped in with a gratuitous statement intended to clarify the situation, thus occupying the tabloids in the run-up to the expected *Daily Mail* revelations. Both *Today* and the *Daily Express* threatened spoiling stories. The latter's was a one-day attack on the 'Fantasy World Of A Hard-Faced Hooker', a volte-face from the sympathetic copy filed when the newspaper was negotiating to buy her story. *Today*'s was more detailed but equally designed to denigrate Bordes and steal the thunder from their rival. Fortunately for the *Mail*, however, Adnan Khashoggi was arrested in Switzerland at the FBI's request and allowed the newspaper to trumpet their 'exclusive' story with the claim they had passed their 'full dossier' to the FBI, but not, unfortunately, to their readers. There was therefore little left to tell of the Bordes story, which the newspaper now ran as the 'morality tale' of her climb to fame and fortune. Its last piece was headed 'Westminster Nights' but the bed was empty of politicians. Bordes retreated into the background, living with her fiancé, visiting museums and planning a trip up the Amazon to satisfy their 'fervent' interest in travel and wildlife. As Auberon Waugh said of the woman who was the girlfriend of the editor of a Murdoch newspaper, who may have met and dined with Murdoch, who was destroyed by another Murdoch newspaper with the offer of Murdoch money and then denigrated by a third Murdoch newspaper: 'I wish her luck'.

The Bordes story was therefore a 'nearly' scandal; with security, sex-for-hire and hints of a cover-up, but it lacked the name of a politician between the sheets to make it all come together. More importantly, the almost tangible desire to link the Bordes story with the Keeler scandal emphasises that the private lives of politicians continue to exercise a strong fascination with the public, a fascination that politicians have long learnt to live with but which many resent or have reason to fear. No-one is perfect, including politicians, but unfortunately for them their predecessors did their utmost to make it appear that they were, thus laying the foundation for scandals surrounding the private lives of today's politicians and sending the media scurrying around looking for evidence of any imperfection. . . .

# Chapter Two

## Is there, One Wonders, no Flaw?

*Too Good to be True*

'Parliament' wrote Liberal MP David Steel in *The Times* in 1976, 'if it is to be the representative mirror of the people must contain its due proportion of homosexuals, lesbians, womanizers, habitual drunkards, card-sharpers, chain-smokers, drug takers and any other cross-section of society you care to mention'.[1]

On the other hand, Parliament makes laws and lays down rules for the rest of society to obey. It may be argued that politicians do not have to be good to know what is good for everyone else. Yet everyone else might take exception to being told what to do, what not to do and how to behave by those who then decide to do otherwise themselves.

Now any group of people can be tolerant of the weaknesses and failings of those in the group because they judge the whole person and weigh up the balance of their worth. Clearly Mrs Thatcher, as Prime Minister and as a friend, valued the political qualities and the personal loyalty of Cecil Parkinson. She was prepared to overlook his affair and the impending love-child (as the tabloids would put it) as a private matter that did not outweigh his political and personal worth to her and the Government, even though it appeared to go against the Government's general stance on the sanctity of the family and the consequences of a permissive society.

When, however, the affair broke publicly and Sarah Keays spoke about their relationship, Cecil Parkinson offered his resignation and the Prime Minister did not refuse it. She was aware, as was everyone else, that this aspect of Parkinson would be the one that would attract the attention, both to the individual and to the Government. In October 1981 a *Times* journalist profiled a rising Conservative politician. In some ways, he wrote, the politician 'seems too good to be true; tall, handsome, charming and likeable . . . the perfect constituency MP, intelligent without being intellectual, self-made, brilliantly supported by a politically-committed wife – is there, one wonders, no flaw?'[2] The politician was Cecil Parkinson.

Why one aspect of a politician should be the focus of attention and be used to assess that politician without reference to all his or her other qualities or behaviour is a historical tradition that was bound up with changes in Victorian political life. The rise in middle class voters – whose values were firmly rooted in the family, the church and the virtues of self-help and respectability – was reflected in the increasing enthusiasm of politicians for adapting their own public behaviour and image to attract these votes. Even then, however, politicians were not prepared to sacrifice their colleagues for personal misbehaviour or financial misconduct as long as the latter were discreet, not too greedy, did not get involved in public criticism and were not seen publicly with those of ill repute; as long, in fact, as they subscribed to the general sentiment that they should reflect those qualities expected in a public person: integrity, honesty and honour. These were spelt out in an important Victorian libel case by a judge who believed that a public person's private conduct was a fair subject for public debate if, in that conduct, he showed himself 'destitute and devoid of these qualities, because they could reflect on his fitness to hold public office' (see Chapter Three).

## Reputation and Image

These qualities were normally expected to apply to the whole man (and occasionally woman) and to all their activities, with the Press – and anybody else – believing they had a right to comment publicly on any private conduct that showed him or her to be 'destitute and devoid' of those essential elements. To a population sternly lectured on the 'beast in man', however, there was a growing prurient interest in, and sanctimonious intolerance of, any behaviour that appeared to suggest that these qualities were lacking. Accordingly, politicians did their best to satisfy public expectations of how they should behave (whatever they did in private) and protect their reputation, a stance shattered by the Profumo scandal (see Chapters Four, Five and Six).

There are plenty of reasons why politicians' private lives are interesting, and even why publication of the details may be in the public interest. Macmillan's knowledge of his wife's lengthy affair with the disreputable Tory MP Bob Boothby may have been the impetus behind his political career and does help explain his mishandling of the Profumo Affair. Reginald Maudling's relationship with John Poulson is central to understanding the circumstances of his resignation and raised important questions about the interrelation between Parliamentary and private business activities.

The link between the details, the public figure and publication, is relevance. A person's private behaviour may well be relevant to a person's fitness to hold public office, and to his or her ability to perform the duties of that office. There is an increasing tendency to use 'relevance' as justification for publishing what the *Independent* calls 'no-holds-barred tales of people's personal lives, relayed as the stuff of entertainment'.

Now entertainment is an end in itself and there are plenty of people who court the attention of the tabloids, including politicians. Unfortunately it is the entertainment value, rather than the issue of relevance or interrelation, which is the motivation of many stories. Furthermore, there has been a tendency to consider newsworthy anyone with political connections, however tenuous, or any behaviour, however petty or manipulated (see Chapters Seven and Eight). It was this that so exercised Jeffrey Archer and persuaded him to offer £2000 to someone he did not know because, as he astutely guessed, 'any publicity of this kind would be extremely harmful to me and for which a libel action would be no adequate remedy'. He was right: £500,000 the richer as a result of the libel action, he no longer holds the highly visible and, to him, deeply satisfying, post of Deputy Chairman of the Conservative Party.

What politicians seek to protect is their reputation, not just as politicians but, as the Victorians determined, as private individuals with those 'essential qualities'. Reputation can cover a variety of personal attributes or essential qualities such as probity, honesty, decency and morality. It is the product of decades of society's high expectations, and the public acceptance of those standards by generations of politicians, and fervently protected by them in public.

This is why, in 1957, the Labour shadow Foreign Secretary, the Secretary of the Labour Party and Labour MP Richard Crossman sued and won £2500 each from the *Spectator* for an article which suggested that, at a conference in Italy, they 'puzzled the Italians by their capacity to fill themselves like tanks with whisky . . . although the Italians were never sure if the British delegation was sober, they always attributed to them an immense political acumen'. With the legal advice of Arnold Goodman, solicitor to the Labour Party, and with the financial support of a 'socialist millionaire' in case they lost and had to pay costs, the trio not only demanded, and got, an apology but also damages. It would appear that not all three were drinking whisky and not all three were drunk, but drinking they had been and, apart from Crossman, sober they were not. This will also explain why Labour MP Michael Meacher thought it necessary to take the *Observer* to court in 1988 for what his barrister called a 'nasty, vicious, mean, despicable, reckless, untrue, bitchy and scurrilous' libel. The cause of such intemperate language was Meacher's belief that the newspaper's political diarist had asked in 1984 whether Meacher's father was a farm labourer rather than an accountant, by writing that Meacher 'likes to claim that he is the son of an agricultural labourer, though I understand that his father was an accountant who retired to work on the family farm because the life suited him better'. Meacher also objected to the diarist's rhetorical remark that, in choosing between

16

Eric Moonman and Meacher, he could only quote Dr Johnson on establishing the 'point of precedency between a louse and a flea' (he objected to using either word). It transpired that Meacher had 'acquiesced' to other journalists' suggestions that he was of modest origins but objected to the *Observer*, a newspaper of 'fairness and accuracy', perpetuating the myth. Meacher lost the case to defend his public image and, in doing so, managed to attract far more attention both to the question of class credentials for the Labour Party and to his own background.

Conversely, it also explains why the media, ever-alert to the possibility of that public facade and that public reputation being exposed as a sham and a lie, were to be found, in October 1983, in packed attendance at the Old Bailey trail of a 37-year-old man accused of raping his former common-law wife. They were there because they were wishing to be enlightened by the defendant's claim that since 1977 he had been framed and 'fitted up' with crimes he did not commit because he intended to reveal five pornographic colour pictures of the woman, an MP, a senior detective and a third man. Sir James Miskin QC, the Recorder, used the 1981 Contempt of Court Act to ban the publication of the MP's identity although the crowded public gallery were treated to all the details. Scenting a good cover-up Labour MPs attacked the Attorney-General for the Recorder's decision. The ban was lifted a few days later at the start of the retrial which allowed the MP, Edward Heath, to make a statement denying all knowledge of the man, the woman and the photographs. He added that there was 'no truth whatsoever in this extraordinary story'. The defendant, who conducted his own case at the retrial, claimed the photographs had been stolen – a copy he produced was dismissed as a forgery – but was jailed for nine months for assault, after the Judge told him that he 'pursued a course of vilifying innocent people in a way which was evil'.

What the media were looking for, and what they thought their readers wanted to read, was the flaw in the otherwise irreproachable public image, the scandal involving that politician's private activities. Whether today's politicians like it or not, this type of story is a headline-maker. Politicians, however, believe that, unlike their predecessors, they should not have their politics and their political position judged by or threatened by their private activities. Nevertheless, there are in theory means to challenge or deal with allegations relating to the latter. If those activities are accurately reported then the hope is that, as a private matter, public interest will die away and there will be no political repercussions. If those activities are inaccurately reported or misrepresented, then we are seeing, increasingly, situations where politicians are winning, either in court or in out-of-court settlements in anticipation of a court case, substantial sums. In 1988 several MPs won damages for allegations in the *News of the World* that they had been castigated by Labour Leader Neil Kinnock for drinking when they should have been voting and, in 1989, Neil Kinnock himself won substantial damages for a libel by a private individual, repeated in the media, over a non-existent incident on a train. In those cases where private interests and public duties overlap there are, again, either the courts or Parliamentary means of inquiry to rule on allegations.

In practice, however, things are not that simple. It is often the allegations, not the subsequent apology or court case, that lodges in the public memory. There are no rules on what is a politician's private activity or on where that activity can be said to be relevant to his or her Parliamentary position. There is also the question of what is or is not an acceptable private activity, and whether or not it is relevant, and that in itself may be influenced by all sorts of perceptions, be they public, party or Parliamentary. Such issues arise over and over again in looking at contemporary scandals and must have been in the Prime Minister's mind when Parkinson first spoke to her. Once aware of the details, she made some adjustment to his visibility in terms of the Party's image but was loath for him to resign his Ministerial office. Some of his colleagues were annoyed that there should have been such pressure for him to resign when he chose not to go and live with his mistress but to stay with his family, one of the more potent symbols in the Party's public image. There was no overt condemnation of his behaviour at the Party Conference during which the crisis broke and his constituency reaffirmed its support for him by increasing his majority from 14,870 in 1983 to 18,106 in the 1987 General Election.

This raises two questions: why did Parkinson's behaviour create a scandal and what were the reasons for his resignation? First there was the question of sex, a subject that is rarely out of the public's eye (or its thoughts) especially when it involves a public figure like a politician. Furthermore, the Conservative Party had made a political issue out of the consequences of permissiveness, the rôle of the family and general moral probity. Then again there is the question of timing. Nigel Lawson had gone to live with a Commons researcher after the birth of their son and did not marry her until both their respective divorces had come through. He was, however, at that time a humble backbench MP and, as Alan Watkins argued when comparing him with Parkinson, might appear to suggest 'an example of the arbitrary nature of political scandals'.[3] Moreover, the status of the politician at the centre of the attention is important and national politicians, particularly Cabinet Ministers like Parkinson, are well-known names, which in itself provides the basis for a good news story. And of course the media attention is usually directly related to the immediacy and drama. The immediacy in Parkinson's case was enhanced because it occurred in a highly-visible environment, the Party Conference, with the attendant media circus and an atmosphere of political excitement, with the details unfolding at the time the attention was focused on the politician involved. The drama was enhanced because it was 'personalised', as both Parkinson and Keays sought to present their interpretation of the facts which were easily identifiable and presentable by the media to their audience. Finally, there is the matter of what interests the public: the public is more likely to be 'scandalised' if the behaviour under scrutiny concerns a politician's private life than, say, the misuse of power or influence-peddling.

There exists also a tradition of mistrust towards politicians because politics is often thought of as a dirty game. Many people believe politicians are in politics for what they can get out of it, while endlessly pontificating and legislating for what is perceived to be good for the rest of society. If politicians are seen to be preaching one set of standards or values while practising the opposite in their own lives, those revelations of the latter behaviour are more than likely to cause a scandal. MPs, therefore, are particularly likely to attract attention if they do anything they are not supposed to do but, of course, they are only human. As Labour MP Austin Mitchell says: 'Any group has its proportion of mavericks, homosexuals, casual adulterers, broken marriages and the House of Commons must by the law of averages have its share of human frailty . . .'[4] Most MPs, he believes, are deeply cautious, terrified of any taint of scandal and very boring. Indeed there are those who, like Dick Crossman, dismiss the ordinary MP because he 'runs nothing, decides nothing, and usually knows nothing . . .' On the other hand they are often very ambitious, publicity-conscious and keenly aware of their highly-visible position in British politics. For an MP, still relatively underpaid and overworked and certainly under-resourced, to make a mark in public, if not political, terms requires ability, hard work and self-promotion (although not necessarily in that order).

*House Rules*

Publicity is double-edged: MPs can give good stories but they also make good stories. If the outside world is often suspicious of MPs and their private activities, and the media always on the lookout for tales about them, then clearly the best way for an MP to behave is to ensure that his or her private activities reflects their public image. If, however, as David Steel and Austin Mitchell suggest,

20

many of them reflect the flaws, foibles and interests of the rest of us, then they have a choice of making those known or of concealing them. Unfortunately in many areas they had no formal guidelines, other than common sense, prudence, caution and an eye to history, on how to behave. As Robert Boothby argued when caught peddling the undisclosed financial interests of a friend: 'I do want to say that I must confess I am not at all clear in my own mind about the duties of a Member of Parliament'. Of course, secrecy and the possible allegation of a cover-up add to the potential scandal if a mismatch is perceived between an MP's private and public lives but the traditions and culture of Parliament have long allowed MPs the belief – and the space – that they can give expression and time to those private activities so long as they don't get caught out or cause embarrassment. Parliament has, moreover, long been governed by the 'gentleman' ethic where, politically, they may be at daggers drawn but personally and privately they tend to mind their own business, not making use of what they know goes on within Westminster, and tolerating a surprising degree of criminal, unethical or silly behaviour on the part of their colleagues. This tolerance – and awareness that those who know what is good for the rest of society may not necessarily be able to live up to those standards because of the pressures of the job or personal weaknesses – depends on discretion and a realisation that, if caught out, they may be disowned by colleagues, party and Parliament.

Thus all sorts of sexual behaviour are accepted, so long as each MP is aware that, if that behaviour becomes public knowledge, those colleagues who tolerated it in private will claim to know nothing about it or will condemn it, because they all know that they need publicly to be seen to adhere to the standards expected of them by society. Said one MP recently: 'In Parliament your private life is really your own affair, and you can do what you like so long as you're discreet about it,' while another MP suggested that 'It was "an unwritten rule" in the House that a member's sex life should be private. It was considered

21

ungentlemanly for a member to look into or discuss such things.'

Attitudes to the private finances of politicians are a little more rigid, but only a little. If those affairs related solely to the politician in his capacity as a businessman then there have been, and still are, no restraints other than a tendency not to offer governmental positions to those whose activities may attract criticism. Thus Edward Du Cann's decision not to accept a position in the Tory Shadow Cabinet in 1975 came 'as a relief to many in the City and political circles who feared that his financial career might be used as a weapon against him and his party. They were all too well aware that in a political climate increasingly sensitive to financial behaviour, the entrepreneurial style typified by Mr du Cann and some of his close associates would no longer be a desirable asset on the Tory Front Bench.'[5] Where there may be an overlap between Parliamentary and private interests there a set of Resolutions concerning the disclosure and register of those financial interests, together with a Select Committee to monitor those interests and publish a Register of them. Ministers are also bound by these requirements and subject to more stringent rules which require the divesting of directorships, controlling shareholdings and other shareholdings where there may be a conflict of interest. The principle behind the rules for Ministers, as Margaret Thatcher affirmed in 1980, was that they should so order their affairs that no conflict arises, or appears to arise, between their private interests and public duties.

This, then, is the world of the MP, a world where image, reputation and standing can be as flexible, uncertain or arbitrary as the few rules and conventions that guide them. It is not surprising that many MPs find themselves in the news for falling short of some ill-defined notion of responsible and respectable behaviour or even, in some cases, for simply being stupid or naive. They are also as likely to appear in the news solely because of who they are, rather than as a result of their behaviour. The words 'Member of Parliament' are valuable to a journalist, or to someone with a grievance or simply to someone who knows that those words will attract attention, however tenuous, trivial, serious or relevant the connection. But why this should be so and how the issue of private interests, public position and the conflict that often arises between the two appears to result in so much controversy is largely the consequence of developments in that era from which the present Prime Minister seems to derive so many of her values, the Victorian era.

# PART TWO

## *PRIVATE STANDARDS, PUBLIC MORALS*

# Chapter Three
## MPs and the Tradition of Essential Qualities

### Respectability and Rectitude

Would the present Prime Minister publicly admit to receiving a letter saying 'I just longed to smack your bottie' (apparently a female friend wanted to smack A. J. Balfour's bottie) or the present Lord Chancellor admit to writing a poem on the death of a beautiful young woman thirty years his junior that ended '. . . and died as those shall die who dare too vividly to live' (F. E. Smith, Lord Birkenhead, about his one-time lover, Mona Dunn)?

Disraeli wisely pointed out that the Victorians, being subject to fogs and possessing a powerful middle class, required grave statesmen. The primacy of the middle-class family with its emphasis on the virtues of honesty and decency and, more importantly, the primacy of the middle-class vote meant that respectability became a key dividing-line in society; it 'consisted in earning a degree of independence by one's own efforts, in self-discipline (especially in sexual and bibulous matters), and in veneration for home and family as the basic social organism from which all other virtues flowed . . .'[1]. To achieve and sustain respectability was fraught with peril and the middle classes were 'obsessed . . . that the weaker vessels among them would inevitably sink into depravity if they departed in the slightest from the rules of respectability'.[2] The underpinning to the striving for respectability was an emphasis on upright personal conduct and the constant need to control the threat posed 'by the beast in man'. The period was redolent with well-intentioned advice and warnings on sexual self-interest, and its attendant vices of gambling, smoking and drink, as the great dissipator of the physical, intellectual and spiritual qualities necessary for advancement up the social hierarchy and respectability within it.

That this image of Victorian society should persist was itself the consequence of the acceptance and persistence of the norms of respectable behaviour by future generations. The Victorians 'wanted to appear to posterity as good, noble, pure in word, heart and deed; and that they have succeeded so well is due not only to the energy with which they tackled this project, but to our own laziness in preferring the easy stereotype to the reality'.[3] It is not difficult to find evidence that that reality was a world which encompassed poverty, drunkenness and prostitution at one end and greed, adultery and decadence at the other. The pretence of respectability and the prevalence of sinners has often been labelled hypocritical, but what was important was the public upholding of decency, honesty and respectability as general standards to govern society's behaviour. Everyone agreed to this in public, including politicians, even if they didn't practise it themselves in private. For that public unity politicians and other public figures were prepared to tolerate all sorts of misbehaviour in private: 'in time, it came to the code above all that mattered . . . if it were departed from, at all costs scandal must be avoided; for if scandal there were, the guilty ones must be punished. And since that punishment was social ostracism, avoidance of scandal rather than abandonment of the conduct that gave rise to it, was of primary concern. This was not so much hypocrisy as a combination of common sense and common charity.'[4]

The imposition on society of middle-class standards had a dramatic impact on politics. The old aristocratic elite could no longer presume to govern as of right but needed the consent of those grudgingly allowed access to the political process. So, while the elite were fortunate that the new voters were prepared to continue to allow them to govern, politicians 'who wanted effective political power had to behave, at least in public, in a middle-class way.'[5] Voters expected politicians' policies and behaviour to reflect the values that were predominant in society at large. Outwardly, therefore, there was pressure on politicians to be respectable whatever their private tastes were. Thus able politicians could find their public careers abruptly ended because of publicly-revealed sexual misconduct, and in the case of two senior politicians, effectively dropped by a colleague whose own private habits were less than normal.

## Courting Dangers

William Gladstone, the Liberal politician who dominated the public stage in the latter half of the nineteenth century, was a man of intense energy and whose appetite for sexual stimulation was fed by a mix of pornography, flagellation and conversations with prostitutes. The conversations were part of his rescue work, undertaken with the knowledge of family and friends and intended to take the prostitutes off the streets and rehabilitate them. But 'it was also clear that for Gladstone rescue work became not merely a duty; it was an exposure to sexual stimulation which Gladstone felt he must undergo and overcome'.[6] He was conscious that 'these talkings of mine are certainly not within the rules of worldly prudence'[7] but persisted with them for many years. His success in rescuing prostitutes was not great and one cynical politician wrote to him that 'he manages to combine his missionary meddling with a keen appreciation of a pretty face . . .'[8]

Nevertheless, his activities were seen in political circles as a sign of eccentricity, with potentially-adverse implications. In 1886 his Private Secretary, Sir Edward Hamilton, and Lord Rosebery, the Foreign Secretary, warned Gladstone that this behaviour would lead to gossip, rumour and the 'misconstructions which evil minds will put on all this'. Accordingly, Gladstone decided that 'there was among some people a baseness and lack of charity which enabled them to believe the worst. Because of this he would cease to visit clearing-houses, brothels or places of assignation . . . and he would promise never again to speak to women in the streets at night'.[9]

Sir Charles Dilke was a Privy Counsellor, Cabinet Minister and potential Party leader who fell foul of such double standards. Widowed for ten years Dilke ran into a contrived divorce action in 1884 engineered by two women. One was his sister-in-law who was married to a fellow MP and the other a widow (she had been his mistress and had hoped to marry him). It is possible that the latter, annoyed at Dilke's intention to marry someone else, may have persuaded the former to tell her husband that she was having an affair with Dilke after he had received an anonymous letter accusing her of having an affair (which she was, but with another man). Dilke's public reputation was not helped by allegations made in court that he induced the MP's wife into a three-in-a-bed romp with a maid, during which he taught the wife 'every French vice'. This the judge condemned as 'a most revolting subject, and one would be glad to believe untrue'. The whole business was made worse by Dilke's reputation as a womaniser – the mother of the MP's wife had also been his mistress – and as a political radical. Gladstone, while privately expressing his regret at doing so, promptly decided not to offer Dilke a Cabinet post because of public opinion and even sought to dissuade Dilke from continuing in public life for the harm it might do to the Liberal Party.

Gladstone was even firmer with Charles Parnell, the leader of the Irish MPs who wanted home rule. In 1880 Parnell had met and fallen for the wife of another Irish MP, William O'Shea. O'Shea's aspirations to be an English gentleman were funded by the allowances his wife received from her aunt. He had already drifted from his wife's bed and life and tolerated her relationship with Parnell so long as it was discreet, that is, kept within political circles. Certainly members of Parnell's party, the secret service and even Gladstone were aware of it. What brought it into the public arena was O'Shea's decision to petition for divorce, with Parnell cited as co-respondent, in November 1889, three months before the appearance of the Parliamentary Report that cleared Parnell of alleged support for terrorism. A year later O'Shea won his divorce – a stunning blow to Parnell, particularly as he had kept insisting his honour would be cleared by the court. This is a reference to Parnell's belief that O'Shea's complicity in the relationship and love of money could lead to an arranged settlement prior to the court hearing. Money is often seen as the basis of the case: O'Shea's longstanding connivance in his wife's adultery was supposed to ensure she inherited her aunt's considerable fortune, and his enthusiasm for divorce was his response to his wife's having inherited the money, in May 1889, in such a way that he could not touch it.

The outcome of the divorce was, in any case, a foregone conclusion. The Liberal Party had decided that Parnell's continued position as Irish Party leader obviated 'any further co-operation' with them while Gladstone made it equally plain that he could not continue political support for Parnell against the force of the 'moral indignation of the lower middle class'. Parnell fought a desperate rear-guard defence but saw both his own career and the possibility of home rule by Parliamentary means rapidly fade.

As the century progressed so attitudes hardened and became entrenched. Even that scion of aristocratic arrogance, George Nathaniel Curzon – politician, civil servant, Viceroy of India – was aware that, although a widower, his long-standing affair with a controversial authoress, Elinor Glyn, was a matter for discretion. Glyn 'had never been introduced to his friends, never been to his house at Carlton House Terrace, never been included in a dinner party or a houseparty. Curzon, though in the political wilderness at this time and living in semi-retirement, was confidently expecting to make a come-back and was being very careful indeed to give none of his political enemies grounds to criticise his public or indeed his private life . . . a notorious novelist, who would have to get a divorce before he could marry her, did not constitute the perfect woman for a man with justifiable aspirations to the highest political office in the land'.[10]

The behaviour of such politicians, while often appearing selfish and hypocritical, was based on an acute sense of self-preservation – 'a terror of scandal, not merely because of the disgrace but because the world came to know of things that should be kept secret to the perpetrators thereof'[11] – but, as long as it was kept private, deviant behaviour was still tolerated among the elite. 'His old games, played with both sexes for years. Curious in a Cabinet Minister, because so risky', wrote Reginald, 2nd Viscount Esher, of Lewis Harcourt after learning that Harcourt had tried to rape his daughter (he had also once tried to seduce Esher's son). Lewis 'Loulou' Harcourt was a highly-esteemed politician and Cabinet minister, a lover of the arts and archaeology, a peer of the realm and an Ecclesiastical Commissioner. He was also a collector of 'improper objects' and a sexual predator. Wrote Dorothy Brett, the young girl he sexually assaulted at her father's house: 'it is so tiresome that Loulou is such an old roué. He is as bad with boys as with girls . . . he is simply a sex maniac, it isn't that he is in love. It is just ungovernable Sex desire for both sexes.'[12] Although his behaviour was known, his attempt to seduce a young boy of twelve led to his disgrace when the boy's mother 'told the whole of society'. That public censure drove Harcourt to suicide (rewritten in *The Complete Peerage* as death by heart failure in his sleep); in the public arena he could not reconcile his position with the ensuing humiliation.

The pressure to tolerate the weaknesses of colleagues grew even stronger as the development of the press and the growth of a reading public combined to provide a ready market for the sins of the great and the good. Press exposés of child prostitution, official reports on the dangers of a mixed workforce toiling half (or completely) naked in coal mines, the increase in reports of divorce cases as a result of changes in the law, spectacular cases like that of Boulton and Park, and the Lord Colin Campbell divorce suit in 1874, were lapped up by the middle and lower classes who were now more likely to be able to read, had more time in which to read, had as a result of new technology more publications to cater for their tastes and, in a society with increasingly rigid codes of behaviour, a craving to learn of those sins and vices that were the downfall of respectable and responsible members of society. The more these involved people high up on the social ladder the better, and there was certainly a growing image presented by the popular press that, for many further down the ladder, 'High Society was, apparently, populated by adulterers and nymphomaniacs, cuckolds and homosexuals, drunkards and swindlers'.[13]

This attitude, this enthusiasm for details of misconduct, for believing the worst of politicians, was emphasised in a 1917 court case. Pemberton Billing, an Independent MP of right-wing persuasion, published the *Vigilante*, the mouthpiece of his Vigilante Society which was dedicated to promoting purity in public life. His assistant editor was a deranged ex-intelligence officer, Harold Spencer, who was convinced of German plots to blackmail important public figures, based on a list of 47,000 perverts in high places. Publication of a libel in the *Vigilante* against a dancer (it accused her of being a lesbian under the title 'The Cult of the Clitoris' and claimed her dance was calculated to deprave, debauch and do more harm 'than even the German Army itself'), and at whose address the list of the names could supposedly be found, put Billing in the dock. Called as a witness, Spencer argued that the list would 'undermine the whole fabric of Government if it was made public'. Since Spencer had been under informal – if unexplained – house-arrest under the protection of Lloyd George's secretary, maybe he knew more than most. The trial degenerated into farce – the trial judge was supposed to be on the list – and Billing was acquitted. He was applauded in court and by the thousands waiting outside and, in acquitting him, the jury 'was seen to have endorsed Spencer's allegations of perversion and treachery in high places. The jury accurately reflected the feeling of the people. Asquith and the old gang, indeed the whole ruling class, were traitors and perverts'.[14]

## Operating The 'Code'

For politicians it became increasingly obvious during this century that they had either to be good or be discreet – and being discreet also meant being careful how, with whom and where, one broke the rules. Both Asquith and

Lloyd George had a penchant for pretty women although the latter's was considerably more rapacious ('which mistress?' Lloyd George's son supposedly said to a telephone inquirer, who asked if the 'mistress of the house' was in). Asquith was sixty-two and Venetia Stanley a 27-year-old friend of his daughter when they began their stream of indiscreet, romantic and voluminous correspondence. Asquith wrote much of his from the Cabinet Room where he was presiding over the War Cabinet planning its World War One strategies. Probably not consummated, the relationship clearly had 'more in it than was apparent to members of Asquith's circle, for all their ready acceptance that the prime minister, as he put it himself, manifested "(perhaps) a slight weakness for the companionship of clever and attractive women". This served as his cover. It meant that his contacts with Venetia needed no apology provided nothing happened to flout the indulgence they were accorded by the two families and friends alike.'[15]

Frances Stevenson was half Lloyd George's age when she was engaged as a teacher for his daughter and so came to share his bed and political life. Lloyd George, who 'believed it was possible to defy respectability provided a certain homage was paid to conventions', had made it plain that nothing, such as a divorce, would threaten his career or the party; he was aware of scandal: 'even in later years, they always had to be careful: careful not to go about in the government car, not to dine together in public; careful not to travel back and forth together too often between London and the Versailles Conference; careful not to be too reckless in going about together in July 1921'.[16]

Lloyd George's relationship was serious and longstanding, and depended heavily on the co-operation and collusion of his staff. It also required the tacit tolerance of those who could control the flow of information to the public arena: 'even with such inside help, however, the affair with Frances would have been impossible if the code governing the private lives of public men, and Press attention thereto, had been in Lloyd George's day what it later became. While he was in active politics, State and Press turned a blind eye to the extra-marital activities of politicians, so long as they were careful to keep out of the Divorce Court. This code was based on two clear principles: that marriage was an institution whose maintenance was in the public interest, and that public men should therefore set an example by upholding it in their own lives. If a politician broke his own or somebody else's marriage, he knew that his career would be broken. But unless he was sued by his wife for divorce, or cited as a co-respondent in another man's divorce suit, he could commit adultery with impunity and without fear of publicity.'[17]

The 'code' worked strongly in the twentieth century, protecting politicians from the consequences of a variety of sins and proclivities so long as they kept them away from the public arena by whatever means were the most convenient. One such example was Duff Cooper, one of those products of the inter-war years who were culturally and socially conditioned for a place in public life that invariably depended on the exploitation of contacts and patrons. Born to what he believed his rightful class – the world of prime ministers, princes, country houses and comfort – he was a fervent patriot who professed to be a practising member of the Church of England and believed women had no place in politics. He, by turn a civil servant, soldier, politician, author and journalist, served as a wartime Minister of Information and roving diplomat before being sacked as Ambassador to France by the Attlee Government in 1947. He wrote his autobiography – *Old Men Forget* – which dealt with his public life: for the other aspects of his life he could only apologise that: 'nor can the dearest and most sacred of them be included'.[18] This is because Cooper, he of the 'would-be fondling hands', 'was intensely sensual. Physically he did not know how to be content with a single woman; even before his honeymoon was over he was seeking diversions outside their marriage. But such diversions were no more than the gratification of a nagging appetite. "My infidelities are entirely of the flesh," he wrote in his diary. "The long habit of promiscuity asserts itself. I feel guilty of no unfaithlessness, only of filthiness".'[19] That he wasn't exposed was in part due to his friends' tolerance and his wife's lack of jealousy over his sexual adventures. It was also due to Cooper's own preference for sex as a 'diversion, a delicious relaxation' with women who 'like him, took their pleasure where they found it with no nonsense about love'. He usually remained friends with former lovers and his 'conquests were usually married women with experience of the world and a complaisant husband; there were rules to the game and he stuck to them'.[20]

At the other end of the sexual spectrum, but with an equally voracious sexual appetite, was Tom Driberg. Discovering his homosexuality and his left-wing politics in his early teens – he was to be expelled from Lancing College for the former – he pursued both vigorously throughout his life. The 'ruling passion' was homosexuality and Driberg was an enthusiastic adventurer with a penchant for 'rough trade'. He worked for the *Daily Express*, mainly as 'William Hickey' during the Thirties, before becoming an Independent Labour MP in 1942. Despite his promiscuity he had only once ended up in court – in 1935 – and was acquitted on the basis of two excellent defence witnesses, Colonel Egerton (who said Driberg had 'a perfectly honourable' character) and Lord Sysonby (who swore to his 'exemplary' reputation).

His employer, Lord Beaverbrook, paid his costs and kept his name out of the newspapers. Political opponents tried to begin a 'whispering' campaign against him but, although his proclivities were well known in the House, he was well-protected by the unofficial code of silence that operated there. On his arrival a fellow homosexual, the Tory MP Chips Channon, took him on a tour of the 'most important rooms' in the Palace of Westminster (the Members' lavatories) – an act of pure, disinterested, sisterly friendship, said Driberg. Surprisingly he 'became more promiscuous after my election to Parliament, relying on my new status to get me out of tight corners'.[21] He had already learnt from his previous brush with the law – 'why didn't you tell us who you were?', the arresting officer had asked him – that his status assisted a tendency not to press charges, a status that was enhanced by his being on MI5's payroll and his possession of an MI5 telephone number that he gave to the police on the numerous times they caught him pursuing his passion in public lavatories.

## Rules of Prudence and Obligation

The middle class saw financial honesty as equally important but MPs were slower to respond. One reason for this was that the election process until the later half of the nineteenth century still required MPs to bribe voters and pay for electioneering. Another reason was the increasing number of private and commercial activities that required Parliamentary approval; this persuaded businessmen, speculators and special interests, if not to secure a seat for themselves, then to have a spokesman to represent them in Parliament. In the great railway boom of the 1840s, over 150 MPs were shareholders in new railway companies in what was then a multi-million pound growth area. Its leading promoter, George Hudson, sat as an MP 'to pilot through both Houses the innumerable railway bills in which he was interested, and to watch over railway interests as a whole in Parliament. To this was attached a considerable amount of committee work, much wire-pulling behind the scenes, and a necessary routine of social duties and entertainment'.[22] Some MPs became increasingly concerned throughout the nineteenth century at the growing intensity and volume of lobbying interests and their attendant MPs – 'not so much a fine art as a perfect scandal', said one MP – as railway, shipping, cotton, telephone and overseas companies vied for Parliamentary attention.

Nevertheless, until 1911 MPs were also unpaid; most, therefore, had substantial business interests and, although there were some rules on not accepting bribes, not receiving payment for advocating matters in the House and not voting on matters in which they had a financial interest, most believed strongly that their sense of honour would govern any conflict or overlap with their Parliamentary behaviour. Thus an out-and-out crook

37

such as Horatio Bottomley could arrive in the House in 1905 in an atmosphere of 'icy silence: a silence cold and contemptuous, which could be felt'. Yet by observing the club-rules in the House and keeping his highly-organised but crooked lotteries and sweepstakes on the outside he could resign seven years later, bankrupted, with F. E. Smith (Lord Birkenhead) saying of him 'he made for himself a position in the House of Commons of which nothing but the loss of his seat could deprive him. His absence from the House of Commons has impoverished the public stock of gaiety, of cleverness, of common sense'.[23]

It was, however, the relationship between Ministers and private interests that awoke Parliament to the need for clearer guidance on standards of financial conduct, when there was increasing concern at the low levels of commercial morality and the use of public figures – particularly members of the House of Lords – to front fraudulent schemes. In 1899 Balfour named the Stock Exchange and public contracts as the 'two great sources of corruption', the *Economist* talked of an atmosphere of money inside the Commons, while the Times referred in 1898 to the 'ugly phenomenon of men of high social position accepting directorships in doubtful companies'. The regularity of financial scandals involving Ministers created a climate of concern that required a political response because Ministers were particularly expected to set a high moral tone in Parliament.

Senior politicians believed in the need to 'avoid the slightest suspicion between personal and public considerations' and the importance of divesting financial interests that might be seen as 'lowering the dignity of public life'. Parliamentary criticism did result in reforms. In 1895 Balfour required that Ministers should not enter into any engagement that took up time that 'would properly belong to the public' or any connection with public companies that 'could be supposed to influence his policy or diminish his usefulness' as a Minister. In 1906 Campbell-Bannerman required all Ministers to give up all directorships other than those involving honorary, charitable or private companies. It was the Marconi scandal, however, which established the principles governing such conduct. In 1912 the British Government signed an agreement with the English Marconi Company to establish an Empire wireless link-up. Its managing director was Godfrey Isaacs who was also a director of the American Marconi Company, the majority of whose shares were owned by the English firm. His brother, Rufus Isaacs, the Attorney-General, Lloyd George, Chancellor of the Exchequer, and Lord Murray the Master of Elibank and Government Chief Whip, each bought in April 1912 (or agreed to buy since they were allowed to pay for them later) 1000 shares in the American company at the pre-issue price of £2 (when put on the market they closed at £4 on the first day). A few days later Murray and Lloyd George sold half their shares and then bought a further 3000 shares between them. Murray then went on to buy 3000 with Liberal Party funds. Political partisanship and anti-semitism then prompted political and journalistic accusations that Marconi had got the contract to push up the value of the shares – the American company could only be expected to benefit from the success of its parent – and that Ministers had exploited their inside knowledge for personal gain.

The escalation of rumours and allegations resulted in the establishment of a Parliamentary select committee in October 1912 to determine whether the wireless contract was commercially imprudent and corruptly obtained. Both Lloyd George and Isaacs had concealed their shareholdings until January 1913, when they were revealed by means of libel action brought against a foreign newspaper by the Minister who signed the contract, Postmaster General Herbert Samuel, who was not involved in the shares transactions but knew of them.

The committee's majority (Liberal) report absolved Lloyd George, Isaacs and Lord Murray while the minority report criticised them for 'grave impropriety' and a lack of frankness, and urged Parliament not to condone their behaviour. Lloyd George fought back strongly; thoughtless, careless and mistaken, but one who had acted innocently, openly and honestly, he argued. Prime Minister Asquith emphasised that the 'rules of prudence', rather than rules of obligation, may not have been 'fully observed'. He argued that the 'rules of obligation' required Ministers not to undertake transactions where private interests conflicted with public duty, to speculate, to use official information for private profit or to accept favours from those seeking government contracts. 'Rules of prudence' essentially required Ministers to 'avoid all transactions which might lead to the belief that they are doing anything which the rules of obligation forbid'.[24] Asquith's support was crucial; Lloyd George threatened to resign if his actions were termed an 'indiscretion'. In that he was supported by party colleagues.

Aware that he was an opportunist (his conscience was 'as good as new. For he had never used it', said one; he knew no meaning in the words 'truth or gratitude', said another), his colleagues were also conscious that he was the Liberal Party's greatest platform asset. While the damage to his reputation as 'a public statesman with serious people' was thought to be irreparable, his 'value as a demagogue was retrievable and it was the business of the party to pull that out of the mess'. Thus that reputation was to be protected by advising him not to use words that could be quoted out of context and 'twisted into an admission of guilt'.[25] In the event a three-line whip was added to ensure the defeat of the Opposition's motion of censure and Northcliffe, the newspaper owner, urged his newspapers not to criticise Lloyd George.

## Paying For The Honour

Even with the introduction of Parliamentary salaries in 1911 (by Lloyd George), political careers often meant financial sacrifice. This was especially true for Ministers who were now encouraged to divest themselves of their directorships and rely on their income from investments and other sources. Some politicians solved that problem through being bankrolled by sympathetic businessmen such as Lord Beaverbrook. Bonar Law and F. E. Smith benefited from share transactions with Lord Beaverbrook (he bankrolled the original investments, paying them any profit and carrying any losses) while Samuel Hoare received cash payments.[26] Winston Churchill's forays into the shares market were underwritten by an American financier. F. E. Smith was also paid some large sums from party funds to compensate for earnings from journalism that Baldwin insisted he ceased on becoming a Cabinet Minister.[27] Others, like Lloyd George, cheerfully traded honours, one of their few official resources, with businessmen, in return for funds to build up their parties' offices as the growing size of the electorate and the increased partisanship demanded properly-organised election campaigns on a national scale. After ousting Asquith from 10 Downing Street in 1916, Lloyd George had no funding and an uncertain political future. Funds meant the opportunity to build a political party around himself and free himself from the Conservative support he needed to stay in office.

He sold honours between 1916 and 1922; the tariff was £10,000 for a knighthood, £30,000 for a baronetcy, and £50–100,000 for a peerage, handing out twenty-six peerages, 130 baronetcies, 481 knighthoods and over 25,000 OBEs until the racket finally crumbled on the award of honours in 1921 and 1922 to a convicted food hoarder, a war-time profiteer, a crook, a 'technical' traitor and a tax-evader. The awards sparked off a major political row, with Lloyd George lying through his teeth and trying to fix the official inquiry to protect himself. Luckily for him, other parties had also found selling honours to be lucrative, so the Conservative Party quietly infiltrated George's team of 'salesmen', pensioned off the most successful to France and insisted that the upright Prime Minister Ramsay MacDonald grant an honour to their fixer, much to MacDonald's disgust. When it was pointed out that some of his own party were involved MacDonald agreed, thus preserving the nation from what he called 'such a filthy sewer as would poison public life'.[28]

The lack of clear or up-to-date rules or guidance on the distinctions between income earned from dubious sources, income with 'strings attached' and 'clean' income, together with the tradition of MPs having private financial interests, meant that during the twentieth century not only the public but also MPs themselves found it hard to know what types of financial interests were or were not acceptable, despite there being a Parliamentary tradition that MPs should not receive money or other financial benefits for doing anything in connection with the proceedings of Parliament. Of course such traditions were not codified, were often the result of intrigue or momentary outrage and were comprehensively ignored when it was expedient to do so. The rule on not voting on matters in which they had financial interests was the only rule that was considered a part of current Parliamentary life; everything else to do with Members' financial interests was assumed to be governed by their sense of honour and the 'gentleman' ethic. As Chamberlain retorted to Lloyd George when the latter taunted Chamberlain about his family arms interests that were supplying the British army in the Boer War: 'I have endeavoured in the whole course of my public life to be in the position in which Caesar's wife should have been – to give no cause even of suspicion to the most malicious of my opponents . . . but they have introduced into our public life methods of controversy which are unworthy, and have made it more difficult for honourable, sensitive men to serve the State.'

For most backbench MPs, however, it was business as usual with no expectation that tney should seek to emulate their Ministerial colleagues unless of course they were publicly criticised. Thus Robert Boothby, a Conservative MP, survived a Parliamentary inquiry into his efforts to secure funds from the Treasury for a Czech business friend, when the Treasury had frozen the London assets of Czech citizens in retaliation for assets seized by the German army of occupation, assets which belonged to individuals and organisations based in England. The idea was that Czechs who could prove they had business interests in Britain but could not get any funds from Czechoslovakia would be able to claim any of the funds held by the Treasury. Boothby's friend then bought an off-the-shelf company as evidence of a British-based business interest. He promised Boothby a percentage of any money he got and Boothby, heavily in debt, used this to forestall his creditors as he began to lobby government departments on the company's behalf. Found guilty of contempt – as well as the lesser offence of failure to disclose his financial interest, the only offence he would later admit to – Boothby refused to resign and, indeed, secured an increased majority at the 1945 elections before going on to become a peer and a substantial, if controversial, public figure.

Nevertheless the contact with businessmen and the lure of money or an appointment to supplement a Parliamentary salary was an ever-present danger for those caught in unsuitable company. J. H. Thomas, the garrulous Labour Colonial Secretary in the National Government, was forced to resign after he told his two business friends, Alfred Bates and Tory MP Alfred Butt, of changes in the income tax rate. What sealed his fate was a large advance from Bates for his autobiography (which comprised at that time a pile of newspaper cuttings) and an insurance arranged with Butt on the date of the 1935 General Election. The £15,000 from the former and £600 profit on the latter outweighed any sympathy for the likely explanation of Thomas talking too much over a few whiskies, a habit of his. As Ramsey MacDonald accepted: 'T's associates may be his undoing. I can see the public interest shifting from whether there was leakage to what is the character of T's friends. On that the "jury of the street" may condemn him.'

Some ten years later an even bigger scandal broke over Labour politicians. Sidney Stanley was a middleman, a broker of political contacts at a time of restrictions, shortages, and controls. He cultivated politicians and officials with gifts and entertainment and exuded an aura of affluent self-confidence. At the same time he tried to sell his political contacts to businessmen, trading influence in return for commission payments. In 1947 Stanley was offering three businessmen his influence to circumvent Board of Trade regulations, persuading them to part with large sums of money; £12,000 from Sherman Pools to avoid prosecution for paper quota infringements, £10,000 from Berger and Sons Ltd, paintmakers, for licences to redevelop premises and £10,000 from Stagg and Russell Ltd to import amusement arcade machinery. One of the businesses involved in the last deal suspected a con-trick and reported Stanley's activities to the police. The pools promoter complained bitterly over the worthless security Stanley gave him in return for his payment to a civil servant who reported the allegation to the President of the Board of Trade, Harold Wilson, who also called in the police. In each case the name of Stanley's contact was Wilson's junior minister, John Belcher, and in each case the payments were allegedly intended to bribe him.

Rumours began circulating of a political scandal. Attlee moved swiftly to counteract them, choosing to set up a public inquiry through a quasi-judicial Tribunal before which three Cabinet Ministers appeared: Charles Key, Hugh Dalton and John Belcher, together with George Gibson, former General Secretary of COHSE and a government-appointed Director of the Bank of England. Key had only reached the early stages of cultivation by Stanley and Dalton argued, to a somewhat sceptical audience, that he had turned down Stanley's blandishments. Both Belcher and Gibson were seen to have succumbed. Belcher was also named as having received favours from other businessmen. While the favours may now appear small – accommodation, drinks, presents, entertainment – they were enough to condemn both men. As the Commons closed ranks over criticism of the severity of the questioning during the Tribunal and the 'unthinking cruelty of modern publicity', Belcher resigned as an MP in 'the very depths of unhappiness and wretchedness'. His departure showed that the Government and Parliament would act firmly but the scandal revealed not only the dangers of links with business but also how easily the press and the public could suspect the worst from such links.

# Chapter 4

## *Setting The Agenda For Today's Scandals*

*Standards? What Standards?*

One may ask, as Lord Beaverbrook asked Chapman
Pincher about Profumo: 'Why in God's name should a
great political party tear itself to rags and tatters just
because a minister's fucked a woman?' The answer as to
why it did lies in the tradition that politicians reflected not
only the predominant middle-class virtues in public (to
secure their vote) but also reflected those values most
prized in a society where the 'gentleman' ethic ruled:
responsibility, selflessness, honour and honesty. The
public expected standards; standards determined how
society should conduct itself and emphasised the patterns
of behaviour through which society reflected its values.
But they were standards concerned both with a politician's
public image and thus his personal conduct. Politicians
were expected to have orthodox private lives, expected
not to use their political position for personal financial
gain and to conduct their political affairs with integrity
and impartiality. When it was discovered that a politician
was behaving in a way that offended – and the popular
press was well aware that sex and sanctimoniousness sold
newspapers – then his colleagues were quick to condemn
or shun the unfortunate colleague. They wanted to appear
to be upholding the values and to avoid being thought
guilty by association – even though they may have been
privy to the very behaviour they had now to publicly
condemn.

While publicly politicians played this game, they were
tolerant of each other's shortcomings and proclivities
within the political world, able to distinguish between

private behaviour and the need publicly to be seen to adhere to the standards expected of them by society. The attitude to the financial affairs of politicians was a little more rigid, but only a little. If those affairs related solely to the politician in his capacity as a businessman he was relatively free to pursue them as he wished. Nevertheless the House did make some effort to avoid MPs and, increasingly, Ministers, profiting from their Parliamentary position, and was only too pleased to drop those who were censured in the public arena – thus it was to be the criminal convictions of Mardy Jones or Peter Baker, for example, which ensured their rapid departure from the House – or were suspected of using their parliamentary position for profit, deliberately or otherwise, and especially if they were Ministers.

MPs were also very keen to protect the dignity of Parliament as the symbol of the democratic process, a triumph of that Victorian concern with outward appearance. The House has always been touchy, however, over allegations which reflect adversely on 'the reputation, character and the good name of the House' and the image of an MP as an honest, truthful and decent individual. Thus MPs who had accused their colleagues of drinking – 'half-drunk and disgusting to look at', on the 'fringe of semi-sobriety', for example – have found themselves rapped over the knuckles or, in the case of Garry Allighan, expelled.

While there were standards, they have often developed unevenly: one can sometimes be surprised at the punishments meted out to those who are found out, considering the greater sins of those not caught.

Tom Driberg (see p. 36) was a Labour MP, journalist and friend to the powerful and influential. Employed by MI5 – and probably by Czech intelligence – he was a rapacious homosexual who ended up in the House of Lords. William Field was a hard-working MP involved in such prosaic matters as the Association of Scientific Workers and the Association of Municipal Corporations. He was fined £15 in 1953 for soliciting or importuning in a public place for immoral purposes. That charge arose because he had smiled and looked at young men ('persistently inviting', the police claimed) in West End lavatories. There was no evidence that anyone objected or responded in a way that suggested his behaviour was homosexually-oriented. He resigned on conviction.

In 1931 T. I. Mardy Jones, MP for the rock-solid Labour seat of Pontypridd, resigned over a thirty guinea fine for sending his wife his Parliamentary travel vouchers so that she could bring papers to him at Westminster. Neither had any spare cash and Jones could not find an opposition MP with whom to 'pair' so he could go himself. For a man with thirty years' service to the Labour movement and whose special hobby was the local government rating system, the decision to resign his seat was inevitable, given the Labour Party's expectation of personal integrity. Harry Deeling on the other hand was bereft of any such quality. A ruthless loan shark and property speculator he cheated the young and debt-ridden Duke of Leinster of his inheritance by agreeing to pay off his debts and give him a fixed sum of £1,000 per annum. The Duke died in a Pimlico bedsit in 1976. Harry Deeling, a pillar of society, Tory MP, magistrate, public benefactor, wealthy business-man, died in 1937 at the Château des Fayeres, near Cannes in France, living off the interest from the Duke's inheritance of over £40,000 a year.

## A Nice Chap, With Murder On His Mind

Now Anthony Eden played the formal game of politics by the book, bringing, as his biographer put it, 'honour and dignity, kindness and loyalty to the often grubby trade of politics'. When the electoral boundaries were redrawn in 1949 Eden chose to remain with his original constituency, even though its composition had shifted in favour of Labour voters. When he was Foreign Secretary he sold his shares in the Anglo-Iranian Oil Company in 1950 – even though they were virtually valueless – because the Government were involved in dealings with it. Said his biographer: 'there is no obligation whatever on Ministers to sell shares on taking Office, but Eden considered that his ownership of a substantial holding in the company could be interpreted as an interest no Foreign Secretary dealing with the future of the company should own. On this, a matter of honour, he would not budge, and the shares were sold, at an appalling loss which he could not afford . . . Had he held on to the shares he could have become rich for the first time in his life . . .'[1]

In 1952 Sir Anthony Eden wanted to remarry; his first marriage had ended in 1950 after both he and his first wife had agreed some years earlier to pursue their own interests and affairs. Concerned at any adverse reaction he took advice from party officials. The *Church Times* had editorialised that 'it is now apparently accepted as a matter of course that those who occupy the highest office in political and public life may breach the Church's law without embarrassment or reproach'. Fortunately for Eden the party faithful were less censorious and the marriage went ahead – after the Conservative Central Office checked with many constituencies to see if there was likely to be any adverse reaction.

Yet only a few years later the same Eden was prepared to deceive Parliament, mislead the US President and ride roughshod over his Ministerial colleagues in his efforts to topple President Nasser of Egypt. What would the public and the press view have been of a man prepared to see a fellow-politician's private life used to undermine his decision to resign from Eden's Government in protest, or a man prepared to consider murder to achieve his political objectives? (Eden had considered some of MI6's assassination schemes, codenamed 'Straggle', as one of the options to get rid of Nasser, and showed 'a toothy grin' at the possibility).

What mattered was what became public knowledge and, more importantly, what interested the public. There were those who saw the Profumo scandal as *the* political watershed, the scandal that set the agenda for future scandals in defining what was likely to galvanise the press, excite the public and panic the politicians: 'British statesmen throughout the centuries have not been notable at all times for their virtuous way of life, but the traditional elite, however they may have laid themselves open to criticism in other ways, can, at least, be credited with having created a stable social system. As a part of the rigid class structure there was the *monde*, and the *demimonde*. The latter provided its comforts and conveniences but, beyond that, it was securely kept in its place, where it could not interfere in any way with good government or, trained in discretion as it was, with the personal reputations of those who frequented it'.[2]

Such behaviour, and the contrast with the public image, was a sure recipe for scandal. Thus Dr Mervyn Stockwood, Bishop of Southwark, could reflect public opinion at the time of Profumo by writing that 'things have happened in recent weeks that have left an unpleasant smell – the smell of corruption in high places, of evil practices, and of a repudiation of the simple decencies and the basic values . . . the smell is intensified in its unpleasantness by the squalid biographies in a particular section of the Sunday press that thrives, no doubt with considerable financial gain, on sexual scandals'.[3]

## Scandals Waiting to Happen

The developments of the nineteenth and the first half of the twentieth centuries set the agenda for how people viewed politicians and how politicians ought to behave. In the case of financial interests, not only was there no major scandal after the Lynskey Tribunal, although it left the Labour Party tainted with a suspicion of seediness, but the post-Tribunal actions of the Government paved the way for a false sense of security. With evidence in the Tribunal's Report that acceptable lobbying was shading into influence-peddling and bribery, Prime Minister Clement Attlee announced a Select Committee to look at such activities. The Committee's Report noted that large firms and trade associations had the staff and contacts to lobby, quite legitimately, the government and the civil service. It did not, however, see any future for the 'intermediary', the private middleman: 'if an individual desires to set up as a professional intermediary, he must be able to attract a clientele, and in order to do so he must be able to offer some services of value to his prospective clients. The only services he can render are a knowledge of the workings of the system, with or without the addition of personal acquaintance with individual officers. It is difficult to see how a private intermediary can acquire this knowledge'.[4]

What it did not, or could not, anticipate, however, was the possibility of those from within the 'system' setting themselves up as intermediaries and selling their knowledge, access and contacts. Although political PR was in its infancy at the time the Select Committee was reporting, there was an increasing number of clients seeking access to the decision-making processes who turned for professional help to those individuals with advertising, public relations and, more importantly, political backgrounds, such as political journalism, government PR work and political careers. During the 1950s these individuals laid the foundation of political contacts and their PR expertise, and they pioneered many of the techniques used today; the provision of detailed briefings, the use of 'fact-finding' missions, the creation of climates of favourable opinion and the hiring of MPs as consultants. While their impact on Parliament was marginal at first, the abilities of PR in orchestrating clients' interests was clearly demonstrated in the mid-1950s battle for the introduction of commercial television where 'the outside interests seemed to have exerted more effective influence than Conservative voters, constituency organisations, or even members of the Parliamentary Party'.[5]

This was clearly an area where the increasingly active role of PR men seemed 'another testimony to the age-old weakness of democracies run by amateur politicians in the face of well-informed and determined professionals . . .'.[6] Furthermore, 'the new post-war Tory MPs were "young men on the make", eager to obtain financial rewards and the hallmarks of status. They were bitterly hostile to socialism, which they interpreted as limiting individual opportunities for personal advancement.'[7] This was their enthusiasm for what MP Francis Noel-Baker described in 1961 as the 'grey zone', the jobs that paid fees and retainers but required no special qualifications or fixed hours of work and where the rôles of advisor and consultant 'need not become generally known'. The growth of so-called 'public relations' and of the power of pressure groups, he warned, 'means that Members of Parliament have themselves become more attractive allies for business interests than they have been in the past. The door, in fact, is wide open for a new form of political corruption . . .'.[8]

Despite the lesson of the 1941 Boothby case, when the late Conservative MP was severely reprimanded by a Select Committee for failing to disclose an interest *and* for speaking in the House as well as lobbying Ministers and Whitehall in expectation of a financial reward, MPs happily signed up for jaunts to Spain, Ghana and the Central African Federation, often organised by fellow MPs employed by PR firms, and threw 'the mantle of Westminster respectability' over their private business affairs. As the late Tory MP Anthony Courtney said: 'I had acquired for the benefit of the firms with which I was connected improved personal contact with the Board of Trade and other Ministers' and, for their activities abroad, 'an aura of official Government blessing through the fact I was now a Member of Parliament'.[9]

On the other hand there was a major scandal involving sex and a politician that did have a dramatic impact. The Profumo affair was also a consequence of its time, blending a sex and spy story with an increasingly cavalier scepticism toward public morality and authority. In the Cold War Britain appeared to be coming off second best, with the disappearance of MacLean and Burgess a decade earlier, the publicity given to Philby in 1955 (and his arrival in the USSR in January 1963), Commander Crabb's disappearance in Portsmouth and Linney's fourteen years' imprisonment on spying charges in 1958. The apparent ease with which the spies were able to perform their activities raised questions about the Government's competence to deal with the threat. The public visibility of sex was probably the most noticeable feature of the period, with increasing allusions to it in the media and on the streets, as the liberalisation of legal restraints and moral prescriptions made it an increasingly marketable commodity and symbol of those who espoused the causes of self-expression, self-fulfilment and a general trend towards more personal freedom, a trend where many 'saw Britain in the kind of light that shone on the later Roman Empire, hurling herself headlong to destruction amid gurglings of degenerate glee'.[10] This later prompted the *Times* to insist that the Profumo affair was a question of morals. Much of the blame for a lack of leadership in this and other areas was laid at the door of Prime Minister Harold Macmillan, of whom Lord Lambton said in 1962: 'he is a temporary leader who has brought the party to its present disrepute and who appears likely to lead it to a temporary oblivion rather than admit that the once bright spark of his leadership has gone'.[11]

Harold Macmillan was an Edwardian character, a laid-back gentleman with a raffish sense of dress, who mixed compassion with cynicism, loved the theatre of high society while being capable of throwing colleagues to the wolves. He was, said Nigel Fisher, 'complex, almost chameleon. He is a shy, sensitive man, reserved and undemonstrative in his personal relationships, unwilling to discuss intimate matters and uneasy if obliged to do so . . . there is a strong sense of irony, partly attributable to his feeling that life is transitory and impermanent. He is a very honourable man of deep and sincere religious conviction and high moral standards, who admires and possesses the old virtues to the point of being straitlaced and almost puritanical in his reactions to modern morals and to the subject of sex, which he dislikes discussing'.[12] This is a reference to his wife's longstanding 'emotional' relationship with the disreputable Bob Boothby, which left 'deep scars'.

That elegant style, the unflappability, and the old-fashioned courtesy was ill-suited to needing to judge when personal behaviour could become a political issue. 'No doubt,' he was to say later, 'Profumo had frequented circles in which, in my youth, it would have been thought inappropriate for a Minister to move. But times have changed, and although I had not myself much knowledge of this new social world I recognised that the distinctions which had ruled in the past no longer obtained. Respectable and disreputable people now seemed to be all mixed together'.[13] Unfortunately Macmillan's powers of recognition were not as good as he thought they were, just as some of his colleagues were to suffer from errors of personal judgement. Nevertheless these were treated as private matters. There was no reason why Macmillan should have anticipated that the convergence of changes in social attitudes, a conflict with the media and the social circles that led Profumo to meet Christine Keeler would precipitate his retirement, hurt the Government electorally and fix once and for all in the public mind that sex and politicians spelt scandal.

# Chapter 5

## Macmillan's Members

*When Feasting With Panthers, Don't Rustle The Bushes: Ian Harvey*

Ian Harvey's steady rise to the front ranks of the Tory Party came crashing to the ground on the night of 19 November 1958, when he and a nineteen-year-old Guardsman were caught in the beam of a park-keeper's torch under a tree in St James's Park, as the court heard, 'misbehaving'. For the 44-year-old Harvey it was the end of ten year's feasting with panthers, as he later quoted Oscar Wilde, conduct he thought to be 'verging on insanity', given his own, 'undoubted political ambitions'.[1]

Born in 1914, his early years were spent in Surrey with his war-widow mother before he attended Fettes College in Scotland and then Christ Church, Oxford. There he devoted his undergraduate life to dramatics, the Conservative Association and the Oxford Union, which resulted in a poor degree in 1937 and a wit, dynamism and facility to communicate that carried him into the advertising firm of Mather and Crowther. At the age of twenty-four he was prospective Tory candidate for Don Valley in Yorkshire. When the war began he enlisted as a Territorial sapper, ending up as a Brigade Major. He lost his first election as Tory candidate for the Spelthorne constituency in Middlesex, in the 1945 Election. He continued his business career – becoming head of public relations at W. S. Crawford Ltd – and took up local politics, first as a Kensington councillor, then as member for South Kensington on the London County Council. He maintained his mainstream political involvement through his membership of the Carlton Club and the Junior Carlton Club.

At the same time he rented a bedsit in Trevor Square, close to the Knightsbridge barracks. Apart from the occasional homosexual encounter at school Harvey had little experience of, although he sensed a predisposition towards, adult homosexuality. From his window he could see soldiers wandering around in an aimless way, as though waiting for someone or something. Harvey was interested. A brief evening sortie into St James's Park opened his eyes to a 'veritable parade' of young soldiers under the trees. A subsequent evening stroll after a dinner party and a pleasurable encounter with a young Scot launched Harvey on a thirteen-year career of regular visits to the Park.

Meanwhile he won the nomination as Tory candidate for the Harrow East constituency and in 1949 married Clare Mayhew, sister of Labour MP Christopher Mayhew, thus satisfying 'my supporters in the constituency who thought it was a mistake to have a candidate who was a bachelor and over thirty'.[2]

In 1950 he turned the 1945 Labour majority of 6770 into a Tory one of 1464 and entered the House with the likes of Enoch Powell, Edward Heath, Ian Macleod and Reginald Maudling, who quickly made their mark as the rising stars. Certainly Harvey, who had not been slow in the past to make his views known to the party hierarchy and been somewhat free with his comments on the shortcomings of others, especially the old guard sitting on the Opposition front bench, was not one to be left behind. He joined the Executive of the 1922 Committee, subsequently becoming its secretary, busied himself in constituency matters and in 1956 received his first Ministerial appointment as Parliamentary Secretary at the Ministry of Supply. Typically this was in spite of his public belief that the Ministry should be wound up.

By 1958 the 'Class of 50' was successful; Macleod was Minister of Labour, Heath was Chief Whip, Maudling was Paymaster General, Powell was a Treasury minister and Harvey was a junior if self-confidant Minister at the Foreign Office. Harvey could have counted himself among those destined for future advancement, until he decided on a 11 p.m. walk in St James's Park on that 'dark and misty' November night after a dinner at the Polish Embassy. With the park-keeper that night was a policeman, who arrested the soldier and politician spotlighted in the rustling bushes by the park-keeper's touch. After attempting to escape on the way to Cannon Street police station and giving a false name on arrival, Harvey revealed his identity and was released pending an appearance at Bow Street the next day. Charged with committing an act of gross indecency (later dropped in court) he resigned his office and his seat and planned to plead guilty at the forthcoming trial. On 10 December he and the soldier were each fined £5 with costs, for behaving in a manner reasonably likely to 'offend against public decency'. Defence counsel for the soldier said he was rather young and naive, went with Harvey out of curiosity and 'as far as could be traced was not addicted in this way'. Harvey paid both fines. His constituency party were willing to support him as MP but Harvey felt the damage was done. He resigned his clubs, only a few of his friends went out of their way to contact him while 'the Conservative Party, quite understandably because of its outlook and make-up, did not want to know anything more about me'.[3]

## A Rather Agitated Manner: Sir Ian Horobin

Sir Ian Horobin's decision to decline the public announcement of his impending life peerage in 1962, on the grounds that he was reluctant to undertake the amount of work involved in being an active peer, received little press comment, other than that the belated decision seemed odd and would be a 'surprise' to Macmillan, who had nominated him. Clearly the Prime Minister was unaware that Sir Ian was due in court as a result of his conduct in relation to his life's work, the Mansfield House University Settlement in the East End of London. Son of the Principal of Homerton College, Cambridge, and educated at Highgate School and Sussex College, Cambridge, Sir Ian virtually refounded the Settlement in 1923. Its warden until 1962, he raised over £500,000 to run it as a young men and boys' club and lived there for the greater part of his time in a bedsit. He had served in the RNVR during the First World War and in the RAF as a squadron leader during the Second World War when he was captured by the Japanese and locked up in the overcrowded Soeka-boemi prison. There he volunteered as the hygiene officer and raised morale as the prison's 'unofficial padre, leader and general wit.' He was also beaten, tortured and made to watch executions in an attempt to force him to reveal the escape route organised by Laurens Van Der Post. A 'person of great courage, wit and humour under appalling conditions', Van Der Post later said of Horobin, who clearly needed medical attention on his release. Nevertheless, rather than recuperate, he quickly returned to the Settlement and public life.

He had been a Tory MP for Southwark Central between 1931 and 1935 and, in 1951, was elected as MP for Oldham East and served as Parliamentary Secretary to the Minister of Power from January 1958 until his election defeat in October 1959. In 1955 he was knighted.

In September 1961 he returned from a holiday in Spain to be greeted by the police, who were anxious to interview him about his activities at the Settlement. In May the following year he and seventeen-year-old Roy Girard were charged with several offences of indecency and assault between 1958 and 1961. Although he was alleged to have told the police that 'if Girard says that, what is the use of me denying it', both pleaded not guilty to the charges at West Ham Magistrates Court. Prosecution counsel was Mervyn Griffith-Jones who had led the prosecution in the *Lady Chatterley's Lover* trial and would be the man to handle the Stephen Ward case: 'he is so ultra orthodox that some aspects of modern life have escaped him altogether', said Ludovic Kennedy.[4] Nevertheless Griffith-Jones had no difficulty detailing the events leading to Horobin's downfall.

One boy was invited to see Horobin's stamp collection and assaulted. Another was taken for a ride in Horobin's Rolls Royce and asked if he wanted to earn ten shillings' extra pocket money. Although he declined a number of invitations to the bedsit, when he finally agreed he was assaulted behind locked doors. He received £2, went again, was assaulted again, but when he refused a third time Girard tried to persuade him to accompany him to the bedsit, arguing it would mean more money if he did. A third, a young groundsman who went to the bedsit for instructions, suffered a serious assault, received £1 and was assaulted every four or five weeks for a number of months, sometimes with Girard present.

A former housekeeper at the Settlement told the court that 'I noticed that he would ask for boys to be sent up. This always happened during the evening meal times. The boys arrived at that time and I noticed that Sir Ian would push his things away in a rather agitated manner and that his voice would take on a higher note and it seemed to me to be almost hysterical.'

The charges had emerged from questioning of Girard by a clergyman who passed the information on to a colleague, the Settlement's Deputy Warden. When confronted Horobin told him that he had had 'sweethearts' for many years and that there had been nothing wrong with his relationship with boys. He offered to resign, declining offers of help on the grounds that it was 'a natural thing for some men to love boys. You must accept me as I am. I am too old to change.' Privately he told his secretary: 'I do not know how they managed to get it out of Girard, a boy to whom I have been virtually married for some years.' They met when Girard was thirteen.

When the trial came up at the Old Bailey in July, Horobin changed his plea to that of guilty to ten charges to indecency and 'grave offences' with young men and boys. He was given four years' imprisonment, the Judge telling him: 'you have pleaded guilty to a number of grave and unnatural offences, two of which were with young boys who were members of the Settlement of which you were Warden. You used your authority and position, as well as what can only be described as bribes, to persuade these young boys to submit to your indecent assaults . . . a man in your position owes a duty to others to set an example, and however unfortunate your own make-up may be, it cannot be allowed to be said that these Courts are prepared to allow this sort of conduct with boys to be carried on by people of education, position and responsibility.'[5]

## Fletcher-Cooke: An Error Of Judgement

As the Vassall affair (p. 61) peaked with the publication of the official inquiry report, the Macmillan Government was faced with another Ministerial resignation – that of Charles Fletcher-Cooke – and was just beginning to pick up the first ripples of the Profumo affair. Charles Fletcher-Cooke had been elected as Tory MP for Darwen, Lancashire, in 1951; he had previously been a barrister specialising in property, taxation and international law. In 1961 he was appointed to his first Ministerial post, Under Secretary of State at the Home Office. During his short career there he had to answer questions on juvenile courts, on current youth delinquency and those appointed to posts in residential youth establishments under Home Office control. In March 1963 a nineteen-year-old youth, Anthony Turner, pleaded guilty at Bow Street Magistrates Court to trespassing on the underground railway at Piccadilly Circus. It was also alleged that he had been arrested in Commercial Road, Stepney, driving a car while disqualified and without insurance, in excess of the speed limit. Back in Bow Street in March his record sheet showed convictions for possessing an offensive weapon and two disqualifications for driving without insurance. He told the police after the Stepney offence that the car belonged to Mr Fletcher-Cooke of North Court, Great Peter Street, Westminster, in whose flat he had been staying until he found a job and who said he could drive the car. Committed to London Sessions for sentence he was fined for speeding and trespass and, in April, sent for borstal training and banned from driving for five years.

In the meantime Fletcher-Cooke had indicated that he had no intention of resigning his seat but wished to resign his Ministerial office, writing to Harold Macmillan in February 1963:

Dear Prime Minister,

A great deal of publicity has been given to the case of a young man who is alleged to have committed a motoring offence while driving a car which I had lent him. At the Home Office I have been particularly concerned with the after-care of delinquents and it was in this connexion, and this connexion only, that I was introduced to and tried to help this young man. On reflection I think that what I tried to do, though well intentioned, was misguided and involved an error of judgement. I do not feel that I should continue my work at the Home Office much as I enjoy it. Moreover, I would like to be quite free to take legal action if so advised. In the circumstances the right course for me is to resign my post.

Macmillan replied at once: 'Dear Fletcher-Cooke, I read your letter with regret. But I am sure that you have taken the proper course in the circumstances, and I feel it right to accept your resignation.'

The Fletcher-Cooke business was quickly over, partly because it was a minor, personal matter, partly because whatever else he was, the young Turner posed no security risk and partly because, for critics in the media, it was not an Establishment issue, nor was Fletcher-Cooke, as Brian Inglis pointed out, one of those close to Macmillan and whom Macmillan could have, if he so wished, retained in office: 'Fletcher-Cooke was a public school product, but not an Establishment-minded man, and his appointment . . . to the Home Office had come as something of a surprise; it appeared that he must actually have been selected for his ability [and] his letter of resignation was precipitately accepted with none of the usual epistolary courtesies . . .'[6]

## The Kindly Politician and the Obliging Civil Servant: Galbraith and Vassall

Thomas Galloway Dunlop Galbraith was the eldest son of the 1st Baron Strathclyde, a life-long public figure who had served as an MP, government minister and Chairman of the North of Scotland Hydro-Electric Board. Galbraith went to Wellington School, Christ Church Oxford and Glasgow University, fought in the First World War, and at thirty-one was elected MP for Glasgow Hillhead: 'a moneyed man who because of his money, his diligence, his competence and his likeability, had found himself a comfortable but not very elevated niche in the Conservative Party'.[21] Galbraith was appointed to such worthy positions as Assistant Whip (1950), a Lord Commissioner of the Treasury (1951), Treasurer of H. M. Household (1955), Civil Lord at the Admiralty (1957) and Joint Parliamentary Under-Secretary of State at the Scottish Office (1959). Galbraith's downfall was the civil servant William Vassall; the circumstances of his resignation lay with the 1961 Navy Spy Ring scandal and the arrest of George Blake.

Michael Goleniewski, a Polish intelligence officer, began leaking information to the CIA in 1958 about Polish agents in advance of his subsequent defection. One name soon identified from the information passed by the CIA to MI5 was that of Harry Houghton. He had been caught dealing in the black market and recruited by the Polish intelligence service while he was working as a clerk in the naval attache's office in the British embassy in Warsaw: he was then taken over by the KGB. Despite a warning from his former office in Warsaw that he might be a security risk (he was a heavy drinker) Houghton was posted to the Underwater Weapons Establishment at Portland, Dorset, where his mistress Ethel Gee helped him obtain secrets about Britain's nuclear submarines and anti-submarine warfare. Covert MI5 and Special Branch surveillance followed Houghton to London – he always went there on the first Saturday of each month – where he met a Gordon Lonsdale who was apparently a Canadian businessman renting out bubblegum machines and jukeboxes. After a search of Lonsdale's deposit box in a Midlands Bank branch in London, Special Branch discovered spy equipment. Lonsdale was in fact Konon Trofimovich Molody (*alias* Colonel Georgi Lonoff) who had assumed the identity of a young Canadian. The real Gordon Arnold Lonsdale had died in Finland in 1932. The new Lonsdale had returned to the USA for his education, went back to Russia for his KGB training and re-emerged in North America in the 1950s. In 1955 the KGB placed Lonsdale in London as resident director and he set up a cover as a flamboyant businessman (he even won a prize at the 1960 Brussels International Trade Fair for a car burglar alarm) with a flat close to Regent's Park. Two other KGB agents, Peter and Helen Kroger, had also moved to London – their cover was a second-hand bookshop in The Strand – and set up a complex HQ in their Ruislip bungalow with a high-powered transmitter, anti-detection devices, expensive photographic equipment, a microdot reader and thousands of pounds and dollars. MI5, under the guidance of Peter Wright, traced Lonsdale to the Krogers' house.

When Goleniewski finally defected, MI5's assumption that the KGB would expect the London operation to be blown led to the immediate arrest of Houghton and Gee in January 1961 in the act of handing over hundreds of classified documents to Lonsdale in Waterloo Road, London. The arrest of the Krogers quickly followed and all five received heavy sentences. Later Molody was exchanged for the part-time spy Greville Wynne and the Krogers for an amateur pamphlet smuggler, Gerald Brooke. Before his defection Goleniewski had also offered another name, this time an MI6 agent working for the KGB who had betrayed agents working in Poland while being based in Berlin. It was clear, from backtracking agents' movements, that George Blake was the prime suspect. Soon after, Blake was arrested. Blake was a Dutch-Jewish refugee who was recruited into SOE, and then Naval Intelligence before joining MI6 in 1946. He learnt Russian, was interned during the Korean War, worked as Deputy Director (Technical Operations) in Berlin before returning to London to work at MI6 Headquarters. He had been involved in major espionage activities, including wire-tapping Soviet bloc embassies. The official version is that during his Korean experience his political views underwent a radical reappraisal and he became ideologically committed to the USSR. Current commentators suggest that he was in fact a longstanding convert to communism but that MI6 never vetted him properly. His return to London to work in MI6's HQ had been engineered to ensure he did not get suspicious and defect. When confronted with his spying he confessed to his covert activities. His trial, held in camera because of the seriousness of his spying and the extent of his betrayal of MI6 agents, resulted in a massive sentence of forty-two years' imprisonment; four years later in 1966 he escaped to Russia. The Government slapped D-notices on the trial but the scope of Blake's treachery was in the air. Says Chapman Pincher: 'Parliament sensed a scandal and the Labour Opposition, which missed no chance to claim that the Macmillan Government was lax on security, kept demanding the facts.'[7]

While this string of arrests and convictions were creditable successes for the security services, the early warning about Houghton and the extent of KGB penetration showed the security procedures and security services in less than a favourable light. The immediate government response was to set up committees of inquiry which, as tends to be their way, used the exposure of individuals to affirm the general integrity and soundness of the institutions for which they worked. The first was the Romer Committee inquiry into the Houghton and Blake affairs, which itself found 'the quality of the security organisation and procedures and the general standard of security discipline is good.' It was, however, somewhat blunt about the failure of security procedures relating to Houghton, in that not only was his drinking problem relayed to Portland but he had been inadequately investigated three times as a probable security risk.

In 1962 a second inquiry, Lord Radcliffe's Committee on Security Procedures in the Public Service, thought that those departments, like the Foreign Office, which had suffered security leaks and where the need for security was obvious to staff had improved: 'the standard of security organisation and personnel and the general feeling of alertness and care impressed us favourably.'

The Radcliffe committee believed that the positive vetting procedures were effective and helped 'to eliminate from sensitive posts persons obviously unsuitable on the ground of a patent character defect', and particularly commended the need to take very great care in the selection of staff who were attached to diplomatic Missions. The report was published in April 1962; in September 1962 William John Vassall was arrested in The Mall. The case was to be devastating for Vassall, Fleet Street, Galbraith and, in the ensuing antagonism between the press and politicians, for the Conservative Government.

Born in 1924 of a devoted Catholic nurse and a rugby-playing Church of England vicar, Vassall had a public school education where he developed an enthusiasm for older males, preferably good-looking, virile with an athletic build, to whom he could look up, and with whom he could fall in love. It was an enthusiasm he pursued wholeheartedly if discreetly all his life. He joined the Admiralty as a clerk after a spell in the Midland Bank and the RAF, and was selected to join the naval attache's staff in Moscow, his report suggesting that he 'should therefore prove a politically reliable clerk and steady character.' He was neither. Disliking the rigid formality of the Ambassador, the coolness of his superior (who complained of Vassall's 'irritating, effeminate personality') and the routine Embassy functions, Vassall decided to find his own way round Moscow's cultural activities. For this he approached a locally-employed interpreter, Sigmund Mikhailski. Such staff had to be hired from a State-controlled agency and, like the others, Mikhailski was a KGB agent, with whom Vassall had a brief liaison and who subsequently took him out to dinner on several occasions. At one restaurant they were joined by two men, one of whom 'looked at me with fire in his eyes': Vassall had just made eye-contact with a KGB 'swallow' – a homosexual agent trained in the act of picking up men of Vassall's proclivities. Vassall, a gregarious if vain social climber with a love of good clothes and a facility for enjoying himself, pursued his relationship with the fiery-eyed Russian who gradually introduced him into a Russian social circle in which the young Vassall was courted and entertained. As Rebecca West suggested later, Vassall worked hard to surround himself with congenial companions and envelop himself in a world where 'he could count himself brilliantly successful, as he was nowhere else, and that by the exercise of more positive characteristics than he apparently found it easy to display at other times.'[8]

The Russian introduced him to another lure, this time with a Mona Lisa smile and black penetrating eyes, who took him to a dinner party where drunk or drugged, or both, Vassall took part in a five-man sex orgy, 'enjoying every possible sex activity . . . oral, anal [and] a complicated array of sexual activities with a number of men'.[9] Vassall promptly forgot both the evening and a subsequent meeting with a senior KGB official to whom Vassall freely talked about his Embassy work; 'I felt compelled to go on, regardless of what I was saying', said Vassall later. Some months later, in March 1955, his Russian friend introduced him to a Russian army officer who wanted to make love to him – 'I was, of course, excited and stimulated by such a proposal . . . I found a kind of sanctuary in his arms', recalled Vassall. It was, of course, a trap; the lights went on and KGB officials waved photographs of the unorthodox dinner party under his nose. 'They had found out my weakest part, my deepest secret which only the people I had met in absolute privacy knew', said Vassall; the KGB impressed on him the gravity of his situation. His source of comfort, and the only person he told, was Sigmund Mikhailski. Thus cocooned, Vassall was regularly invited to meet KGB officers who courteously and solicitiously indicated their interest and concern for him; 'they appeared to want me as a kind of friend', said the incredulous Vassall. Vassall continued to lap up local culture and talent, went on a KGB holiday, pursued the round of embassy functions and performed his official duties without any sign of stress or tension. All the time the KGB patiently massaged his ego, eased his conscience and gave him money until he returned to London after his two-year tour of duty.

Back home, he was offered, and accepted, a post in the office of the Director of Naval Intelligence. He began supplying his Russian contact with information and documents: the Russians not only told him to buy a camera but also suggested he buy it abroad. The obedient Vassall trotted off to Hamburg via a Swiss holiday to buy one – and managed two holiday romances at the same time. A year later, in June 1957, Vassall was appointed Assistant Private Secretary to the new Civil Lord at the Admiralty, Tom Galbraith. Vassall's ingratiating and deferential manner, his enthusiasm for running around after his master, brought the sort of rewards he enjoyed. Galbraith invited him for lunch and drinks in the family home in London; Vassall got to carry official papers to Galbraith's Scottish mansion. He moved into a flat in Dolphin Square, (costing £400 a year on a £700 salary; the KGB were apparently paying him an equivalent amount), entertained, travelled abroad two or three times a year and continued his homosexual encounters. When he felt tense or depressed he went to talk to his Russian contact who 'helped me most, being the only person who knew how I felt . . . he was a man of the world and understood and had respect for my feelings.'[10] In October 1959 he was posted to the Naval Secretariat in the Admiralty, where he had access to armaments and radar materials as well as tactical and operational information. There were claims he even went out of his way to obtain classified information that his contacts did not realise he had access to when colleagues went on holiday and left keys with him.

After the Houghton arrest, Vassall was rested from spying by the KGB but reactivated in December 1961, the month Anatoli Golystin defected from Helsinki's KGB office and gave evidence that pointed to several spies, including Vassall. He was arrested in September 1962 after confirmation about his activities came from a further KGB defector. The DPP apparently went to see the Attorney-General with the cryptic message: 'we have arrested a spy who is a bugger, and a minister is involved.'

Once arrested Vassall made a full confession, although he later thought that '[I] was not necessarily to be held totally responsible for my actions. The authorities would have had to make out a good case that they were not partly responsible for the events which made this night-mare situation possible.'[11] He believed that his homosexuality, the effect that its admission may have had on his career and the unfriendly attitude of his superiors forced him into the KGB's arms. Even more incredibly he assumed that the security officers would see he was a 'victim of circumstances' and discreetly release and relocate him for a few years. Unfortunately for him the prosecution and judge had little time for him. Lust and greed, said Lord Justice Parker, prompted Vassall to attend the fateful dinner party and gave him eighteen years' imprisonment for some six years' spying.

The political storm that then engulfed Galbraith had been steadily building up a head of steam after the Houghton case. Labour MPs, with evidence of security shortcomings and the political target of Ministerial responsibility, wanted Lord Carrington, first Lord at the Admiralty, to resign. This he offered to do but Harold Macmillan declined to accept it. A civil servant at Portland was sacked and reforms were promised after the official inquiries but when Vassall was sentenced the press went to town on the Government. It was, according to Macmillan, 'terrible, without any sense of responsibility. They want sensation.'[12] Now, not only had the Romer Report's censure of inadequate security procedures been confirmed, not only had the promised reforms failed to catch Vassall but, to the simple minds of the public and press, Vassall the homosexual (and therefore axiomatic security risk) should have been easily identifiable (reflecting the climate of that time the *Sunday Mirror* ran an article 'How to spot a Homo'). An internal inquiry (the Cunningham inquiry) comprising civil servants, was set up in October 1962 to look at breaches of security arangements, failures in supervision and Vassall's employment on security work.

The press called again for Carrington's resignation on the grounds that this would demonstrate that the Government not only took the matter seriously but that it accepted political responsibility for what had happened. The Labour Opposition demanded an inquiry, partly on the grounds of Ministerial responsibility but largely about the 'position of the former Civil Lord, who seemed . . . to have social relationships with a minor official of the Admiralty which were quite inappropriate'. The implication, Ministerial culpability resulting from some 'unusual' personal relationship, was reiterated by George Brown, who told the House he had letters which 'indicate a degree of Ministerial responsibility which goes far beyond the ordinary business of a Minister in charge, being responsible for everything which goes on in his Department. The Lynskey Tribunal was set up to deal with a junior Minister for far less than is involved in this'. Brown, industrial adviser to the *Sunday Pictorial*, had obtained this correspondence from a *Sunday Pictorial* journalist and Vassall's solicitor. Since the Lynskey Tribunal involved bribery, influence – peddling and fraud, the Opposition were managing to imply much more serious misconduct, unnamed if alluded to, that in turn served to build up the atmosphere of innuendo and suspicion. It was made plain by the Labour Opposition that the letters would be made public if Macmillan did not act. He did, by referring them to the inquiry.

Galbraith had been on holiday when Vassall was arrested. On his return he faced a series of door-stepping journalists who not only emphasised the closeness of the relationship but suggested Vassall had used his visits to the Galbraith house to insinuate himself with his superiors and develop his 'all-round knowledge of Admiralty procedure'. The imputation was that in the rigid hierarchy of the civil service a government Minister and a member of the landed gentry would not normally entertain socially a mere clerk. The implication was that Galbraith was contributing to the activities of a spy and, worse, that that relationship had been concealed. As one Labour MP claimed, none of the charges against Vassall included spying during his time working for Galbraith; 'on the face of it, it certainly looks a little odd. We would like an explanation of why the courts did not refer to that period.' If press rumours about an alleged homosexual liaison weren't bad enough, there were even wilder allegations that the pair intended to run off to Russia together, that

Tory politicians were 'sheltering traitors in the Admiralty and almost of treachery itself.'[13]

On 8 November 1962 the letters, twenty-five of them, were officially published as the Cunningham inquiry's interim report on 'the relationship between Vassall and those for whom he worked'. This appeared restricted to Galbraith and his wife. Vassall worked for him between June 1957 and October 1959; Galbraith left office in October 1959; the letters are dated between September 1957 and April 1962. They began by revealing Galbraith's pleasantness to an incipient Jeeves – asking for papers to be taken to his home, arranging for Vassall to clear his office, to obtain Admiralty china, not to be bothered at home by official business, arranging meetings, and thanking him for his loyal service and friendship when he left office. The post-1959 letters were clearly responses to Vassall's attempts to keep in touch and to see if Galbraith could help his career, via holiday postcards and seasonal greetings. They were, as Rebecca West pointed out later, 'over-emphatic and twaddling because the writer was trying to discharge a moral obligation to be interested in a person whose interest for him was very slight indeed.'[14] The most that could be said against Galbraith, said the *Annual Register* later, 'was that he had suffered a socially pressing and plausible junior colleague a trifle too gladly'.[15]

The publication of the interim report led immediately to Galbraith's resignation on 8 November 1962. He announced: 'I am glad that their report has made clear that any imputation against me is unfounded. But it is apparent to me that my accustomed manner of dealing with officials and others who serve me has in the circumstances become an embarrassment to you and the Government. For this reason alone I feel that my only proper course is to tender my resignation.'

Galbraith's resignation was accepted immediately, although Macmillan would have preferred him to wait for the final outcome of the inquiry. Nevertheless, 'having tasted blood, the Press was thirsty for more. After all, this is the stuff that sells papers', said Randolph Churchill.[16] In any case the press were now attacking Lord Carrington, and Macmillan chose to end the 'dark cloud of suspicion and innuendo' by setting up a Tribunal of Inquiry in November.[17] This took over from the Cunningham inquiry to consider issues about neglect of duty by those responsible for Vassall's work and conduct, breaches of security arrangements, allegations against the honour and integrity of those involved in the case, and if other ministers knew of the existence of another spy at Portland. Under the chairmanship of Lord Radcliffe, Lord of Appeal, it first met in January 1963 and saw 142 witnesses. It was critical about Vassall. Although it accepted that he was not an ideologically-motivated spy it believed that he was defective in the power of judgement and had limited intellectual capacity. He was, nevertheless, 'pleasant to work with, a discreet, reserved and obliging man, well-spoken and in appearance neat and well-dressed.' On the other hand he was 'a weak character, with little sense of responsibility, little power of resistance to pressure and susceptible to appeals to his vanity'. He was 'captured' by the Russians and controlled by a mixture of criminal and social menaces, and skilful persuasion. Nevertheless the discretion with which he pursued his homosexuality, the even tenor and helpfulness of his work, the lack of clear evidence of extravagance (Vassall always alluded to family means and legacies to explain his circumstances) and the lack of suspicious characteristics that may have been discovered by the vetting procedures, all suggested to the Tribunal that no-one and no system was particularly at fault for letting him get to where he was.

On the other hand the Tribunal was scathing about the press's happy knack of turning surmise into fact and invention into headlines. It found no evidence for their allegations that he 'strutted round Moscow like a dressed-up doll', that his conduct was notorious, or that a senior official helped Vassall avoid the vetting procedures and get promotion. It was equally dismissive of the press's attempts to insinuate a relationship between Vassall and Galbraith. Vassall was a 'namedropper', a 'somewhat insinuating young man who liked to develop any social contacts' which came his way but had also formed a genuine admiration and attachment to Mr Galbraith who

71

'was a kindly and considerate head of his office who liked to encourage some personal relations with those who served him as his staff'. The contents of the correspondence 'are never more than trivial and are always correct.' The Tribunal accused the press – and that included most Fleet Street newspapers – of fabrication, chequebook journalism, speculation, innuendo and gossip-mongering. When it tried to prise some of the journalists' sources of information out of them, it took action against three who refused to reveal them; two were sent to prison for contempt.

Macmillan himself understood the consequences for the Government and himself. He wrote: 'It will be seen, therefore, that during this period, by an extraordinary combination of circumstances or an exceptional run of ill-luck, Parliament and the public were being continually stimulated into a sense almost of hysteria . . . It infuriated Fleet Street, at every level of activity, and made the newspapers anxious to seek and exploit any possibility of counter-attack.' Wearily he noted in his diary the first murmuring of the Profumo scandal: 'Unhappily, another wave of painful and damaging rumours had begun to circulate. This time, however, although cloaked under the cover of security, they were moving into the realm of scandal.'[18] The majority of the Press was certain that the Radcliffe Tribunal had been set up as a political means to chastise them and were somewhat aggrieved at the censure and jail sentences handed out. Editors were convinced that only their persistence made the Government take security seriously, and that their vigilance was the only protection against the erosion of democracy and 'predatoriness of officialdom'. There were others, however, like Macmillan, who believed that the press had been left 'resentful at the way in which its less reputable methods, of building a tower of innuendo upon a foundation of rumour and labelling the result a house of fact, had been exposed. There could now be little doubt that the man at the head of the Government which had put them on such public trial would, if he was ever caught in their trap, be shown no mercy.'[19]

The Profumo affair begins with Christine Keeler. She was a tomboy who, at fifteen, decided to escape to London, away from a drab existence in a converted railway carriage in a rundown part of the Buckinghamshire village of Wraysbury, a dull job in Slough and a stepfather she couldn't get on with. Within months her looks and self-confidence took her from being a waitress at a Greek restaurant to some modelling assignments and a job as a £8.50-a-week topless dancer at Murray's Cabaret Club. There she met Stephen Ward, thirty years her senior, a thin, elegant man, a talented artist who qualified as an osteopath at Kirksville, Missouri. He combined his profession with his social charm and gregariousness, expanding his Harley Street practice to cater for politicians, royalty and showbusiness figures: he was the 'society osteopath' in the Fifties. He liked company, he liked doing favours for people, he liked new experiences – with a particular preference for attractive young women, often prostitutes, pleasing status figures he could mould and display in public. He himself said: 'I would say I was one of the most successful men in town with girls . . . I'm not handsome and I've no money. What is it then? . . . I know I understand a woman's mind.'[20] The girls were there to impress his circle of friends but also expected to join in the circle's enthusiasm for sex and parties.

Ward 'was, in a sense, a beatnik; smooth, charming and intelligent but none the less a scavenger of experience . . . any man powered by an uncontrollable desire to fulfil his image of himself would be inclined to accelerate the search, at a time when more stable men are coming to terms with themselves. And Ward's beatnik side was beginning to require stronger kicks'.[21]

Those kicks primarily concerned soft drugs and up-market sex orgies at which Ward was an enthusiastic onlooker: 'I think', said one girlfriend, 'it gave him immense excitement and satisfaction to watch someone else making love to a girl of whom he was fond. And the more passionate or violent the sex act the more it seemed to satisfy him.' Not that he was averse, as Christine Keeler said later, to joining in one 'mass of heaving bodies', but his preferred relationship with the girls he picked up was that of a paternal Professor Higgins with a streak of sexual deviance thrown in. Part of that streak manifested itself in his asking them to make love to men he invited to his flat sometimes for free (or fun) and sometimes for money.

He also took them to a cottage he rented for £1 a year from one of his patients, Lord Astor, in the grounds of Cliveden estate. The cottage was Ward's pride and joy, a rural retreat in upper-class surroundings to which he invited a cosmopolitan mix of weekend guests, spiced with 'chases in the woodlands, the childhood games played by adults in the nude, the fishing of girls from the Thames by rod and line.'

One of his favourite guests was Eugene Ivanov, Assistant Naval Attaché with the rank of Lieutenant-Commander at the Russian Embassy in London since March 1960. In April 1961 Colonel Oleg Penkovsky, a senior GRU officer, was being debriefed by MI6 and the CIA in London, which he was visiting as part of a Soviet Trade delegation after offering to supply information to the West. (He was allegedly executed in 1963; his British contact, Greville Wynne, went to prison). Penkovsky named Ivanov as a GRU intelligence officer with a decided leaning toward Western decadence. By that time Ward was seeing Ivanov regularly, after meeting him at the invitation of Sir Colin Coote, editor of the *Daily Telegraph*, over lunch at the Garrick Club. (Coote was Ward's patient; Ward wanted to go to Russia to sketch the politicians and Coote knew Ivanov). A recent suggestion is that Coote, a friend of Sir Roger Hollis, then head of MI5, may have arranged the meeting to introduce Ivanov to Ward and thus to the delights of Ward's demi-monde. MI5 already knew that Ward was 'the provider of popsies for rich people' because they had a section that monitored the 'mood' of people in influential circles. Ward and Ivanov got on well together, going to play bridge at the Connaught Club and working on the garden at Cliveden. There Ivanov met Christine Keeler: 'to me he was an exotic, glamorous figure, with impeccable manners.' On a journey back from the cottage they went to Ward's Wimpole Mews flat to drink vodka and then 'he gave me the kiss we had both been waiting for and we made marvellous passionate love. He was gorgeous, so utterly masculine, we were for a while totally swept away.'[22] There is some doubt whether Keeler and Ivanov actually ever consummated their meeting but that was less important than the fact that others thought they had or could have done so. During that weekend, however, Keeler had also met another man, Jack Profumo.

Then forty-six, Profumo was definitely a rising Tory star. Son of a successful barrister, with a considerable family income invested in an insurance company and a country squire's lifestyle, Profumo moved from Harrow to Oxford to a world tour and the beginnings of a political career in East Fulham, whose MP was Bill Astor. In 1940, as a young army officer, he won Kettering with an 11,298 majority before ending up a Lieutenant-Colonel on Field Marshal Alexander's HQ staff. Losing his seat in 1945 he stayed with the army until 1947, joined the Conservative Central Office as the Party's broadcasting adviser and won Stratford-on-Avon in 1950. He got his first Ministerial post in 1952, married the actress Valerie Hobson, then playing the lead in *The King and I*, in 1954 and in 1960 was appointed Secretary of State for War. He had charm, enthusiasm and all the right connections.

In July he had accepted a house-party invitation to Cliveden. On the Saturday evening he and Lord Astor were strolling past the swimming pool as the naked Keeler clambered out. A game of chase was followed by drinks at Cliveden House, enlivened with a later chase around the rooms for a kiss and 'a little surreptitious grope.' The next day Profumo asked Keeler for her telephone number. Later Ward egged her on to meet him, and, within a week, Profumo drove her to his Regents Park house for the first 'very, very well-mannered screw of convenience', repeated later in Ward's flat and, athletically, in a Mini Minor. He gave her presents and 'money for her mother' – what Lord Denning later called in his Report 'a polite way' of paying for her services.

At this point the different strands collided. After learning of Ivanov's KGB status MI5 trailed him to Ward's flat and considered mounting a blackmail or entrapment operation against him.[23] In June 1961 an MI5 officer had contacted Ward about his relations with Ivanov and learnt of the Cliveden weekend. MI5 told Ward to keep in touch but were worried that Profumo's presence might complicate any entrapment. Through the Home Secretary, Sir Norman Brook, Profumo was first warned of MI5's interest and then asked to help in the operation. He refused, but in the mistaken belief that MI5 knew of his affair with Keeler, hastily sent to her in August the notorious letter saying he would be unable to see her for some time – 'something's blown up tomorrow night and I can't therefore make it ... please take great care of yourself and don't run away.' The affair was effectively over and it would appear that Profumo may have assumed that, warned to behave, the matter was being decently buried through the old-boy network. Certainly his future conduct would suggest that he believed any evidence, if any existed, was never likely to be used to contradict him.

Ward, in the meantime, had egged on Keeler to stay with her two new-found friends because he saw a new game, telling her 'Eugene on one hand and Jack on the other, you'll be ruling the world next or starting the next war.' At that time he allegedly asked Keeler to find out 'when the Germans get the bomb' from Profumo. Ward's politics were liberal and, as far as they took any definite shape, were pro-Russian because he was anti-American. Ward believed that, with his wide circle of well-connected friends, his contact with MI5 and his friendship with a Soviet agent (who may have encouraged him in his belief), he could play at being an unofficial but influential go-between, first over the September 1961 Berlin crisis and then over the October 1962 Cuban missile crisis. Using MP contacts, and Lord Astor's aristocratic old-boy network, he sought to impress on the Foreign Office and ministers that he could assist in the efforts for world peace. MI5 were approached for information but did nothing other than tell the Foreign Office in November 1962 that 'it would be most unwise to trust him.' One recent theory is that both Ivanov and Penkovsky were messengers for Kremlin 'doves' who wanted to warn the West that Krushchev could not sustain a nuclear war and to try and persuade Kennedy through influential intermediaries that he should seek a negotiated settlement of the Cuban crisis.[24]

In November 1962 Profumo clashed with George Wigg, the dogged, self-appointed security-minded Labour MP with a deeply-held passion for the army and the serving conditions of its men. Wigg had been concerned over a June 1961 exercise to protect Kuwait from a belligerent neighbour and test the army's response time to an overseas crisis. The exercise resulted in stories of heat exhaustion, seized-up machinery and showed up gaps in the War Office's deployment strategy. Wigg, who considered that the blue-blooded Profumo had no affinity with the ordinary soldier and his needs, got hard evidence of the Kuwaiti errors and he and Profumo agreed a means of airing them in Parliament. In November, however, Profumo procedurally outmanoeuvred him so he could not debate the issue or repudiate Profumo's counter-claims. Wigg was, in his own words, 'trussed up and done.'

In February 1962 Christine Keeler had moved from Ward's flat to a flat in Dolphin Square, in the Chelsea heartland, to indulge in her favourite pursuits, primarily as good a time as possible. After a short spell living with Lucky Gordon, a West Indian jazz singer, she went off to the United States with a friend, Mandy Rice-Davies. As 'Miss Austin' at the Earls Court Motor Show, Rice-Davies attracted sufficient attention to encourage her to desert the Birmingham council estate where she lived and move to London. On the advice of a girl she met at the Show she auditioned for and was hired by Murray's Cabaret Club where she shared a room, and later a flat with Keeler. Through Keeler she met Peter Rachman, a displaced Jewish-Pole who had experienced the Russian labour camps and settled in London after the war as a tailor's assistant.[25] On the suggestion of a prostitute he set up a flat agency, renting flats and sub-letting them to her friends and more orthodox clients, working for local landlords as a sub-letter and rent-collector before deciding to deal in property.

Business contacts with other dealers, and building societies and solicitors with access to loans and mortgages, brought him into the world of end-of-lease and rundown freehold properties where vacant possession, ignorance of the law and cheapness combined to give Rachman a fortune and a reputation for running noisy, overcrowded, poorly-furnished flats in rundown areas. Certainly his ramshackle empire was protected by a labyrinth of companies, creative accounting and muscle-bound employees not known for their customer relations. He loved women, as many as possible, and Rice-Davies was one in a long line of mistresses. He installed her in a luxurious flat – with expensive presents, clothes and horseriding to keep her happy – although she kept her contacts with Ward and Keeler and moved back to Ward's flat in the summer of 1962. She remained there when Rachman died in November and was there when one of Keeler's lovers, Johnny Edgecombe, tried to shoot open the door in December.

Keeler had been alternating between two lovers, Edgecombe and Lucky Gordon, who fought over her in the All-Nighter black club in Wardour Street in October. Gordon got his face slashed; Keeler went to live with Edgecombe but soon tired of life in Brentwood and returned to Ward. Edgecombe was reluctant to let her go. Just how reluctant he showed when, in December 1962, he turned up at Ward's flat where Keeler was discussing her future with Rice-Davies, and shot up the door. After Edgecombe's arrest (charges were later dropped), whether through panic or to build up her own importance, Keeler began talking. Those who listened were to include the police and John Lewis, a former Labour MP, who disliked Ward intensely because of Ward's appearance on his wife's behalf in their 1954 divorce and because of a subsequent, abortive libel action. Lewis repeated the story to George Wigg in January 1963. Wigg had been alerted the previous November by a mysterious phone call the previous November which had told him; 'forget the Vassall case; you want to look at Profumo.' Lewis kept him informed of developments, including the security issue that was the spark of Wigg's sustained interest – the suggestion Keeler was asked by Ward to find out from Profumo about the nuclear arming of West Germany. Wigg went to Wilson who was reluctant to raise the issue publicly at that time; 'if it emerged that a rich Tory MP with a responsibility for security had been guilty of a serious indiscretion, it would document Wilson's allegations more vividly than tens of thousands of words. But if Wilson or the Labour Party were thought to be smearing a Minister for a moral dereliction, of interest only to his wife, it would rebound against them.'[26]

In the same month that the Labour Party were learning the details of Keeler's life, Fleet Street were preparing them for print. Her life story, together with the 'don't run away' letter from Profumo, had been bought by the *Sunday Pictorial* in January 1963 for £1000 but publication was delayed pending her signature verifying that the letter was genuine. Both Ward and Profumo were interested in stopping publication for different reasons although neither were prepared to go so far as to pay Keeler the 'recompense' that her solicitor asked of both, in return for non-publication (he wanted £3000 then £5000, a claim that seemed to some of the Government Ministers who were to become involved with the allegations against Profumo that this could be a blackmail attempt). Ward, who managed to kill the story by claiming it was inaccurate and threatening to sue, made desperate efforts to use his contacts to stop publication. The allegations now reached Government Ministers, either from a Tory MP who was a barrister or a newspaper executive who was once a Tory Party official (or both). The Attorney-General and the Solicitor-General questioned Profumo. He denied the rumours, pointing out that using 'Darling' in a letter was not synonymous with an admission of adultery and that the Christine Keeler he had met in 1961 was a very different person from that of 1963. He also saw the Director-General of MI5 in the vain hope that a D-notice could be served. Meanwhile the police had visited Keeler in connection with the forthcoming Edgecombe trial and learned that Ward was a 'procurer' (Keeler was somewhat upset at Ward's interference) and that he had asked her to obtain 'atomic secrets' from Profumo with whom she had had 'an association'. There followed a lacuna of official distribution of information. The police gave their information only to Special Branch. Nothing was passed on to the Home Secretary and no follow-up interviews were conducted: 'an unfortunate decision', said Denning later, 'another failure in coordination', and he was concerned that the police believed that 'in so far as it concerned private morals it would not be for them to report it to anyone.' As far as the security aspect was concerned, the police felt they had fulfilled their duty by informing Special Branch. Special Branch had informed MI5 who had in any case learnt of the story and the letter from the *News of the World*'s general manager, and the former director of research at the Conservative Central Office, who also passed on the story to Macmillan's Principal Private Secretary; he then checked with MI5 and decided to ask Profumo about its validity. MI5's Deputy Director-General had already told the Prime Minister's PPS he knew of the background to the story and, despite the concern of Ward's case-officer that they could be criticised for failing to bring the story to light, agreed with MI5's Director-General, Sir Roger Hollis, that there was nothing further to do. Even after Special Branch's visit, MI5's bosses decided: 'no action on this at present.'

Consequently the senior government officers had little to go on but rumours, and Profumo's version of events. Profumo had several meetings with senior Government officers, including the Attorney-General, the Solicitor-General and the Chief Whip, at the end of January and beginning of February. Each time, despite invitations to be absolutely frank, Profumo denied any sexual association and made it plain he was prepared to take legal action. He argued passionately that 'in the particular climate of opinion then prevailing . . . there would be those who would disbelieve him, but that it would be grossly unfair that he should be driven from public life and into ruin when he was totally innocent . . .'[27] Later, questions were to be asked about why such senior, experienced and politically-sensitive officers allowed themselves to believe that Profumo could satisfy them that he was totally, unequivocally, innocent, particularly as the Solicitor-General had told Profumo that the Tory party was in the business of winning and keeping power: it would have no scruples 'in sacrificing any of its servants should interest demand it'. 'It seemed impossible to doubt the man', journalist Iain Crawford suggested later of their attitude. 'He had vigorously denied the most scandalous rumours and was energetically setting about taking legal action to stifle them. No man who was not innocent and who had so much to lose would dare behave in this forthright way unless he was guiltless. Suspicion quickly melted into sympathy for a colleague who had been wrongly and disgracefully abused.'[28] Similar concern was later expressed over the passive rôles of Special Branch and MI5. The former felt it had done its duty by informing MI5; the latter would argue that, without Ivanov, who had returned to Moscow, the issue of security had evaporated and that little credence could be given to either Ward's or Keeler's 'nuclear arming of Germany' tales. Moreover, according to their rules of operations, even if Profumo had had a relationship with her, as now seemed probable, it was no concern of MI5's; 'a Minister's private life was of no concern to MI5 if it did not endanger the safety of the realm.'[29] More jaundiced critics, who believe Roger Hollis to be a Soviet agent, assume it was a plot to starve politicians of information and ensure maximum public embarrassment when the row broke.[30]

The row did break publicly in March when Andrew Roth's weekly insider newsletter, *Westminster Confidential*, reported the outlines of the cancelled press story, the letter and the security aspects, as a filler after the collapse of his intended story on foreign exchange rates. His source was Henry Kerby, a right-wing MP with MI6 connections. Shortly before its publication, the Edgecombe trial, postponed since February because of a witness's illness, surfaced in the Old Bailey, without its star witness. 'She had disappeared', said the prosecution counsel. In fact, Keeler had had enough and gone off to Spain with a boyfriend. That sparked off more rumours that she 'had been got out of the way for political reasons', rumours strong enough for the Attorney-General to ask Profumo again if he was involved.

Macmillan had heard the outlines of the story in February on his return from an official visit to Italy, and also his Chief Whip's warning that it was a potential scandal. It appears that Macmillan knew of the allegations from American sources but, because the Radcliffe Tribunal was then savaging the press for rumour-mongering, because there was no security risk and because Profumo was adamant about his innocence, chose not to make an issue of the story – a decision that reflected his dislike of discussing such matters personally. 'Profumo,' he wrote, 'has behaved foolishly and indiscreetly, but not wickedly. His wife . . . is very nice and sensible. Of course, all these people move in a selfish, theatrical, bohemian society, where no one really knows anyone and everyone is "darling". But Profumo does not seem to have realised that we have – in public life – to observe different standards from those prevalent today in many circles.'[31] Now, with Keeler's disappearance, Macmillan was forced to pay more attention to this 'silly scrape' being talked about in 'the whispering gallery of London'. But before he could decide what to do to protect the reputation of the Party and Government the Labour Party stepped into the affair. Despite what in retrospect might appear as a planned attempt by Labour politicians to attack the government, their early efforts were relatively uncoordinated. Wigg wanted to act to anticipate the impending climax forewarned by *Westminster Confidential*; Wilson wanted to 'play it cool'. Indeed, when Wigg raised the story, Crossman, Castle, Foot and Shore 'all advised Harold very strongly against it and in a way rather squashed George'. Wigg knew Castle was going to raise the rumours of the disappearing Keeler during the debate on the jailed Vassall journalists on 21 March, so he and Crossman 'thought we had better get in first'[32] because Wigg, alleging Castle was being briefed by a newspaper to 'spill' the scandal, thought she would 'do it wrong.' Both men called for a Select Committee to dispel rumours and protect the honour of the Minister concerned 'from the imputation and innuendoes'. Forty minutes later Castle popped up to say her piece – in 'a manner maladroit and unfortunate', said Wigg: 'nothing could have been more helpful to the rattled Government than to drag the red herring of Miss Keeler's disappearance across the trail'.[33]

Wigg and Crossman believed they had 'blown the story'. Even so, the Conservative hierarchy determined to deal with the allegations at once: the MPs who raised the matter in debate 'really helped Profumo', thought Macmillan, because there were now allegations to repudiate, something Profumo had promised to do. That night Profumo was hauled from his bed at 2.45 a.m. to meet the Leader of the House, the two Law Officers and the Chief Whip. Rather than a further inquisition – they now believed his denials of adultery with Keeler and such denials removed the basis for believing the further allegations of his being a security risk and spiriting away a court witness – they wanted to prepare a firm statement of rebuttal 'publicly to scotch the rumours and nail the lies'. From a man with two hours' sleep induced by sleeping pills this was unfortunate: 'The meeting of Ministers, convened in haste and panic, was a disaster. Profumo was in no state to take part in discussions which would obviously have far-reaching consequences . . . Extreme states of sleep deprivation can cause disturbances in understanding, perception, attention awareness . . . statesmen and officials are rarely allowed the luxury of quiet reflection and adequate time in order to weigh the pros and cons in moments of crisis . . . long past the normal hour for retiring these officials, in varying stages of exhaustion, irritation and exasperation, were compelled to draft the fatal speech that cooler heads and clearer minds might have made less incriminating for the unlucky Minister.'[34] The Solicitor-General, however, said later that he had no impression that Profumo was drowsy or that there was any lack of understanding.

The speech, delivered at 11.08 that morning, 22 March, was concise and explicit: Profumo accepted that the rumours involved himself and that he knew Ward, Keeler and Ivanov. He denied any involvement with disappearing witnesses and stressed that there was 'no impropriety whatsoever in my acquaintanceship with Miss Keeler', threatening to sue anyone who said otherwise. His colleagues were happy: no-one, particularly a Tory gentleman, would have the effrontery to lie so blatantly.

Since the Labour MPs' charges, particularly Castle's, specifically mentioned the court case, Profumo may have assumed that 'the nature of the charges against him, once they were made . . . led to his resolve to lie his way out of his actual sin by being given the opportunity to answer groundless allegations with absolute honesty.'[35] Wigg was furious: 'I left with black rage in my heart . . . I had been trussed up and done again'. Profumo's absolute denial of any involvement with Keeler or her movements had made it appear that the Labour MPs had used Parliamentary privilege deliberately to smear a Minister. Profumo's 'categorical statement' settled the matter for Macmillan, a confidence confirmed when Profumo later successfully sued two foreign newspapers for repeating the allegations. For Crossman it was a defeat: 'we were extremely isolated. I think the people on our own side much disliked what we had done. George and I both felt that it was now absolutely vital to lie low.'[36] Nevertheless Wigg made one last statement that was the direct cause of the scandal's dramatic climax. He went on *Panorama* the following Monday and baldly stated that Ivanov and Ward were security risks. Wigg and Wilson were now convinced, largely through the latter's intuition, that security was still the issue and in the debate on the Vassall Tribunal on 25 May Wigg made it plain he was not giving up the chase. As Crossman said later: 'one man can do incredible things if he works hard enough and is sufficiently tenacious and unrelenting and singleminded.' Certainly the *Panorama* programme gave him the evidence he wanted. Ward called Wigg and, looking like 'a shivering jelly', arrived at the Commons to make a long rambling statement that Wilson later described to the House in June as 'a nauseating document taking the lid off a corner of the London underworld of vice, dope, marijuana, blackmail and counter-blackmail, violence, petty crime, together with references to Mr Profumo and the Soviet attaché.'

Wilson sent Macmillan a copy, only to be fobbed off with the reply that he would 'get in touch with you later on, if it seems necessary', and, later, 'there seems nothing in the papers you sent me which requires me to take further action.' Macmillan believed he was 'engrossed in far more important issues' and, in any case, the Home Secretary had already elicited from MI5 and the police on 27 March an assurance that any security angle was not worth pursuing because the witnesses were too unreliable and that Ward's private life was no matter for the security services. Nevertheless that meeting did precipitate police inquiries, alleged by some commentators to be intended to shut Ward up or to charge and thus discredit him by insinuating the possibility that he was living off immoral earnings, inquiries that Ward considered so damaging 'both professionally and socially' that he had a meeting with Macmillan's PPS and wrote letters to several politicians, including Wilson, arguing that, as a result of protecting Profumo, he was being persecuted. As subsequent investigations have shown, Ward was right in his assumptions. Whether by a direct order or because the police and the judiciary sensed that Ward was *the* malign influence who had caused all the furore, it was Ward alone who was arraigned and convicted on the flimsiest evidence as the appeasing sacrifice.[37] The Labour Opposition used the existence of these letters to force Macmillan into setting up an inquiry under Lord Dilhorne, the Lord Chancellor, to review the security issues. Profumo was called back from holiday to be interviewed and decided to own up. Why he chose to do so at this stage is still unclear. The various recent allegations – that MI5 wrote anonymously to his wife, that government sources warned him that the contents of Ward's letter would severely implicate him or that the same sources warned him of the existence of a tape made by Keeler – are based on a belief that Profumo had been compromised and that his continued tenure of office would only be an increasing embarrassment to MI5 (trying to conceal its role in recruiting Ward) and the Government. Therefore he was persuaded to go or realised he had no other choice.

On 5 June journalists were informed of his letter of resignation: 'rumour had charged me with assisting in the disappearance of a witness and of being involved in some possible breach of security. So serious were these charges that I allowed myself to think that my personal association with that witness, which had also been the subject of rumour was, by comparison, of minor importance only. In my statement I said that there had been no impropriety in this association. To my very deep regret I have to admit that this is not true, and that I misled you and my colleagues, and the House.'

The resignation released the restrictions on press comment and gave the politicians a far more useful means to attack the Government – not the security issue but the issue of who was to blame for Profumo's longevity with the lie. The five Cabinet Ministers who helped Profumo draft the fateful statement were the subject of accusations of deceit, gullibility or incompetence but Peter Rawlinson, the Solicitor-General, was to say later that the late-night meeting was not an inquiry but a 'council of war' about how best to exploit the opportunity of rebuttal. Rawlinson believed that he was completely deceived both professionally and personally by 'what was not only a wicked series of lies, but was also a most brazen and convincing performance'. Between the resignation and the debate on 21 June the scandal erupted; said Bernard Levin, the 'flood waters poured, unchecked, into the valleys of public life, sweeping everything before them in a great release of joy in the depravity of others.'[38]

On 5 June the Old Bailey trial of Lucky Gordon began, with charges of assault against Christine Keeler who arrived at the court in a chauffeur-driven Rolls Royce. On 8 June Stephen Ward was arrested for living off immoral earnings. On 9 June the *News of the World* ran her £23,000 life story. Between these events and the great Parliamentary debate the rumour machine went into top gear. Apart from the nine High Court judges supposedly involved in an orgy, there was a Minister who nearly rented another cottage from Astor (he prudently pulled out of negotiations in April) which was translated into his having 'close relations' with Ward and his girls, another who was supposed to be an organiser of orgies at Ward's cottage, a third Minister apparently seen with Keeler in a London nightclub and a fourth attending orgies wearing nothing but a small lace apron around his waist and a black mask over his face.

Probably the silliest, but most revealing, rumour was the photograph of the body of a naked man used as evidence in the Argyll divorce case, which was claimed to be that of a Minister who paid money through Ward to keep his name out of the trial. Not only did Denning later decide to investigate this rumour during his inquiry but, with the Minister's agreement, checked both his handwriting and bank balance to prove he had not handed over any money and then got a Harley Street consultant to inspect him to make sure it was not his body in the photograph. As Levin suggests: 'even in years so copiously provided with material on which madness could feel fat, there was one episode which stands out from the decade, and still stands out, as a monument to the willingness of man to suspend the operation of reason . . . how it came about, almost exactly two-thirds of the way through the twentieth century, and in a country as advanced as Britain, that a judge should have been obliged to ask a doctor to examine the penis of a politician, is something so extraordinary, and in many ways so significant, that it deserves examination as detailed as that which the Minister underwent.'[39]

The next, more public, examination was that of Macmillan by the Labour Party. Harold Wilson had gone off to Moscow warning Macmillan that 'there is such a background of rumour, innuendo and suspicion that we think the right thing is to clear this up with a direct confrontation with the Prime Minister as soon as the House resumes.' This time the 'cool and collected' Wilson and Wigg planned the preparations for the confrontation in the Commons, stopping Labour MPs airing their views on TV, planning the order and content of speeches, ensuring Macmillan would not be able to feed off heckling and interruptions when he spoke – all intended to undermine the public image of the Conservatives and 'so assist the conditions for a Labour Party victory at the next Election.' In the event Wilson offered a restrained recital of the events surrounding Profumo's resignation, pointing up Macmillan's 'unflappability and unconcern' as evidence of ignorance or collusion and taking a sideswipe at the effects of Tory leadership: 'the sickness of an unrepresentative sector of our society should not detract from the robust ability of our people as a whole to face the challenge of the future. And in preparing to face that challenge, let us frankly recognize that the inspiration and the leadership must come first here in this House.'

Macmillan's poor response reflected the deep personal hurt he had felt at the affair – the lies, the deception, the lack of information – but he pinned his hopes on the argument that in acting as he did, 'honourably and justly', then he should be believed to have acted 'with proper diligence and prudence'. He was, he argued, 'entitled to the sympathetic understanding and confidence of the House and of the country.' Unfortunately, among his silent colleagues, his 'reply commanded the respect due to frankness, but hardly the confidence which can only be earned by the addition of activity to integrity, and of judgement to faith.'[40] Unfortunate, also, was the contrast between his resigned defence of the affair and the spirited response of ministers like Hailsham, who had hissed out his contempt for 'a woman of easy virtue and a proved liar' and Selwyn Lloyd who demanded 'courageous and confident leadership not based on expediency but upon obedience to high moral standards'. The plaintiveness and lack of firm leadership, so different from his Cabinet reshuffle the previous July, only served to unlease 'the fury and discontent' in the Party, as Crossman put it, or 'one of those attacks of hysteria' as Macmillan called it, that the Parliamentary Party underwent both during and after the debate.

Although he later regained control of the party and his confidence – telling Wilson not to 'try on the crown early in his life' – his decline was inevitable, particularly when his prostate problem hospitalised him, and he chose to resign in October. Had he not then he would still have to take the full brunt of the fading scandal. On 3 August Stephen Ward committed suicide, before Mr Justice Marshall, 'a Cornwall congregationalist and non-Conformist Liberal, reared and nurtured in the great English Puritan tradition',[41] could sentence him for living off the immoral earnings of Keeler and Rice-Davies, adjudged by the jury to have been prostitutes. Both decisions were based on an 'admittedly tenuous and delicate balance of probabilities' but were inevitable after a trial which revealed to a still-fascinated public a world of promiscuity, perjured evidence, flagellation (at £1 a stroke), two-way mirrors and the occasional orgy. The following month the official end to the affair (the political world was now more interested in Philby, Rachmanism and Macmillan's successor) appeared in the all-time best-selling HMSO publication – the Denning Report – which suggested that immorality and discreditable behaviour were only security risks if the circumstances could lead to blackmail or undue pressures. Homosexuality and perverted practices with prostitutes were risks but clandestine adultery with someone not likely to resort to blackmail less so: 'in short, every case of immorality and discreditable conduct must depend on its own special circumstances.' Denning believed that what was at issue in dealing with allegations of such behaviour was less that of the fact than the reasonable belief of the fact. He suggested that 'it was the responsibility of the Prime Minister and his colleagues' to deal with rumours involving such circumstances, and theirs alone. No single politician, he concluded, was to blame for the Profumo affair other than the failure of the Prime Minister and his colleagues for not acting on a reasonable belief that Profumo was misbehaving. But the report never touched on the context in which it happened and, as Wayland Young suggests, Denning's Report had to be both personal and inconclusive, otherwise it would 'have led to a wholesale condemnation of certain structures of loyalty and complicity which are hard for anyone to see and understand, and especially hard for those who, like the judges, live and work at the heart of the establishment which sustains those structures'.[42] Whether Profumo was ultimately pushed or ditched by his colleagues or by MI5, or whether he went honourably and of his own volition, is less important than the fact that, once he and therefore the major source of public embarrassment had gone, Ward could be arraigned and convicted on evidence that did not relate to Profumo but which could effectively portray him as evil and immoral, as well as criminal, and thus thoroughly discredit him in an act of public exorcism. By focusing all the attention on Ward as the sole cause of Profumo's downfall – and that in itself caused only by his stupidly coming into contact with and being contaminated by Ward's world – the whole business took on an act of public exorcism reminiscent of the old treason trials. When Ward committed suicide Denning was able to publish his Report as the final chapter that protected the workings of the Establishment from being asked to explain who was using whom for what purpose. Nevertheless, the Tory Party knew that, in terms of sexual escapades at least, they did not want any further embarrassment and they moved swiftly to sort out the last scandal of the Macmillan era.

## The Sexy Tale of an Old Sea-Dog: Anthony Courtney

The dying embers of the Profumo scandal flickered briefly in the same constituency where the first scandal of the Macmillan era began, to extinguish the political career of one more Conservative politician. Harrow East's reaction to the embarrassment of Ian Harvey's resignation was to choose his intellectual and social opposite – an ebullient, middle-aged former naval officer with a bluff no-nonsense manner. Unfortunately for Harrow East, Commander Anthony Courtney also had a penchant, if not for feasting, then nibbling with the panthers. 'What more natural than that a widowed sailor should in the course of his travels take a pretty woman friend to a hotel bedroom?' asked former MP Donald Johnson.[43] What indeed, unless the KGB are on the other side of the bedroom wall with a camera and the intention to teach one of their critics a lesson in security matters. Anthony Courtney's interest in Russia began in childhood when his father was exporting machine tools there before the 1917 Revolution. Before entering Naval Intelligence Courtney had become a fluent Russian speaker. He ended up in the British Naval Mission in Moscow during the Second World War. In 1946 he was put in charge of the Russian section of the Naval

Intelligence Division, which involved both co-operation with Russian officials in London over the disposal of German naval assets and an assessment of the Russian naval capabilities as the possible enemy of the future. His work also involved providing cover for Foreign Office staff attending a special Russian course at Cambridge University and discussions with the head of MI6 over the use of submarines and other craft in its activities. On retirement, when he was almost recruited into the Secret Service, he took his first steps to find a Tory constituency and set himself up as Eastern Trading Group Consultancy Services, which involved numerous trips for industrial clients to Poland and Russia (and may have been used as an intelligence cover, a favoured MI6 method at that time). In 1958, after the resignation of Harvey, he was nominated as Tory candidate for Harrow East and won the by-election the following March. His election, he accepted, helped his business affairs because of the aura of official Government blessing through the fact that, as he said, he was now a Member of Parliament.

A few months after his election in 1959 he returned to Moscow, conducting his business from his hotel, the Hotel Ukrania, where he met Zinaida Grigorievna Volkova, an Intourist official who ran the hotel car service for visitors. During his visit he became concerned at the 'moral ascendancy' the Russians had over the Embassy by harassing staff and making life uncomfortable for them. Harold Macmillan's lack of interest prompted a Parliamentary campaign by Courtney and others to persuade the Government to stand up to the Russians. In 1961, two months after his first wife's death, Courtney went back to Russia for the British Industrial Exhibition where Zina, the Intourist car renter and graduate of the Marxist-Leninist Institute, had given up her holiday to work for a British firm. Evenings found them together where she responded, Courtney thought, to his sadness while he clearly responded to her hazel eyes, fair hair and the 'new pleated blouse, in pale blue nylon, with its buttons up the back'. After one particular dinner with dry champagne she, according to Courtney, took the initiative and guided him up to his bedroom where he undid those buttons.

The sex was not a success and was never repeated, to Courtney's lack of surprise. On his return to England Courtney remarried – to Lady Elizabeth Trefgarne – and renewed his criticism of the Foreign Office, which he thought 'excessively gullible', over security matters and the Russians' strength in intelligence and espionage affairs. He attacked the Diplomatic Privileges Bill in 1964 for trying to extend the diplomatic immunity to the entire staffs of the Russian Embassy and those of three East European countries, which he suggested would be misused for espionage: he accused the Russians of leaning on British diplomatic staff in Moscow to ensure such concessions. In July 1965 he asked Harold Wilson 'when the Government were going to stop behaving like a lot of hypnotized rabbits in the face of the efficient Soviet espionage organisation.'

A month later an anonymous broadsheet arrived headed 'I'm not a Profumo but . . .' with three pictures of a very plump and undressed Courtney, two with a woman on a bed and one of those a picture of unbuttoning the buttons up the back. It was Zina, the MI6-listed KGB seducer. They were sent to the *News of the World*, Labour and Tory MPs, and constituency officials. While the details in the broadsheet did not emerge in the press the immediate consequence was the break-up of his already shaky second marriage – a fact presumably known to the KGB after he and his second wife had discussed their deteriorating relationship over a Moscow telephone line. A second effect was that the new Labour Government, on the advice of George Wigg, dissuaded Courtney from any further visits to Moscow, which effectively curtailed his business activities. The announcement of impending divorce proceedings on grounds of adultery – Zina was named – resulted in a *Daily Telegraph* article in October 1965, written with Courtney's help, that referred to a 'scurrilous' broadsheet which, it claimed, was designed to deflate pubic sympathy for Courtney. With the story now pushed into the public arena, leading party figures became alarmed at the divorce petition and the effect of the 'Profumo subconscious' on the party's image. The Conservative leader, Edward Heath, warned Courtney that any Parliamentary statement defending his position would be disowned by both sides. Courtney believed that the Party wanted him to keep quiet and were none too pleased with the *Daily Telegraph* story. When the story first surfaced before the General Election it was plain to Courtney that 'any publicity concerning a Conservative MP which might be even remotely associated with the Profumo scandal must be stifled at all costs'. His meeting with Heath was chilly and Courtney reported later of 'my impression of the complete absence of that human quality of personal involvement . . . towards a colleague in trouble'. But Courtney was already in trouble with his constituency party who used the allegations to persuade him to step down. In November his constituency association deselected him and, despite a special constituency meeting that reinstated him, he was to lose the 1966 General Election.

# Chapter 6

## *Profumo, Scandal and The Media*

Denning's report on the Profumo affair was important for several reasons: it gave the public a 'racy' insight into the world of politicians and high society which it had never had before. It therefore provided a sense of things not being quite what they seemed behind the public appearances. Second, it personalised scandal, making it easily understandable and associating it with private, personal, often sexual, behaviour. Third, it appeared to be storing up trouble for politicians in the future by formally, if unconsciously, spelling out the 'code'. Denning said that he had refrained from investigating immorality or discreditable conduct that did not amount to a security risk because he was not conducting a witch-hunt and because such an inquiry into private lives would be repugnant 'to the great majority of our people'. There was therefore a clear ambiguity in the report about such conduct that may have reflected Denning's belief in the privacy of the individual and his awareness of the frailties and weaknesses of others, but which provided for a conflict of interpretation: whether the conduct of a politician was acceptable did not depend on the behaviour but on its context – what may be acceptable for a backbencher may not be acceptable for a Cabinet Minister. If there were no all-embracing essential qualities by which all politicians could be judged as a whole, then there could be a danger of any behaviour coming under scrutiny and of different views taken of the same behaviour by different people about different politicians at different times. If Denning was mildly critical of the way politicians allowed the scandal to develop he was harshly critical of the press. The scandal happened through their 'trafficking in scandal for reward' rather than 'a decline in the integrity of public life'. Scandalous information about well-known people, he argued, had become a marketable commodity. What was unpublishable became rumour 'swelling all the time.' Without the original purchase of such information 'it might never have got started on its way.'

The assumption would appear to be that the acceptability of what politicians do in their private lives is a matter for any Prime Minister to decide. 'No doubt', Macmillan believed, 'Profumo had frequented circles in which, in my youth, it would have been thought inappropriate for a Minister to move', with the implication that without the old social distinctions that kept respectable and disreputable people apart anything could and did happen. Thus Macmillan himself blamed the 'strange environment in which men of some importance, sometimes even holding high positions, were led to mingle with crooks, charlatans, pimps and courtesans. In my youth, good manners, although not necessarily good morality, made such a confusion impossible.'[1] The problem is that such revelations tend to reinforce the belief that what politicians do in private is at variance with their public image and the public's expectation. Telling a lie is one thing; deliberately telling one *and* being caught, particularly about sex, offended not only those who believed that the 'gentleman ethic' was a fundamental characteristic of politicians at that time but also those for whom sexual immorality was both cause and consequence of the sense of moral decline in society. Dr Mervyn Stockwood, Bishop of Southwark, could reflect public opinion at the time of Profumo by talking of 'the smell of corruption in high places', of a repudiation of simple decencies and basic values that was exploited by the press in its enthusiasm for sexual scandals. His concern over the behaviour of the press was shared by Macmillan who saw in it the press's revenge after the Vassall affair. Even before the censure debate he wrote: 'every part of the Profumo story . . . was used against the Government by an exultant Press, getting its own back for Vassall . . . Day after day the attacks developed, chiefly on me – old, incompetent, worn out'[2] Crossman, too, saw the scandal firmly rooted in the 'hostility between the press and the Government, which makes the press willing to leap at anything. A secondary interest is the sleaziness of those Tories who get mixed up with this kind of society.'[3]

Other commentators saw a lethal mix of rumour – 'a dark, dangerous and uncontrollable form of communication', public cynicism and a tradition of scandal-journalism, exacerbated by the failure of politicians 'to bring out the truth while the rumour was still small enough to be extinguished [and] the subsequent disaster could have been averted.'[4] As Macmillan himself intuitively recognised: 'to disapprove was one thing; to turn this incident into an extravagant campaign, which by its very lack of proportion became ridiculous, was to destroy rather than sustain respect for all established government. Perhaps also some of the people who were affected by these revelations had themselves a certain sense of shame at the apparent weakening of the old ties. They required a sacrifice to appease the offended gods, if not of morality, at least of convention.'[5]

Bernard Levin, ever the man with a perspective, thought this cathartic experience was the result of a direct clash of attitudes to personal conduct – the private lusts of politicians are neither new nor always well-contained but never so easily publicised – where 'the tensions of the decade . . . had their common origin in the fact that the Sixties saw an old world die and a new one come to birth . . . it is a fact of history that in every age of transition men are never so firmly bound to one way of life as when they are about to abandon it, so that fanaticism and intolerance reach their most intense forms just before tolerance and mutual acceptance come to be the natural order of things. If this is what was happening in the Sixties, then Mr Profumo was the last victim of the old, unpermissive standards . . . sacrificed on their altar in the most public, brutal and bloody fashion imaginable . . .'[6] On the other hand it may have been just 'the simple human failing of taste for scandal, especially that concerning the great and famous . . . these rumours, progressing in a trice from hint to certainty, travel so fast and far that the origin – which may have been invention, misunder-standing, ingenious deduction or sheer malice – is soon irretrievably lost.'[7] It was, however, a taste that both the media and the public was not likely to forgo easily and indeed, as a result of the Profumo affair, became an increasingly prominent means of viewing politicians. With the attendant issues of security, suspected cover-ups, ambiguity over acceptable behaviour and the belief of differential standards for politicians as opposed to every-one else, the Profumo affair ensured that the minefield of public life was most fraught with danger to one's career or reputation, with the likelihood of attracting media attention, when the behaviour involved the social or personal life of the politician.

# PART THREE

## *BEHIND EVERY STORY LURKS A HEADLINE*

# Chapter 7

## A Decade of Parliamentary Gossip, Scares and Scandals, Part One

*Wanting to become a Member of Parliament*

Being an MP has increasingly entailed publicity and press attention. From that focus, however, spreading out like ripples, that publicity and that attention has come to encompass anyone who is connected or related to an MP, anyone who has been an MP and anyone who wants to be an MP, as stories drawn from the last ten years will amply illustrate. Gwilym Jones was clearly aware of how far the press could delve into a prospective MP's background and later embarrass him or her – one only has to think of the old photograph of Paul Boateng in unusual fancy-dress that duly appeared on a tabloid front page when he was elected a Labour MP – for him to decide to take pre-emptive action. At thirty-eight Mr Jones had been chosen as prospective Conservative parliamentary candidate for a Cardiff constituency in 1983. Deputy leader of the Tory Opposition on Cardiff City Council, a successful businessman, director of the Welsh-based part of an international insurance brokers and married to a JP, he felt it best to announce to his constituency selection committee that at the age of thirteen he helped set fire to his headmaster's study, an offence for which the juvenile court put him on probation for two years. 'I can offer no . . . justification for what happened,' he said, 'I know what I did was very wrong and I have remained very ashamed about it ever since. It made a tremendous mess of my early life, much worse than the actual punishment of the court, and I had a very hard lesson to learn.' It turned out, however, that not only did Jones win the seat, but he polled 2000 more votes than the previous Tory victor.

Sometimes, however, the media can perform a useful function in warning potential politicians that some types of behaviour are not acceptable despite what they might think. In August 1979 Secretary of State for Industry Sir Keith Joseph wrote to a colleague at the Home Office that Martin Bendelow was 'knowledgeable about drug abuse and had views which he should put to officials.'[20] In fact he was so knowledgeable that in December 1981 the courts gave him six years' imprisonment for smuggling kilos of cocaine into Britain. The son of a Harrogate vicar, Bendelow hitched round the world and made money in the early 1970s importing Afghan coats and then dabbling in property development. He was successful, accumulating a gold Porsche, a Chelsea flat and a financial base from which to indulge his interest in politics. This had begun with a part-time course at the London School of Economics where his economics lecturer introduced him to free-market economics. It continued with his involvement in the Tory Bow Group and the Centre for Policy Studies. There his self-confidence and enthusiasm captured the attention of Sir Keith, to whom he acted as an informal personal assistant and who subsequently recommended him as a prospective Tory candidate. Chosen as Tory candidate for the Huddersfield East constituency, Bendelow reduced the Labour majority from 8414 at the 1974 Election to 3095 at the 1979 Election. Between 1977 and 1980 he made several trips to Bolivia, ostensibly on business, but cocaine was later found in his house by customs officers. Bendelow's explanation was that he had been forced to smuggle the drugs because of threats against his family; he then said he did it to finance Bolivian friends seeking exile abroad. 'I now think that he is a compulsive liar', said one journalist friend. The *Sunday Times* alleged that, according to the US Drug Enforcement Administration intelligence files in El Paso, he was a known associate of drug smugglers from as early as 1972 and travelled to drug capitals of the world. Sir Keith was 'devastated', and Bendelow never got to be a Cabinet

Minister within five years, as he had once promised a journalist in 1979.

On the other hand, and as is more likely to be the case, the media are more interested in stories that fit their perceptions of what their readers want to read and explains why Peter Tatchell's life was turned upside-down in December 1981. James Wellbeloved MP asked Margaret Thatcher what she thought of the prospective Labour candidate for Bermondsey's comments in the *London Labour Briefing* pamphlet which called for 'extra-parliamentary opposition' and 'a siege of parliament to demand jobs'. Thatcher fudged her answer, leaving the confused Michael Foot, leader of the Labour Opposition, to anounce that 'the individual concerned is not an endorsed member of the Labour Party, and as far as I am concerned, never will be.' For the next fifteen months, until he lost the Bermondsey by-election to the SDP, Tatchell's life became a rich source of press inquiry. A 29-year-old Australian who came to England ten years previously, he was a painter and decorator before taking a degree at the Polytechnic of North London and then a job as a housing advice worker dealing with single homeless people. He joined the Bermondsey Labour party in 1978 when the GLC allocated him a 'hard-to-let' flat on the Rockingham estate. It was a moribund constituency party dominated by Labour MP Bob Mellish and ripe for take-over by a broad-left coalition. With battlelines drawn over local property redevelopment, ideological splits between local councillors and party activists, and Mellish's departure to the Docklands Corporation, the coalition took over the local Party; Tatchell was elected as Party Secretary. Its control was first evident when the Party refused to re-nominate some sitting councillors and then selected Tatchell as Parliamentary candidate in preference to the veteran Arthur Latham by thirty-seven votes to thirty.

Whether prompted by leaks from dissident Party members or by Tatchell's frank announcement that his Parliamentary salary would be used to fund constituency work if he won, or by his support for gay rights, the press responded to Foot's repudiation with enthusiasm: 'like vultures descending on a prey', said Tatchell later, 'the hacks and seedy scribes of Grub Street gathered . . .'[1]

At first they thought they had found, if not a Militant supporter, another politician, like Ken Livingstone, to taunt with extremism. Much more newsworthy, however, was Tatchell himself: 'a rather exotic Australian canary who sings some odd songs', said the *Daily Express* as it and others began 'a process of trivialisation, ridicule and personalisation of the issues', with particular reference to his appearance – 'a symphony in brown', two-tone shoes, knitted ties – and allusions to his sexuality. There Tatchell made his mistake. In the belief that as soon as he put his sexuality on public record, 'it would then become in the eyes of Fleet Street a matter of legitimate public interest and justification for them to publish the most intimate details about my private life [and] the issue of gay rights would be manipulated by a hostile press to dominate the inevitable by-election',[2] he refused to discuss it.

The Labour Party's decision not to endorse Tatchell as candidate, and the likelihood of his being re-selected by the local party, returned the press's attention to Tatchell's private life. The fact that his importance was as a candidate for a by-election, and in London, meant that Fleet Street could easily concentrate their attention on it. Personality plays an important part in a by-election – it adds 'colour' – and Tatchell had plenty of that to add to the other stalking-horses of the media at that time. Neighbours and garbage cans were sifted for evidence – one journalist knocked on doors pretending to be a long-lost cousin – of homosexuality, boyfriends and exotic holidays; the search was even enthusiastically extended to Australia. When Tatchell was re-nominated, the anti-gay campaign was taken up by his political opponents. Tatchell lost heavily, the Liberal candidate having nearly 6000 votes over all the others combined. He stood down as candidate. Although he had intended to declare his sexual preferences after his election, his decision not to do so before, because he feared a succession of 'kiss and tell' stories, underestimated Fleet Street's capacity to work on the basis of supposition and suspicion, for which he paid the price.

This enthusiasm stretches out to the fringes of the world of politics and invariably attracts the media, many of whom arrived promptly in Middlesbrough from where 'the whiff of a political sex scandal hovered tantalisingly', as the *Daily Telegraph* put it hopefully, 'over the . . . courtroom which heard the bizarre and lurid story behind the "perfect murder" carried out by the surgeon Paul Vickers.'[3] Vickers was a politically ambitious medic. Leaving Westminster public school with four 'O' levels, he took his 'A' levels at Sunderland Technical College and squeezed into Cambridge to read veterinary science before switching to medicine. He climbed up the medicine tree, became a nationally-elected member of the GMC, the BMA and the DHSS Central Manpower Committee, travelled regularly abroad for conferences and, at the time of his trial, was head of the accident unit at the Queen Elizabeth Hospital in Gateshead. He became involved in medical politics through the campaign for shorter hours for junior doctors and in the Conservative Party through his membership of the national council of the European Movement. He was keen to find a candidature for Parliament, either in Westminster or in Europe. He was unsuccessful in both, 'an ambitious and unpleasant personality', said one party agent.

In 1976 he met Pamela Collinson at a European Movement congress in Brussels. She had joined the Movement with her parents, working first as a local branch secretary and then joining the national executive. She had become involved in Tory politics while an undergraduate and became infatuated with the world of politicians and academics. A woman of expensive tastes, she had a fierce, dominating personality which, combined with an elegant charm and an amoral childish innocence, made her attractive to men: 'she prides herself in being able to twist them round her little finger. Once she has them hooked she won't let go', said one friend. She worked for Michael Heseltine as a researcher and then travelled widely in Europe as a national official of the European Movement as well as becoming involved in the Bow Group. She found politics – and politicians – fascinating, boasting of affairs with them (one letter discovered by police was from a politician alleging he had contracted VD from her, an accusation Vickers also made). She, too, had ambitions to be a Euro-MP.

Vickers himself had an active sex life, haunting tea dances in Newcastle's Oxford Galleries and devoting his spare time to at least four mistresses who were given candlelit champagne dinners, expensive pieces of jewelry and secret foreign holidays. Vickers fell heavily for Collinson in a tempestuous, passionate affair that began in 1977, replete with pornographic photographs and letters, dominance and submission romps and dressing-up games. At his later appeal, which he lost, Vickers' counsel described her as a 'femme carnale'. Vickers was clearly proud of her, introducing her openly to friends while she revelled in the attention with lowcut dresses and expensive furcoats. She clearly had every intention of marrying him; Vickers saw her as his perfect partner for his political ambitions. There was one problem: Margaret Vickers.

Vickers had met and married Margaret in 1962. A Cambridge maths graduate, she was shy and friendless. She was also schizophrenic, exhibiting signs of mental disturbance, including hearing voices in her head and thinking transistor radios were implanted in her teeth. At the outset of his affair with Collinson, Vickers decided to divorce his wife but was warned of the political damage it might cause. He chose instead to murder her, choosing a rare and dangerous anti-cancer drug CCNU, one of the side effects of which was to destroy the body's bone marrow function while leaving no trace of its use. On the argument, advanced in his defence at the trial, that her schizophrenia might be due to a brain tumour, Vickers began feeding CCNU capsules to his wife, giving her twice the maximum recommended dose over a nine-month period. He concealed his prescriptions by writing them for five fake patients at medically-approved intervals. By 1979 Mrs Vickers was hospitalised and finally died in June that year.

After her death, Collinson demanded that Vickers redecorate and refurbish the house but Vickers had had enough of her, pulling out of the proposed wedding and then the relationship. Collinson was not pleased and stormed off to a London police station in May 1980 where, 'looking like Margaret Thatcher's double', said an officer, she accused Vickers of murder (another lover who dumped her was to be reported to the Yorkshire police as the Ripper). Both were arrested in October that year. Collinson stage-managed her arrest by telephoning the press and telling her mother: 'Mummy, please tell Gerry Vaughan [then Health Minister] I have been arrested'.

The packed press ranks in Middlesbrough were at the trial because Vickers had alleged she had had affairs with prominent politicians and had taken great delight in describing the affairs in detail to Vickers in bed. Much to their regret, Vickers was firmly warned not to drop names by the judge. Vickers was found guilty and sentenced to life imprisonment with a recommendation he serve seventeen years. Collinson received a suspended six-month sentence for illegally obtaining CCNU tablets for Vickers; she was acquitted of murder.

## All in the family

Whether they like it or not, MPs make other people's stories or behaviour newsworthy and, however much they might wish that the media concentrate on their politics or even their own private lives, no newspaper appears willing to pass up the opportunity of a story that has in it, however tenuous or accidental, a politician's name. Brian Walden, Labour MP for Birmingham Ladywood between 1964 and 1977 and later frontman for *Weekend World* on commercial television, provided a cautionary lesson from the Seventies, once in relation to his financial interests attracting the attention of the serious parts of the media and once through a 1977 front page article in the *News of the World* that began: 'The former wife of a prominent MP has written an amazing article in a sex magazine.' In the article Jane McKerron, Walden's former wife, described various affairs with MPs, including an (anonymous) Cabinet Minister who apparently dived on her with 'the intensity of a lapsed vegetarian attacking a T-bone steak.' As a weary Walden, who divorced her in

1975 on the grounds of her adultery, told the newspaper: 'I not only have [no] control whatsoever over what she writes, I deplore that such an article should have been written . . . My error is to have married this woman, a decision that has never given me anything but embarrassment and grief. Sanctimony is an odious quality, but exhibitionism and a desire for notoriety are worse . . . None of us is perfect, but to advertise our imperfections without regard to the feelings of others is the mark of the truly selfish person.'

Nevertheless such stories sell copy. A mass-circulation women's magazine began such a story: 'One is brilliant and ebullient, an ambitious man with drive and power. A Member of Parliament. The other is slow and easy, a quiet, friendly, affectionate man, totally without ambition. A bricklayer. One is my husband. The other is the man I love.' Bill Price, Labour MP for Rugby between 1966 and 1979 read it when his wife Joy decided to tell *Woman* magazine why her marriage to Price, a Coventry journalist, foundered on her rivals – his constituents, colleagues, reporters, broadcasters, agents and 'all the people he met in a very busy day' – and ended in divorce. As a junior Minister in the Callaghan government he was, she claimed, uninterested in the trivia of domestic life – not bothered enough to buy Christmas presents, too tired to make love, and lacking in tenderness. A few years later in October 1987 Robert Hicks, Tory MP for South East Cornwall, had to endure a *Daily Star* banner headline that read: 'SWINE: NO, NOT THE PIG . . . MY HUSBAND THE MP'. The front page was dominated by a photograph of a pig accompanied by Mrs Hicks. Although already separated from her husband, whom she was in the process of divorcing, the reason for the story was Mrs Hicks' annoyance over her husband's 'insensitive and indiscreet' relationship with an Australian civil servant who, she claimed, was living in the family home with the MP and appearing at constituency functions. And the more senior the political figure the more the attention is given to the behaviour of the spouse.

Denis Thatcher's business life began with the family paint and wallpaper firm of Atlas Preservatives Ltd, of which he was managing director. It was sold for £560,000 to Castrol in 1965; Thatcher joined Castrol's board. Months later Castrol was taken over by the Scottish oil firm, Burmah Oil. Thatcher joined its board and became Planning Director. He also picked up directorships with Chipman Chemical Company, Halfords Ltd (the car parts retailers), Quinton Hazell Ltd (vehicle parts manufacturers), Edwin Cooper and Co. Ltd, and a consultancy with IDC, a building firm. Until then Thatcher had been portrayed in parts of the media, despite his war record, his MBE and his rise through the ranks of British industry, as an amiable old man with a penchant for golf and gin-and-tonics.

This last appointment developed from a Lamberhurst golfing friendship with Ron Monk, director of William Ellis (Etchingham) Ltd, an IDC subsidiary. IDC was a civil and commercial building firm whose chairman, Howard Hicks, had a track record of employing directors with a political background. He agreed that Monk, wanting an adviser with wide business experience, could employ Thatcher from 1971, on a small salary (£2000 in 1981), to promote IDC among various industry contacts and take part in general management meetings.

At one such meeting in 1980 Thatcher learnt from IDC's deputy chief executive that a planning application of one of its subsidiaries had run into delays. This firm, Housing Development and Construction, had bought twenty-four acres in Harlech from the local authority with planning permission in 1979. It intended to build a motel and sixty-three houses, but the Snowdonia National Park Planning Authority saw that incompatible with the small town set on a rocky promontory overlooking Cardigan Bay. Hicks was furious. He felt that the local authority had cheated him by selling the land at a commercial value when the key to that value, planning permission, was unavailable for his purposes. He wrote complaining to the Welsh Office and a South Wales Labour MP he knew through interests in rugby; both told him to appeal. Although there are recognised appeal procedures which in theory should reach a conclusion within months, IDC heard nothing for eleven months. When Thatcher learnt of the delay he volunteered to write to the Conservative Welsh Office Minister, Nicholas Edwards, a Welsh MP since 1970 and whose long tenure at the Welsh Office was a consequence of his being one of the few Wales-based Tory MPs. Thatcher wrote in December 1980:

Dear Nick

First, I always hesitate before bothering busy Ministers with 'problems'. They have too many from other sources. Second, I have to declare an interest in this for I am a consultant to IDC Ltd., whose wholly subsidiary Housing Development and Construction Ltd. is the appellant.

The relevant information is set out in letter (2) of this file, the core of which is that it has taken 11 months to set up a planning appeal hearing. Officials will doubtless advance good excuses but I would doubt good reasons. Obviously nothing can be done to advance the hearing but I thought you might be interested and concerned at this sort of incident.

The cost of these prodigious delays to the construction and building industry is enormous: in this particular case hundreds of thousands of pounds have been locked into an unproductive asset.

Instead of minuting his officials to hurry up the procedures Edwards sent the letter with IDC's file to Cardiff in a Minister's correspondence dossier with a note: 'The explanation had better be good and quick – i.e. this week.' His London officials also telephoned Cardiff to alert them to the dossier's arrival. In March the appeal was held; the inspector supported the appeal, a decision endorsed by Edwards in August 1981. The Thatcher letter disappeared in December 1980 then emerged in photocopied form in September 1981. The press were alerted to its existence by reference to internal searches for it in a Welsh Office officials' newsletter before it appeared in the hands of local press agencies and radical magazines. Plaid Cymru MP, Daffydd Thomas, quickly criticised the Edwards note and Thatcher's use of 10 Downing Street notepaper.

Edwards, on the other hand, dismissed the criticism as 'exaggerated and absurd', arguing that 'it is a very quaint idea in this modern world that because you happen to be married to the Prime Minister, you cannot write a letter from your home, or draw the attention of a Minister to an unquestioned delay in the setting up of a planning enquiry.'

The press was more concerned over Edwards' note, which appeared to invite 'the comment that the treatment you receive at the hands of a government department depends on who you are' and believed that 'the slag heap of supposed scandal was a mouse-dropping' but increasingly paid more attention to how far the husband's business interests might have repercussions for the Prime Minister. Blakedown Chipman worked as landscapers in Saudi Arabia; its activities were run by Blakedown Landscapes, which owned half the company. The other half was owned by Chipman Ltd, whose chairman was Denis Thatcher. In 1983 Blakedown Chipman was in the news for allegedly using non-permit British workers on Saudi contracts. The headline in the *Sunday Times* read: 'Why Thatcher workers are Saudi outlaws.' In 1980 Chipman Ltd was in the news for selling 'Chipman Brushwood Killer' for large-scale use in plantations and industrial sites. In 1983 Thatcher joined Attwoods, a firm that specialises in waste disposal, and sand and gravel excavation for motorway-buildings, at the invitation of David Wickins, owner of British Car Auctions. 'I was invited onto the board', said Thatcher later, 'because I have certain skills. I can add and subtract.' Between then and 1986 the firm began buying into US waste management firms, an industry that is not unknown for its links with the Mafia and attracted the headlines such as – 'Denis Thatcher firm indicted by US Jury' (*Daily Telegraph*) and 'Denis Thatcher co-directors in "Mafia link"' (*Observer*).

It could be argued that adults are well able to look after themselves, whether or not they deserve the attention they get. Children, on the other hand, might be thought to deserve more careful handling, but children of public figures are considered fair game for press attention, particularly if their behaviour is somewhat at variance with the policies and prescriptions being dished out by their parents to the rest of the population. 'Their fathers run the country. But despite all that power there is one thing the dads cannot control – the oddball lifestyle of their own children', muttered the *News of the World* in 1984 about the antics of the poor little rich kids with too much time, too much money and not a little self-indulgence on the part of the parents. Thus the newspaper happily photographed Katherine Hogg in suspenders and stockings and Alex and Annabel Heseltine out on the town, while taking sideswipes at their lifestyles – 'pintswilling' Lisa King, 'Queen of hellraisers' Nigella Lawson and the 'debagged' Bernard Jenkin. Even those who tried to work were viewed sceptically: 'Alec [Howe] knows all about the problem of getting jobs – he has had lots', while Jeremy Prior's catering at No 10 Downing Street was won 'because of my connections.'[4] Alec Howe even managed to reach the back pages of the *Guardian* when he joined CND's press office and was asked if he was 'about to hand a loaded gun to his father's political enemies . . .'[5]

Often the fact that a parent is a politician is enough to justify a story. In October 1987 *The People* managed to devote three pages to the eighteen-year-old daughter of Cabinet Minister Kenneth Clarke. The story lovingly worked its way through tattooes, pet rats, animal rights, friendships with junkies and visits to 'way-out' clubs to the scruffy flat where she lived. Father appeared as a tolerant, supportive person and the daughter a less-than-stupid teenager keen to pursue her own individuality. Almost as a throwaway line, however, Sue Clarke did note that politician-parents are so busy that 'most of the time they didn't know what the hell I was really up to'. Certainly there have been a number of stories about the children of politicians who have often become involved in sex, drugs and drink lifestyles that their parents were unaware of: drugs in particular appear to be a major attraction. Mrs Thatcher has herself been at a dinner party with one of her ministers where an offspring has coped with the situation by getting thoroughly stoned. Certainly, the tragic consequences of such behaviour have the media displaying their ill-disguised curiosity about the activities of the offspring of politicians, most notably following the death of 22-year-old Olivia Channon in June 1986. As the *Daily Telegraph* said charitably: 'Olivia Channon's passionate enthusiasm for adventure tipped over into extravagance, and finally into tragedy.'[6]

Daughter of Paul Channon, Tory Minister of Trade, she was in her final year studying history at St Hilda's, Oxford. Well brought-up, with a penchant for the unusual in clothes and travel, she was called 'a weak character who had fallen in with the wrong crowd'. This included drug-taking, wild parties and mixing with those to whom moderation in their personal lives or political views were anathema. It brought the press to town, raking over the activities of the 'Brideshead' set whose correlations, as Richard Hoggart put it, 'between family background, school, the right sorts of connections . . . are so close that, plainly, actual ability can be a virtually disregardable element.'[7] She died of a lethal cocktail of heroin, drink and amphetamines which slowly poisoned her at a party to mark the end of her final examinations. She died because no-one around her noticed that she was slipping into a coma rather than falling asleep. She did care about her work – part of the post-exam indulgence was a response to her fear of failure – but the surroundings and lifestyle in which she died attracted the full attention of the media. In her own £45,000 Oxford house, on an annual allowance of £25,000 and with total assets of £500,000, she ordered heroin from an unemployed pop musician who used a radio pager to stay in touch with his wealthy patrons. At the subsequent trial, the girlfriend she asked to go to London to collect the heroin, the supplier and another user, her cousin Sebastian Guinness, all received prison sentences, to act, as the judge said, as a warning to the 'rich and privileged' that it was not acceptable to dabble in hard drugs.

There are those who would say that, with their background and connections, the offspring of politicians should neither need such habits nor find it difficult to make their way in the world. But, as Mark Thatcher was to discover only too well, it is the background and the connections that can be the problem. Mark 'was very much the apple of his mother's eye, as he always had been. He didn't abuse that position in that he was devoted to her and always totally loyal, but she did become quite worried that he might get into deep water. "You know, the trouble with Mark is he just can't pass exams," she told a friend over a drink in her room at the House of Commons one day. "And the difficulty is, people are offering him jobs right and left. And you know I cannot accept a job for him just because he's my son"'.[8]

If she was worried for Mark, Mark was aware of what the rise to public prominence could mean for him. After her election as Leader of the Opposition in 1975 Mark said: 'I used to think, "what makes me so special to be the son of the Leader of the Opposition. I've done nothing to deserve it, nothing at all." I realised that suddenly I was in a different league where I was expected to behave in a certain way otherwise I'd get crucified by the world outside. So I try and fulfil other people's expectations of me.'[9]

Unfortunately he was less than careful of his own caution in pursuit of his own career: 'some people think,' he said in 1980, 'that just because I'm Mrs Thatcher's son, it's plain sailing, but it isn't because at the end of the day I've got to earn my own living like everyone else . . .'[10] That, however, was the problem. Mark Thatcher's career was, as the *Observer* unkindly put it, 'a model of relentless mediocrity' until his mother became Prime Minister. After 1979 he managed, the newspaper alleged, to 'extract spectacular advantage from the one special asset he possessed – his name.'[11] Leaving Harrow at eighteen in 1971, he worked for Jardine Matheson, the Hong Kong trading company, for a year. After a few months with a London stockbrokers he spent four years with accountants Touche Ross before leaving without a qualification. He joined a firm of jewellers in 1977 and the London office of an Australian freight company, IPEC, in 1978. In 1979 he left to devote himself to motor racing and to setting up an international consultancy firm, Monteagle Marketing (London) Ltd, with a racing colleague, Steve Tipping. His own scheme, Mark Thatcher Racing, soon ran into financial difficulties. His racing career was only noteworthy for several expensive crashes, a period lost in the Sahara that had his mother in tears and two controversial offers of sponsorship – from a soft porn magazine and Japanese clothes – which managed, as one newspaper noted, to achieve the impossible – to unite both his mother and the textile unions in criticism of the offers.

The real row broke in Jaunary 1984 when the *Observer* alleged that Mark was acting as a consultant to a British civil engineering and building firm, Cementation International, a subsidiary of Trafalgar House. In 1980 the Sultan of Oman announced his intention of building a university for his country of 1.5 million people. In March 1981 an official plan emerged which stated that 'a reputable establishment renowned for its experience in building universities will be selected.' It also proposed that the competition for the contract would be by sealed tenders, a legal requirement in Oman since 1975, and that the successful firm would work under the supervision of an independent, government-appointed architect. Internally there was no unanimity of the type of firm being sought and the design to be used; the design study had in fact been carried out by a Canadian firm. It was, as Cementation said later, a 'critical' period.

In April 1981 Thatcher undertook a six-nation tour with her husband and daughter in the official party. She landed first in Abu Dhabi. Mark met her there. He was with Jamil Amyuni, Cementation's Middle East director, where Cementation were pressing for the contract to build a multi-million pound irrigation scheme in the desert oasis of Al-Ain (the firm won a test-well boring contract which showed there was insufficient water after the visit). Off went Mother to Oman with the official party, Mark arriving two days later to join her. There she pressed for the contract to go to a British firm, 'batting for Britain' as she put it: several were interested in the contract but none, apart from Cementation, had got as far as conducting informal negotiations with the Sultan's officials.

In May 1981 Cementation's London bankers, Morgan Grenfell, were applying to the Export Credit Guarantee Department in anticipation of Cementation's success. In

September 1981 Cementation won the £300 million building contract without tendering and by direct personal negotiations. No government-appointed architect was required; Cementation won the design contract as well. The ensuing row over Mark Thatcher's involvement in winning the contract and over how much mother knew of his activities was prolonged and fed during 1984 while the Prime Minister and son stayed silent; in an April 1984 *Panorama* interview Margaret Thatcher avoided two questions: did she know her son was in the employ of Cementation when she went to Oman and did officials warn her of any conflict of interest when he joined the official party in Oman, unannounced? But by this time the media interest in her son's business activities had uncovered other examples of his unfortunate capacity to attract controversy.

At the end of January 1984, Thatcher's name again showed the value others attached to it. The *Mail on Sunday*, not renowned for its anti-Thatcher stance, felt the need to warn of the dangers of the fast-money, up-front world of international deals: 'The trouble with Mark, say acquaintances', intoned the paper, 'is not who he is but who he knows. Impatient to make a financial killing, he is less wary of those with whom he is prepared to do business than one would expect of someone in his position.'[12] Mark met Leon Walgar, a 39-year-old Argentinian, through motor racing. Walgar had made and lost a fortune gambling on commodity futures, the money he used to fund his racing. Shortly after, Walgar used Thatcher's name without him knowing in attempting to set up an arms deal for the Peruvian Government (his wife was the grand-daughter of a former Peruvian President). The telex to an American arms dealer read: 're: certain particular countries in which we are well connected and in which we might be able to help selling your ideas and/or equipment. I would also like to point out that I am a close friend and associate in some particular deals of Mr Mark Thatcher who, for obvious reasons, is also highly well connected in other parts of the world.'

Two of the dealer's associates went to London to see Walgar and his lawyer who alleged to the newspaper:

'Mark Thatcher was being used simply because of his name and the credibility it held. They said Thatcher was not very bright and had to be instructed on what to do.' That deal collapsed as Mark Thatcher became increasingly aware of the criticism he was attracting. On 12 February 1984 Mark spoke to the *Sunday Times* about being a 'very insignificant cog in a very big wheel.' Believing his business affairs to be 'entirely private' he accepted that a Prime Minister mother was an advantage but, on the other hand, it was impossible to assess his career without that advantage. He thought that the 'politically motivated attacks' on him came from those hostile to big business but that his role in Oman was very small and in any case he exercised considerable discretion because he was aware that he had become 'a public figure.'

In March 1984 the *Sunday Times* published an interview with Steve Tipping that revealed his own uneven business career and the curious operations of Monteagle Marketing. It did not have an office and its telephone number was ex-directory. The activity of the firm, said Brenda Sanger, Mark Thatcher's personal assistant, was catering: 'by catering we mean that somebody who knows somebody can put somebody in touch with somebody else.' She added: 'we don't talk about the business for the single reason that we are not trading on Mark's mother's name.'[13] The *Sunday Times* discovered that one of the three signatories on the firm's Barclays Bank account (overdrawn by £12,000) was Denis. That brought a squawk of protest: how did the newspaper discover the account, the deficit and the names? ('You know who that is, don't you . . . right in one!' said the obliging bank clerk) The Prime Minister called the methods used – paying in £25 to the account to check the names on the receiving account – impersonation and deception and the bank rushed off to complain to the Press Council that the confidentiality of client's accounts was threatened. The bank claimed that the journalists used aliases, the newspaper retorted that the story was 'based on hard fact confirmed by reputable journalistic methods'.

What the newspaper had learnt in an earlier story was that Thatcher was representing Monteagle in Oman and that the expected commission payment – £50,000 – would go into Monteagle's bank account. During that inquiry they learnt that Denis's name might be on the account. Accordingly on 1 March they filled in a paying-in slip for £25 in favour of 'Monteagle Marketing, Denis Thatcher, S.W. Tipping, Mark Thatcher' and demanded both the account number and all the possible names were verified. They were. The signature on the paying-in slip was false: the journalists were Barry Penrose and Simon Freeman. The newspaper's rationale were that Cementation had claimed no connection with Mark and Monteagle had said that there was no connection with Denis. Since neither would comment the newspaper decided to find other ways to check the veracity of their suspicions. Said Andrew Neil, the editor: 'allegations have been made that the Prime Minister's son benefited from the Prime Minister's work. Public figures have to live by different standards of disclosure than the rest of the country. They must not only be clean, but be seen to be clean. As the Prime Minister's son, Mark Thatcher, is a public figure.'[14]

While the Press Council were unhappy at the newspaper's suggestion that Denis could be a beneficiary of, or sole signatory to, the account, it rejected the bank's complaint. It accepted that the Oman story was a matter of public interest and that confirmation of the account was a permissible subterfuge when it appeared that money from the Oman deal would be paid into it. Subterfuge, it agreed, could be used only 'in the pursuit of information which ought to be in the public interest, and where there is no other reasonably practicable method of obtaining or confirming it.'[15] The *Sunday Times* story pushed the Oman business into the public arena; the Monteagle aspect had raised the issue of whether members of her family had benefited financially from the Prime Minister's batting for Britain in Oman.

Ministers are bound by the Members' Register, which requires information on relevant pecuniary interests. In addition, Ministers are required to be more circumspect and divest themselves of any interests in such a way that, as Thatcher said herself in 1980, 'no conflict arises, or appears to arise, between their private interest and public duties.' The requirements do not, as in local government or the public sector, extend to disclosure of family or non-pecuniary interests.

The questions that lay at the core to the political criticism of the Prime Minister were posed by the *Observer* in its original article of 15 January 1984: was she aware of her son's involvement with Cementation when she was in Oman, did she discuss the contract with him and did she know he would be in Oman at the time of her official visit; did she see any conflict of interest and did she take official advice; did she think it prudent that her son work for a firm that 'benefits from British influence overseas' and whose contracts may be underwritten by public funds; did she not think it desirable that the arrangement should be made publicly known? On 5 February the newspaper returned to what it saw as the grounds for criticism, arguing that Mark 'was secretive about his activities, in circumstances where there is legitimate public concern that the office of Prime Minister may be at risk of being abused' and that his mother 'appears to have come close to confusing her role of mother with that of British Prime Minister.'[16] Additionally there was the question of the Middle Eastern assumptions that the appearance of mother and son in Oman might awaken.

For, as one businessman with Omani interests told *World in Action* in July 1984, it was normal practice for the Omanis to assume that if the relative was present then the head of government would expect the contract to go to the relative: 'they would say that it's normal part of business, if one starts with the point of view that it is recognised as normal in the Arab world for people in positions of authority to use . . . that position for their own business interest they would regard that as perfectly normal for other people as well.'[17]

Thatcher's arguments that she was 'batting' for Britain in general terms and that the activities of her son were a private matter left Labour MPs somewhat sceptical. Their first tactic was to place a series of Parliamentary questions about the contract and her involvement in it (seventeen in all) and then refer to her failure to register her interest – and failure to declare that interest in responding to the questions – to the Select Committee on Members' Interests. Neil Kinnock, Labour's leader, stayed out of the row but, in February, Peter Shore, a long-serving Labour politician with a substantial Ministerial background and not an interest to speak of, stepped up the pressure with a published exchange of glacially phrased letters. Shore's first letter tried to entice her to support the need for high standards of conduct and then issued his challenge: 'the central issue of principle that the Oman contract raises is how far the standards of conduct expected of Ministers of the Crown, designed to ensure that the use of Ministerial power and patronage does not promote their financial interests, should extend to close members of the Minister's own family: and in what circumstances . . .' Thatcher was having none of it. The central point to her was that she did not 'bat' for a single firm in which her son had a direct financial interest in the outcome. His complaint was therefore unjustified and 'the rest of your letter has no relevance.' Shore quickly replied, asking her whether or not she knew that it was 'widely known in Oman that Cementation was the only British firm in negotiation for the contract' and whether or not her son told her of his and Cementation's interest. The reply was equally swift and terse; she was briefed to raise Britain's general interest in the University contract. Furthermore since she was not pursuing the interests of an individual company her son's movements and business affairs were 'irrelevant to the issue.'

Labour continued to exploit the evasion and stonewalling they saw as her response to their questions, while some Tory politicians were in favour of a fuller disclosure of the facts – something to which she reacted 'incandescent with rage.'

During this period the Select Committee on Members' Interests issued its first report.[18] After a series of votes the Committee had come up with a report that essentially refused to give Brian Sedgemore, a leading left-wing Labour critic of the Oman contract, a platform for his allegations. It also refused to censure the Prime Minister for not having 'a more forthcoming attitude' to the allegations. It ruled that there was no requirement to register the financial interests of close relatives or to declare an interest in relation to Parliamentary questions. While there may have been some muttering at the 'lack of candour' from the target of Sedgemore's criticism there was also a desire not to let the Committee be used as the stalking-horse of the irate left. When the *Sunday Times* bank account story appeared Willie Hamilton, Labour MP, asked her why she had 'degraded the high office of No. 10 into a rather squalid seedy family casino'. She retaliated by accusing the *Sunday Times* of deception and impersonation and arguing that, in Oman, she raised British interest in general – 'I did not raise the interest of any individual companies which, at that stage, could have had an interest in securing the right to negotiate on all aspects of the university project'. Despite Labour pressure to try and coax from her what expertise her son had to offer the firm, she countered by referring to the jobs the contract created and her clear insistence that 'at no time did she promote a single firm.'

By mid-March there was stalemate. While Labour Leader Neil Kinnock still kept clear of the row and used available debating time for other issues, other Labour MPs pressed for a further meeting of the Select Committee on Members' Interests. Some Tory MPs officially tabled their support for her stance but others were concerned that their official support of *her* might be interpreted as endorsing her son's activities and precipitate a full-scale Parliamentary debate.

Sedgemore, however, was still battling to have the issue raised in Parliament. This time the Select Committee on Members' Interests was persuaded to re-examine the case on the grounds that the Prime Minister had a financial interest, indirectly through her son and directly through her husband's involvement in a company, Monteagle, on whose behalf the son was acting in a consultancy capacity. The Committee did not respond; it believed it was unnecessary 'to investigate the validity of these allegations' and reaffirmed that there was no evidence of any financial benefit to the Member of Parliament concerned, Margaret Thatcher. There was no case to answer, said its

Report, although it managed to place on record the full account of Sedgemore's allegations.

It was a story now running out of steam. As one *Observer* executive put it: 'there was a vein of truth, everyone knew, but several weeks of digging failed to lay it properly bare.'[19] The object of the attention had already departed for the USA when in March 1984 Thatcher got a £45,000-a-year job as a director of Lotus Performance Cars, the US front for the Lotus Group controlled by British Car Auctions. Thatcher's job was to build up Lotus dealerships, a job won by 'his knowledge and contacts on the American sports-car and racing circuits', said Wickins. Thatcher said that he accepted the post 'not the least to show how sorry I am for the totally unnecessary aggravation all this business has caused my mother . . . I suppose the lesson I have learnt is that even though I had done nothing wrong, I must not give people a chance even to think I have, and even then not to be able to connect it with her in any way.' At the same time he announced the end of his links with Cementation and moved out of 10 Downing Street for New York. 'Only a fool', he said, 'and I am not one – would claim there to have been no advantages in having the name Thatcher. I now know some of the disadvantages.' On 1 April 1984, Mark surfaced in New York to tell the *Daily Mail* 'why I must move away from mother' and why he was naive: 'naive not to see that people I regarded as friends would try to use an association with me for their own ends. I see now how wrong I was. Naive to think that this business was just to do with me and my partner and nothing to do with my mother. I see now how they have used me to get at her.'

## Former politicians: gone but not forgotten

Even retirement from public life (or to the House of Lords, which is often the same thing) does not mean the media will readily drop any decent 'human interest' story that can be hung on the peg of the magic letters 'M.P.' John Ryman, the fox-hunting barrister Labour MP (who defeated Eddie Milne, the Labour MP for Blyth, himself forced out of the Party for campaigning against corruption in North East Labour councils) resigned in 1987 only to emerge in the *Mail on Sunday* two years later as the former MP 'Who's a Legend in His Own Love Life'. This was a reference to the attack on him by his fifth wife for spending her money before disappearing. Jack Surgenor, on the other hand, tagged Anthony Barber, a Tory Life Peer and former Chancellor of the Exchequer, as 'Rat of the Year' in 1989 for 'stealing my wife', who was formerly engaged to Barber during the war. Barber told the tabloids 'this is none of your business' as his solicitors announced the forthcoming marriage. Barber's ditched fiancée (over thirty years Barber's junior) then appeared in the tabloids alleging 'he just wanted me as a sex toy' and that he was impotent ('he would be tearful after hours of our trying to put some sexual life into him').

And, if media allegations about MPs are risky while alive, they have no compunction about thoroughly libellous comments concerning those not able to answer back. Even the arrival of AIDS, the latest sexually-transmitted disease, has meant that it was only a matter of time before the press began to look for AIDS-affected politicians. As every competent libel lawyer knows, however, to suggest that someone has a contagious disease that would lead to their ostracism from society is actionable *per se*; that is, virtually undefendable unless true. This has not stopped the media ghoulishly lurking among the obituaries to make any such suggestions. Lord Avon, 54-year-old son of former Prime Minister Anthony Eden and his first wife, died on 17 August 1985. The *News of the World* decided AIDS was the cause of death; he was treated by a specialist in the virus, he lost a lot of weight, he suffered a series of illnesses and he was a 'confirmed bachelor' (journalese for homosexual). He served in the army, became a city banker and invested in showbusiness ventures. He worked almost anonymously in public life after the death of his father in 1977, first as an aide-de-camp to the Queen and then a junior Minister at the Department of Environment before his resignation on health grounds in March 1985. 'Monstrous', came the comments of Lord Denham, the Government Chief Whip, on the story, to which the *Daily*

*Telegraph* added that his cause of death, inflammation of the brain, was a common ailment among AIDS sufferers. A few months later Martin Stevens, the large, florid-faced Tory MP for Fulham, died of a coma in a Paris hospital in January 1986 after a West African holiday. He was an alleged homosexual – he was a former vice-president of the Campaign for Homosexual Equality – and a busy Parliamentary consultant. His death – from a heart attack and blood poisoning – was enough to prompt journalists to ask if he died of AIDS. No he didn't, said his staff, which was enough for its headline: 'TORIES' GAY MP "DIDN'T DIE OF AIDS"'.

# Chapter 8

## A Decade of Parliamentary Gossip, Scares and Scandals, Part Two

*Motes, Beams and Bullets*

That the focus is on politicians is undeniable and it is discernible in the extraordinary range of stories – drawn from the past decade – on a wide range of activities that an MP may argue to be his or her private concern. Members of Parliament will fill the media from a paragraph in a gossip column to banner headlines on the front page for behaviour that ranges from the most harmless to the most bizarre, from the most innocent to the decidedly criminal. Where the line between privacy and publicity, between behaviour that only attracts attention because it involves an MP and behaviour that may be stupid, unethical or unacceptable for someone in a public position, is drawn is, unfortunately for MPs, not for them to decide.

From their hobbies to their politics, MPs can be in the firing-line of media attention, as were a gamekeeper and the chairman of Cherry Valley duck producers, Sir Joseph Nickerson, when Viscount Whitelaw slipped in August 1984 and peppered them with gunshot as he aimed at a grouse on the South Durham moors. 'The incident', said Sir Joseph, 'was really a non-event and has been grossly exaggerated.' Willie Whitelaw was reported as being 'extremely upset.' Left-wing MP Kevin McNamara, a Hull MP from 1966, came under fire in 1980 from his constituency party for sending his son to Ampleforth, a first division Roman Catholic public school, to which he had won a music scholarship. He had been criticised two years earlier when another son also won a music scholarship to the same school and a grant from the Tory-controlled county council to help pay the fees (£750 a term). McNamara was 'not penitent but proud of his son's achievement', but his local party was clearly divided by what they saw as a personal rejection of party attitudes to private education.

Another MP in someone's firing-line was Norman Lamont, whose friends suggested that he had 'a habit of dropping in on friends late at night.' One night he dropped in on Olga Polizzi (eldest daughter of Lord Forte), said to have separated from her husband, airline sales manager Alessandro Polizzi de Sorrentino, in 1980. Present also was Richard Connolly, a 43-year-old art dealer. Asked to leave the house in Clarendon Close, Bayswater, around midnight, because they were arguing, Connolly was alleged to have punched Lamont in the eye. Lamont has had a mainstream rise through the Tory ranks – President of the Cambridge Union, personal assistant to Duncan Sandys, chairman of the Bow Group, merchant banker at N. M. Rothschild and Sons, MP for Kingston-on-Thames since 1972, Minister in the Departments of Energy and Trade and Industry. At first he said he had walked into a wall (or door) until the *Daily Mail*'s Dempster's Diary printed the story in July 1985. Lamont said the background to the incident was 'innocent but complicated', an attitude accepted by Mrs Thatcher on the grounds that it was a personal matter. Lamont thought the incident 'so trivial and so minor, it does not justify my comment' but the flesh-coloured patch over his eye was a temporary source of amusement for his colleagues and Opposition MPs.

Much of the behaviour is often no different from the minor offences and crimes that are committed by a large number of people every year. Michael Fallon, the Tory MP for Darlington, who is the joint Parliamentary scourge of quangos, was banned from driving for eighteen months in July 1983 for having more than twice the legal amount of alcohol after driving his car into a lamp-post. Winston Churchill was fined £100 in May 1983 for driving at ninety-eight mph in a sixty mph speed area; Michael Brotherton, Tory MP for Louth, was banned for three years from driving and fined £600 for driving his car into another lamp-post after being found with more than three times the legal limit; he had been disqualified for three years and fined £300 for a similar offence in 1977. In 1984 the late Sir Anthony Berry, Tory MP for Southgate, a JP, and a former deputy Chief Whip and treasurer for the Royal Household, was fined £1350 and banned for two years for reckless driving and driving while unfit through drink. He was also ordered to pay £24.56 for damage to police uniforms. When stopped in Chelsea by police and asked to step out of his car he replied: 'Not bloody likely. I'm getting out of here'. He drove off, brushing aside the policemen (who tried to stop him by hitting his windows with their truncheons) narrowly missing pedestrians and other cars, and jumping a red light. His QC argued that 'He really can't believe that he could have conducted himself in this way. This was an immediate and uncharacteristic reaction, to totally panic, realising he was over the limit. It was almost like a brainstorm.' In 1980 James Dunn, Labour MP for Liverpool Kirkdale and a former Northern Ireland Under Secretary (he later joined the SDP and disappeared from view) was conditionally discharged and ordered to pay £100 costs on two shoplifting charges – a 60p map, two ties, two armbands and a sweat top worth £14.53 from the Army and Navy Stores, Victoria Street. His defence was that he was being watched when he took the map, and that the other articles were in a shopping bag given him by an assistant to replace one that had split. At least the judge accepted that he was 'acting entirely out of character, which was attributable to [his] appalling state of health.'


*Safe Bets*


Business interests, which MPs may continue on becoming an MP, or take up once they have entered the House (provided these are included on the Register and declared, where relevant, in any Parliamentary context) may also be the subject of comment or criticism because business works by a different set of rules from politics, and views fellow-businessmen in a completely different light from that in which politicians see each other – which may not always be good news for politicians in the business world. Casinos, for example, might be a newsworthy pursuit, because the Gaming Board has itself to ensure that directors of companies buying or running casinos are fit and proper persons. This means that one's directors are given a far more searching examination than other businesses. During the clean-up of the London casinos at the start of the 1980s, Playboy director Clement Freud, the Liberal MP for the Isle of Ely since 1973, whose lugubrious face fronted TV dog food commercials and whose lugubrious voice often appeared on the radio, was alleged by the police to have gambled at a Playboy casino, something specifically forbidden by the 1968 Gaming Act. At the end of the 1980s Tory MP Barry Porter found his name in the press because the firm of which he was a director was apparently being investigated 'reaching back into the Seventies' for company associations, to ascertain whether or not his business colleagues were fit and proper persons to run casinos.

Business interests with a political or public sector dimension will also attract media attention. In March 1980, the House of Commons Public Accounts Committee published a critical report on the Underwater Training Centre at Fort William, Scotland. In 1974 an inter-departmental Underwater Training Task Group, appointed by the Department of Employment, considered that advanced training facilities should be provided to train divers for the expanding but dangerous offshore British oilfields. The Manpower Services Commission felt that the development of training standards should remain in public rather than private hands and that a centre thus funded should be set up as soon as possible. In late 1974, the MSC awarded a five-year contract to establish, operate, and manage the Underwater Training Centre at Fort William to a private bank, Shenley Trust Ltd, with the MSC paying all overhead costs and expenses attributable to the contract, and an annual fee of £35,000. The MSC also funded the purchase of assets – classrooms, barges, equipment, and so on – which were vested in a Shenley

Trust company, the Underwater Trials Centre Ltd, for the duration of the management contract.

At the same time Shenley Trust had taken over the land and assets of UEG Trials Ltd, another contender for the management contract that found itself in financial difficulties, and renamed it Underwater Trials Ltd. In 1975 Peter Emery signed the five-year management contract with the MSC on behalf of the Shenley Trust and then, some months later, signed another contract with the Centre on behalf of Underwater Trials, to provide the land and other facilities for the Centre. This latter contract was for twenty-five years and included a compensatory break-clause, worth three years' fees to Underwater Trials, if that contract was broken. In 1976 Shenley Trust ran into difficulties and the management contract was transferred to Shenley Trust Services Ltd, run by Peter Emery.

The PAC was concerned at the 'alacrity with which public funds were provided to set up and run the Centre', the failure to elicit the oil industry's involvement or financial support, and what it saw as the 'large' profit margin accruing to Shenley through the management contract. Media interest was awakened by the fact that Emery was a Conservative MP and had held junior Ministerial posts in Industry and Energy during the Heath government. Labour MP John Prescott was quick to raise questions about the 'cosy relationships' between civil servants and the North Sea oil industry and said: 'A matter of major concern to me is that a minister could come out of office and be involved in bidding for a contract in these circumstances which also involved civil servants from his former department'. Emery was furious with the Report, complaining that neither he nor his company were called to give evidence and that profits alleged were incorrect. The PAC met again in November to hear further evidence from, among others, Emery, the MSC, and the Minister then responsible for such matters at the Department of Employment, the latter stating that Ministerial approval for the MSC's actions had not been sought. The Committee, however, 'saw no reason to change its views', including those on the profit margin of the management contract.

The question of private interest and public decisions, on the other hand, was so sensitive that a *New Statesman* article headed 'FORMER MINISTER'S COMPANY MAY GET £¼ MILLION FROM PUBLIC FUNDS' cost it damages and a public apology for the imputation of undue influence and the suggestion that Emery would receive any financial benefit from the ending of the twenty-five year contract. That apology stated that the article had not intended to convey the impression that he had used his influence as an ex-Minister to obtain the management contract but had intended to raise 'the question of potential conflicts of interests where ex-public servants accept positions in industry and commerce both generally and in this specific instance'.

More seriously, such business interests may cost an MP his career. Tom Benyon was a former insurance executive who joined the Rossminster Group of companies in 1973. Rossminster marketed tax-avoidance schemes which had no other purpose other than exploiting existing tax laws by reducing liability on income. The complex company structure was run from London through a network of offshore companies based in Britain's tax havens. It was highly successful, appealing to those in the higher tax brackets who were increasingly hit by the Labour Government's tax policies and finding moral support from Conservative Party circles that made no secret of its belief in the right to enjoy the material rewards of success and of its dislike of the 'authoritarian' behaviour of the Inland Revenue and the Customs and Excise. In 1979 Benyon won the candidature of the safe Tory seat of Abingdon after the assassination of Airey Neave. Ironically, Tim Yeo, his competitor for the seat, had been criticised a year earlier by the Stock Exchange, something that 'created an embarrassment for Yeo which encouraged his decision to stand down.'[1] Benyon, who had severed his links with the company, was not the only Tory politician to have had dealings with Rossminster. John Nott, a barrister and a former merchant banker, once worked for a subsidiary as a consultant. Peter Rees, a QC, often acted as tax adviser to Rossminster. All were subject to increasing media attention as financial journalists and the Inland

Revenue began to look hard at Rossminster's activities. Rees in particular was criticised as poacher turned gamekeeper, being able to pronounce on the legality of schemes to avoid tax and later to become a Government Minister with responsibilities for Inland Revenue policy. Nevertheless it was Benyon who was to suffer, as a former managing director of Rossminster went onto *World in Action* to allege that he ordered Benyon's affairs 'so that he did not pay a penny piece in tax.' Benyon's seat was merged with another, Wantage, and he had hoped to be the only candidate. The programme, together with the possibility of criminal prosecutions following the Inland Revenue's raid on Rossminster, stirred up local opposition to his candidature. 'A very bitter Benyon, suspecting that he was unlikely to get the nomination, stood down and announced his retirement from politics. He blamed the Rossminster taint stemming from the still unresolved Revenue investigation. "It had been difficult to know how to rebut the inevitable cloud which developed over everyone involved," he said.'[2]

With the rules on business interests stricter for Ministers than the ordinary MP, Ministers are more likely to attract greater attention. In 1986 the *Observer* was soon knocking on the door of another Tory politician, the then Transport Minister Nicholas Ridley. It wanted to ask him about the purchase of Jaguar Car shares following its privatisation in 1984. His broker bought 2000 shares at £2.15p and then sold them at £4.15p some sixteen months later, almost doubling the return on his initial investment. The newspaper also checked with other Ministers on their attitude to private investments and found that there was a degree of variation on what they felt was acceptable. Ridley's attitude to the newspaper's questions was to label them an 'intolerable intrusion' into his privacy. Privacy and the value, material or otherwise, of one's property, however, are just as much subject to scrutiny for the same reasons as business interests – to find out if any Minister could not be seen to be using his or her position for personal benefit. Thus, in 1988, as Secretary of State for the Environment, Ridley was again having to face intrusion into his privacy, this over attempts to build houses behind his Cotswolds Queen Anne house. Ridley had been warning fellow Conservative MPs against NIMBY (Not In My Back Yard) attitudes to new housing developments in their constituencies ('this, I am afraid, is rather selfish') when he was asked on Radio 4 about his own backyard. He stopped the interview, he said later, because he 'could not reasonably be expected to remember details about letters written many years ago'. He was referring to letters of objection he had written in 1980 'in my capacity as private citizen' to the local council about plans to build houses in the meadow at the back of the former rectory. Mrs Thatcher ignored attempts by the Leader of the Opposition to provoke a reaction from her and professed that her colleague 'does his work excellently and in a very distinguished way'. In 1989 Ridley did win his appeal to protect the view behind his Cotswold home. The planning inspector said that 'very real harm would occur to the fundamental character and appearance of the village' if the houses were built. This brought to three the number of planning permissions that involved the various Ridley homes. In the same year as the Cotswold case he was asking permission to build an extension to his Cumbrian home, across a public right of way, and in 1985 he had objected to penthouses being built on a row of houses in one of which he once had a flat.

## Private Lives and Privacy

In October 1987 the *Sunday Mirror*'s headline read: 'SHAME OF MP'S NIGHTS IN GAY BAR'. John Cummings, former miner and leader of Easington District Council, had won the rock-solid Labour seat of Easington with a majority of nearly 25,000 in 1987. In London Cummings visited a Soho pub, the Golden Lion, where his briefcase went missing while he went to the Gents. In it were non-transferable travel warrants whose loss he immediately reported to the police and Commons staff. Unfortunately one of the warrants turned up in the possession of a young homosexual who went to the newspaper with a tale of £30 sex services and of a travel warrant as a gift. Notwithstanding the unlikelihood of the story, the fact that the newspaper had an interview from a self-confessed rent boy and that the pub had a degree of notoriety – mass murderer Donald Nielsen met some of his victims there – meant that the story was worth running. This was guaranteed when Cummings, who denied all knowledge of the man, admitted that he had visited the pub knowing its reputation – 'I know the sort of place it is, I'm not that daft', he supposedly said – and allegedly telling the newspaper when pressed about his sexuality that 'I'm bisexual, my sexual preferences are both ways'. The case of John Cummings and his appearance on the front page of the *Sunday Mirror* was, said Yvonne Roberts, a 'tribute to the power of innuendo. It was only made possible by that lethal combination in Fleet Street – sharp reporters and a naive member of the public'.[3] Now Cummings was not just a member of the public, he was a politician – but he certainly was naive. Interviewed alone, after midnight and after several pints of beer at his local pub in Durham, by two *Mirror* journalists, he unwittingly provided the basis of a carefully structured story that 'read as if he volunteered information without questions and implicitly was admitting guilt which he emphatically was not.' More interestingly, the male prostitute who provided the story later denied ever meeting the MP, admitted he took money from journalists to pay for drugs and was later sentenced for stealing the travel warrant. By that time it was too late for Cummings to recover his reputation and peace of mind from a simulated scandal. Nevertheless he apparently must now accept that the press don't overlook such weaknesses: in October 1989 the same newspaper was back with a small story about the suspended jail sentence for the MP's former chauffeur-cum-research assistant for deception. 'What happened was unfortunate', said Cummings' agent, 'I'm sure John doesn't feel good about it'.

Dr Roger Thomas came late to Westminster, elected as Labour MP for Carmarthen in 1979 with a 1154 majority at the age of fifty-three. A doctor since 1948, married with two grown-up children, he was watched by two plain-clothes policemen in lavatories in the Llansamlet area of

Swansea one afternoon in October 1983 and arrested for importuning for immoral purposes. He told the officers: 'Oh my God, no. This is the end. Oh God, what about my family? I just called here off the motorway. There is no toilet there and I had heart palpitations.' He was fined £75. He continued to sit in the House, speaking out on the need to protect individuals from disclosure of information, including that relating to their sexual lives and criminal offences, held on computer data banks. Despite support from Labour MPs and constituents, his local party disowned him in July 1984 after he announced he was reconsidering his promise to resign – 'there is a growing feeling in the constituency that this is not a resigning matter', he argued. He subsequently retired at the 1987 General Election.

It was a *News of the World* reporter, the experienced Ron Mount, who ventured into the gloom of the Buddy Club in Duisburg Strasse, Berlin, in February 1981. The club seemed to contain a leather and chains clientele in an atmosphere lit only by red lights and candles behind the black leather drapes over the windows. If the mirrors, posters and TV video didn't upset Mount, the sight of men kissing the American barmen certainly did: 'I can only say I wouldn't like my MP to go anywhere near the place', wrote Mount. Unfortunately Bootle's Labour MP, Allan Roberts, a former teacher, social worker and Manchester city councillor, did. *Private Eye* picked up the story of a visit to the club in Easter 1980, alleging he was dressed in a dog collar and whipped, club activities that led to an overnight visit in a Berlin hospital. Roberts admitted to a drunken spree in the club and an accident that involved hospital treatment but dismissed as rubbish the *Private Eye* details. Nevertheless the *News of the World* found a member of the party of six that included Roberts that had flown to Berlin. In a signed statement to the paper's reporters he alleged an assault on Roberts by himself and two Germans at the club which resulted in an injury that required medical attention. Roberts, who received a unanimous vote of confidence from his constituency party, refused to talk to the newspaper. His solicitor Rex Makin called their inquiries disgraceful although a

134

week later he announced that Roberts regretted being involved in a drunken escapade.

Maureen Colquhoun's brief tenure as Labour MP for the new constituency of Northampton North from 1974 to 1979 was noteworthy for focusing attention on how the media would handle a new aspect of political sexuality: lesbianism. As any good media lawyer would learn from his work bible, Carter-Ruck on *Libel and Slander*, imputations of unchastity (sic) against women under the 1891 Slander of Women Act were actionable *per se* – and unchastity included allegations of lesbianism. Colquhoun put herself in a position where she had no defence against allegations of her private life and, as a consequence, suffered from the 'leering innuendo and lip-smacking suggestions' of the *Daily Mail*.

Colquhoun, an uncompromising commentator on some of society's more sensitive issues – abortion, cannabis, the police, prostitues – was never comfortable with the role-playing and intrigue that is an integral feature of Parliamentary life. Public support for Enoch Powell's contention that MPs were not paying enough attention to immigration issues hardly endeared her to her political colleagues. Another issue, female representation on the membership of quangos, led to a meeting with a feminist lesbian writer in December 1974. The sequel was sincere if somewhat melodramatic. The two went to the ICA to see *Fanshen*, a play about revolutionary China, and then on to Soho for supper. Colquhoun looked into her companion's eyes and announced: 'what on earth are we going to do about us?' 'You, too?' was the reply. After that, said Colquhoun, 'neither of us could eat a thing. So there we were, two middle-aged women, ridiculously, totally and very much in love, and there wasn't anything that either of us could do, or even wanted to do, to change that.'[4]

While her companion was aware of what might happen if the story reached the press, Colquhoun was not: 'private lives were private and that was that, and it was nobody's business except her own and our immediate family.' Colquhoun left her Fleet Street journalist husband and the two set up home together. A party invitation found its way to the *Daily Mail* whose editor immediately spotted a good story and passed it on to his political staff. They refused to develop it and it was placed with Nigel Dempster, the newspaper's gossip columnist. The tone of their approach to the story was set when the newspaper interpreted the use of interlocking feminist symbols incorporating the two women's faces as 'two intertwined females.' The publication of details of the break-up of her marriage and her subsequent decision to share a house with 'a close woman friend' exposed Colquhoun to the paraphernalia of media interest – persistent phonecalls, journalists in the garden, lurking photographers. Her response was to complain bitterly to the Press Council.

The *Daily Mail*'s defence was that 'any area of the private life of a public person is open to investigation.' The editor, David English, argued that the story had been published 'out of a sense of public duty' and that, by not co-operating in this, Ms Colquhoun 'was depriving the newspaper of its right to access to information about the private lives of public people.' Its defence went so far as to suggest that, by complaining of harassment and invasion of privacy, she was being vindictive and 'trying to get her own back.' Surprisingly the Press Council only reprimanded the newspaper for harassment and for printing the name of Ms Colquhoun's companion. Otherwise, it argued, she had brought it all on herself because she took 'a very strong stand on feminist issues and had not been loth to publicise her views upon them.' As a consequence, 'this brings the breakdown of her marriage and the fact she had left what had been her matrimonial house to share a house with another woman, into the area of those matters which the public is entitled to know as being capable of affecting the performance of her public duties, or affecting public confidence in her views as a Member of Parliament.'

While supported by some of her Labour colleagues for the 'flagrant' intrusion and the 'typically male' approach to her complaints, the damage was done. She was seen to be susceptible to provocation and her actions open to ridicule. Her behaviour was misrepresented or paraded as examples of loony feminism, such as asking to be addressed as 'Ms' in the House. When she had a row with a car park attendant in Northampton over the right to park in the council office car park, the subsequent fisti-cuffs and the claim for damages to the car park barrier by the council quickly found their way into the newspapers. In 1977 local activists and moderates combined to chal-lenge her reselection – and pass a motion of censure. Typically she threatened court action while dismissing the charges against her as 'trite'. Nevertheless she knew by now that her lesbianism was an issue ('I am gay and I am proud of my private life', she announced) because, although not an issue to her, it was 'identifiable in the minds of others.' The consitutency party's general man-agement committee voted twenty-three to eighteen in September to ask her to resign because they did not wish to readopt her as their candidate. She appealed to the Labour Party NEC on procedural grounds and won back the nomination before losing the seat in the 1979 General Election.

## As A Consequence Of the Actions of Others . . .

When your 1973 *Who's Who* entry lists your recreations as making love (as well as making ends meet and people laugh) and enjoying life, then publicity for some if not all of those activities will surely grab the headlines. Nicholas Fairbairn's life has been rich and varied: a poet, broad-caster, painter, bon viveur and wit which, said former Tory colleague Tom Benyon, were talents in short supply on the Government front benches and totally absent among his critics. A barrister in 1957, a QC by 1972, he was actively involved in cultural and social organisations and, in 1974, entered Parliament as Tory MP for Kinross and West Perthshire. In 1978 he was divorced: in 1979 he was appointed Solicitor-General for Scotland. In 1981 his public position and private life collided embarrassingly.

Late in December 1981, newspapers carried reports of the attempted suicide of Pamela Milne, Ian Gilmour's Commons secretary until 1979. The story alleged Ms Milne had been found hanging by her neck from a lamp-post outside Fairbairn's London home; the more prosaic reality was an attempted suicide in his bathroom. Milne says the affair had begun in 1974 when Fairbairn pursued her with roses, 'fanatical' letters (addressed from 'Bee' to 'Ant') and proposals of marriage in a stormy on-off relationship. Fairbairn, on the other hand, says it was a happy relationship but that 'I never wanted to marry her, although she wanted to marry me.'

The announcement of the attempted suicide by 'a vicious, priggish and pseudo-priggish press', as Fairbairn labelled it, was followed by concern expressed by senior MPs at the incident. Nicholas Fairbairn retreated to his Scottish home, Fordell Castle in Fife, where, armed in a blue and white dressing-gown, he held an enthusiastic press at bay, using both his daughter and a phonecall to the police to drive back their assaults.

Margaret Thatcher herself learnt of the incident from Michael Jopling, the Chief Whip, after a spate of press inquiries about it, but took a 'relaxed' view of the matter because she felt it was a private matter and had no security implications. Fairbairn accused one of his colleagues – 'allegedly an officer and gentleman about whose sordid private life I had first-hand knowledge', said Fairbairn – of sneaking behind his back to the Whips.

Prime Minister Margaret Thatcher chose not to do anything on the grounds that, as a divorced man, an affair with an unmarried woman was not grounds for dismissal or resignation or even a friendly word of caution. On the other hand the whole episode was wholly unwelcome to the party managers and whips – 'I really don't think we can be helpful on this one' was the official line; privately, warm hands were keen to reach for several throats for 'winning the party so much unpleasant publicity'.

Unfortunately for Fairbairn the stories of his private sex-life were superseded by his handling of a much nastier issue – rape. The courts' and police treatment of rape cases had been under attack in the media at that time because it was felt that the masculine approach appeared somewhat cavalier and indifferent to the severity of the offence and the effect on the victims. Clumsy interrogations, light sentences, particularly on the grounds of 'contributory negligence', created a level of concern in which the decision not to prosecute a Glasgow gang for raping a woman was greeted with outrage. In the ensuing row Fairbairn resigned on 21 January 1982, largely because he had announced the reasons for not prosecuting the case to the press before he had officially informed the House.

Retreat to the backbenches did not, however, entail oblivion as Pamela Milne told the press of her 'FIERY AFFAIR WITH "BEE", THE ROMEO MP' with its talk of rages, fights and rows. This was rapidly followed by the announcement of Fairbairn's relationship with the forty-year-old wife (nicknamed 'Sambo' according to Milne) of a wealthy businessman. He, Alasdair MacInnes, an investment consultant and member of the Turf Club, alleged in headlines that 'TOP TORY STOLE MY WIFE'. He claimed that he had had suspicions they had been having an affair in Edinburgh which he thought had ended when they moved to London. Fairbairn retorted that he and Suzanne MacInnes had met in Scotland when he had been asked to help deal with some of her marriage problems. 'I was bowled over by her', he announced, 'but we were forced apart by her moving to London with her husband. When she came back and I met her again, it was love at second sight'. Fairbairn stuck to Suzanne MacInnes and his values, riding out the criticism on the grounds that he had no intention of being part of a world in which people are expected to be 'faceless, headless, meaningless, sexless, mindless and useless'. In 1983 Alasdair MacInnes was granted a divorce on the grounds of his wife's adultery with the former Solicitor-General for Scotland, whose latest Who's Who entry gives his interest as ornithology – the study of birds.

One man's attempt to protect his liberty was the direct if wholly unexpected cause of the destruction of another man's reputation. The link between them was a woman who 'walked like a Slinky toy.' From one journalist's description of her it is hardly surprising that she never failed to attract attention:

Five feet four inches tall, she had a heart-shaped face with large, limpid blue eyes, black hair, a complexion like a cake of white Dove soap, and pale, sensuous lips. Her eyelashes were long and uneven, giving her a wild exotic look. She peered out from under her eyelids, heightening her sex-appeal . . . Everything about her, including her chest, seemed larger than life.[5]

This vision was Sandra Daly. She grew up with her mother and grandparents in a terraced house in Leicester. She went to work in London as typist and night telephone operator, giving birth to a daughter, Kim, after an affair with an American serviceman. When her mother won a holiday for two in Paris in a *Daily Mirror* essay competition she took Sandra with her. In Paris Sandra met a young Arab businessman. She went to work for him as a secretary and then, in 1961 in Beirut, she married him. So Sandra Daly became Soraya Khashoggi. Khashoggi was the son of the doctor to the Kings of Saudi Arabia. He was educated in Egypt and then the USA, where he first discovered the benefits of a business career. A talent for spotting the market potential of his rapidly-industrialising home country, shrewd negotiating skills, the ability to act as both a man of the West and the Arab world, and his close ties to the ruling feudal royal family, all combined to make his career flourish. He was successful in starting up businesses in Saudi Arabia, importing supplies and, crucially, acting as intermediary to the multinationals chasing the Saudi petro-dollars. His clients offered the best in the sophisticated hardware for an acquisitive nation, from cars to jetfighters, and included Lockheed, Northorp, Westland, Marconi, Fiat, Chrysler and Rolls Royce. His speciality was the arms trade and his world the executive boardrooms, Pentagon inner sanctums, presidential residences and royal palaces where 'megabuck' deals made him extraordinarily rich. Between 1970 and 1975, Lockheed and Northorp were allegedly to have paid him $160 million in commission. He invested the money in a range of commercial and banking schemes and indulged himself in little luxuries like a £22 million yacht and a $31 million McDonnell-Douglas DC-8 (with a ten-foot wide bed). He acted the playboy, moving between Las Vegas, Paris, Cannes and Beverly Hills in a flurry of ostentatious wealth and a circle of prominent friends, associates and servants. In 1989 he was arrested in Switzerland at the request of the FBI to face charges that he had been involved in laundering the money that President Marcos stole from the Philippines.

One person who was less than happy with the glamorous lifestyle was Soraya, who had given him five children but was divorced, Islamic-style, in 1974, through an intermediary. Soraya still had use of the Eaton Square house in Belgravia and the £200,000 country mansion in Somerset but often clashed with her former husband over access to the children and her maintenance. From her housekeeper's memoirs published later – which she tried to block in the High Court – she was still able to maintain a gossip-column life, which included friendships with Tory MP Jonathan Aitken and singer Jack Jones. She was to achieve international fame in 1979 when she hired Marvin Mitchelson, divorce specialist to the stars and inventor of the 'palimony' settlement. They instituted a £1,135 million alimony suit against her husband on the grounds that she had been an equal partner in his spectacular rise as an international businessman. That soon paled (she got an alleged £2 million in 1981) when, within months, her name was the focus of another trial in London.

In 1977 she claimed that £150,000 worth of jewelry had been stolen from her hand luggage on a flight from Paris to Heathrow. Heathrow, which had a reputation as 'Thiefrow', had its own Scotland Yard clean-up squad to whom Soraya Khashoggi took her complaint. If the theft was from her hand-luggage – a necessary fact for insurance claims – then the most likely thief would be a Heathrow porter. A porter was in fact arrested and then subsequently cleared; part of the jewelry was found in the home of a Paris airport worker, which suggested that it had been in Soraya's other luggage. The insurance company claimed back the money they had paid and three detectives from the Heathrow squad tried to suggest that £6000 was the price for not pursuing perjury charges against her. Creditably she told her solicitors and allowed Scotland Yard's anti-corruption department to wire her up with concealed microphones to obtain the evidence.

She did; the three officers were arrested and were charged with conspiracy to corruptly obtain £6000 and of demanding the money with menaces. One of them, however, decided to speak to Soraya's housekeeper about her employer's lifestyle and so learnt of her longstanding affair with a Tory politician. Whether or not he intended to use the information to buy her silence in court, he did claim at the trial that he had previously visited her London home not to demand the money but to investigate her relationship with a married politician that could have defence implications. The affair was not particularly clandestine. It was 'common knowledge' in the Soraya household, the CIA knew about it, as did MI5 and, apparently, Prime Minister Margaret Thatcher. Notwithstanding the unlikelihood of a Heathrow police officer being entrusted with affairs of state, the security aspect woke up the media and opposition Labour MPs.

James Wellbeloved, the Labour MP who made the running in the Lambton affair, called on Mrs Thatcher to refer this court-room allegation to the Security Commission. The mystery politician had only been referred to as 'Mr X' in court although his name had been written down and passed to the judge and jury. 'The whole area of security in respect of the Ministry of Defence', argued Wellbeloved, 'is a very important matter . . . Parliament is entitled to the assurance that the politician concerned did not have access to sensitive defence material.' With that the ubiquitous Lord Goodman stepped forward in December 1979 to announce that, 'to avoid further speculation affecting other members of Parliament Mr Winston Churchill MP has instructed us to state that the name written down in recent criminal proceedings at the Old Bailey, but not published, was that of Mr Churchill.' An MP since 1970, and Opposition deputy spokesman on defence from 1976 to 1978, Churchill had blotted his copybook and been sacked by Thatcher for voting in favour of the immediate ending of the sanctions against Rhodesia instead of abstaining when the Labour Government proposed a motion to continue their sanctions policy. Since it was six months before the 1979 General Election, he had blown his chances of Ministerial office but, conversely, had therefore never been in a position to see classified information (a right only for Ministerial and not Opposition officeholders).

Although Thatcher saw no official consequences in the announcement, the media galloped after the details of the affair. It appeared that the affair began in the early 1970s when Soraya met Churchill at a party on her return to live in England, and lasted for four or five years. Although neither side saw the affair ending his marriage she signed herself 'Mrs Churchill', appeared openly with him, and spent a lot of time with him. Her daughter, from Soraya's affair as a teenager (and whose boyfriend Soraya briefly married) claimed that Churchill was 'the love' of her mother's life. One version suggests the affair ended by mutual agreement to protect his marriage and children; Soraya claimed she sent him home to his family despite 'his flowers and his pleas still to see me.'

Once in the open, Churchill's wife declared him 'a man of integrity' for announcing his involvement and said that, while not condoning his actions, the affair was over and the family more united than ever. The media took up the 'happy Churchills' story as his constituency party endorsed his courageous action in speaking out. One official went so far as to assert that 'any ill-feeling is reserved for Mrs Khashoggi for making her affair public.'

In November 1986 Elizabeth Browne was expecting to be sent to prison. In 1965 she married John Browne, who became Tory MP for the safe Winchester seat. In 1984 she divorced him on the grounds of his adultery. As a result of inheritances she had acquired substantial assets during the time of her marriage: a £335,000 Belgravia house, a £430,000 trust fund in Jersey and property in the South of France. In the financial settlement her former husband was awarded £175,000 in maintenance and costs. With a shortfall of some £65,000 still outstanding, which she claimed she could not pay, Browne's solicitors took legal action against her that could have led to her imprisonment. She said her former husband was 'motivated by spite'; the judge, in staying the threat of prison, said that her husband had acted entirely properly and suggested that her tactics, including hiding her assets of nearly

£800,000, were intended to pressurise and try to break Mr Browne financially. He also suggested that her evidence was suspect and unacceptable.

Browne then ran into constituency problems, partly as a result of the 'adverse publicity' and partly over allegations that, in trying to tell his side of the story, he had been selective in the material he provided. The full documents relating to the settlement were obtained by Browne but both TVS and the *Observer* then alleged that, in trying to present himself in a favourable light, Browne had omitted those parts that referred to his 'life of affluence', the judge's comments on his frankness and the judge's suggestions that Browne had 'felt temptations in other ways to improve the financial status of himself and his wife'. His conduct was discussed at two constituency meetings in 1987 – a reselection meeting and the Party's annual general meeting – and he was reselected comfortably. In May at a constituency public meeting, however, he was questioned about his business interests, details of which had been obtained by the *Observer*. Browne, a former Grenadier Guards officer and an adviser to Barclays Bank International and the kidnap specialists Control Risks, also had a company called Falcon Rose whose major asset appeared to be Browne himself. This firm acted as a consultancy and he declared it in the Register of Members' Interests. He did not mention that one of Falcon Rose's clients was Selco East Consultants which had hired him at £2400-a-year to promote its interests as a Middle East intermediary business seeking contracts for large industrial concerns. One of these was Davy McKee, a large British engineering firm that wanted to build a chemical plant in Bahrain. Browne's role was to assist in this and he urged Margaret Thatcher to visit Bahrain to promote British interests as well as writing to Cecil Parkinson, then the Minister of Trade, that political influence may 'well prove decisive'. He clearly had the support of Davy McKee, one of whose directors wrote to him that 'it would certainly be beneficial if the maximum political assistance could be made . . . at all levels of government influence'. In the event he was unsuccessful; the contract went to an Italian firm and Barclays persuaded him to drop his Selco deal on the grounds that there was a 'conflict of interest'. Browne, who remained as MP for Winchester, was annoyed at the publicity. The Selco consultancy had required contractual secrecy and Browne obtained an injunction to stop the *Observer* printing any more of the document it had obtained about his activities for them.

At the end of 1988, Browne's divorce settlement was sorted out, retaining the £175,000 he had previously been awarded. Said Lord Justice Butler-Sloss: 'the suggestion is, I believe, that he was a man hoping to live off a rich wife. The facts are very different. This was an application by a husband for financial relief of a capital nature, for redistribution of family assets after divorce – an application which this husband made of right'. Mrs Browne was ordered to pay the £95,000 legal bill.

Rather than let the publicity he had received subside, it was given fresh impetus by Browne coming first in the Private Members' legislation ballot for his Protection of Privacy Bill. This would allow anyone to seek damages for invasion of privacy, whether the facts were accurate or not and against which the only defence would be whether the publication was a matter of public concern and for the public benefit. Together with the Labour MP-sponsored Right of Reply Bill (establishing a quango to enforce a statutory right of reply in cases of misreporting and extending legal aid to libel cases) the Bills attracted substantial attention in the wake of the tabloid stories on the private lives of, among others, TV presenter Russell Harty, the businessman Ralph Halpern, and the singer Elton John. The Bill failed in January 1989 to gather enough support to continue; the Government expressed its sympathy for its aims but doubted it provided a practical, workable answer while receiving cross-bench support, as MPs spoke out against tabloid harrassment: Labour MP Dawn Primarolo recalled tabloid journalists seeking 'sordid and unsavoury' details about her private life, George Galloway opposed the bill but complained of 'rampaging rat packs' while Tory MP Gerald Howarth said that a story about Harvey Proctor had been a pack of lies but 'to this day the "News of the Screws" had failed to retract that story'. Part of the bill's failure might have been caused by 'an active dislike' of Mr Browne which 'may have played a fair part in seeing off his bill'. The Bill reappeared in February, however, as the *Observer* returned to allege that Mr Browne had not made full disclosure of payments from abroad in the Register. In May 1989 Browne withdrew his Bill (the Right of Reply Bill had been 'talked out' a few weeks earlier) because it was unlikely to proceed further and because the Government had decided to act by setting up an independent inquiry into media activities. That month, however, the Registrar of Members' Interests had decided Browne should be investigated after complaints by journalist David Leigh and a constituent for not disclosing certain financial interests. These were followed by more allegations from the *Observer* (the MP's solicitors unsuccessfully tried to stop publication) and *World in Action* about undeclared foreign payments and his support for cable television while failing to declare any financial interests. Mr Browne was the first MP to have his personal financial interests investigated by the Committee. (see p. 312)

## . . . And Putting Your Foot In It.

Occasionally, however, some MPs seem to become involved in highly complicated and embarrassing personal circumstances. Gerry Bermingham was selected as a compromise candidate by the St Helens constituency Labour Party in 1981 after a successful career as a Sheffield solicitor. Unfortunately he went on to win the seat for Labour in 1983 with a majority of 9662 in a constituency about to indulge in a prolonged bout of internecine warfare between the left and the right. Allegations of financial irregularities, packed meetings, vote-rigging, intimidation and membership chicanery have resulted in legal hearings, court cases and NEC inquiries. In the middle of all this Bermingham's love-life became significant, as the left adopted an unexpected interest in sexual standards in its efforts to deselect him. The first row erupted at the end of 1983 over his involvement with 35-year-old Ruth Harrison, his former political assistant. A month later a prominent Liverpool solicitor with a fearsome reputation, Rex Makin, who also handled Allan Roberts' case (see p. 134), announced he was seeking maintenance for the son of 24-year-old nurse Janet Ball. His party called on him to resign, less for his private life than because, as they put it, his recent conduct and handling of the allegations against him seriously damaged his and the party's credibility. Janet Ball then appeared in the local press to announce that her pregnancy stemmed from the first night they slept together after a miners' club social; 'it just happened and it was nice', she said. Not to be outdone, the local commercial radio station managed to obtain a tape of the MP speaking to Ruth Harrison on which he allegedly told her that 'I want to be part of your world . . . I accept willingly the obligation of caring and supporting you.' That was played in December 1983 as part of the station's news bulletins. Bermingham went to ground as his constituency party began to distance themselves from him. Nevertheless, despite admitting in January 1985 paternity of Ball's child, he managed to retain his candidature and the seat because the NEC imposed him upon the constituency and suspended the local party. A few years later the party was readmitted into the fold and, in October 1989, voted to deselect him.

George Galloway decided to reveal hitherto untold revelations about his private life to unsuspecting journalists at the time that the tabloids had discovered 'bonking', a popular euphemism for sex. Galloway, former leader of the broad-left grouping that took control of Dundee after the discrediting of the old guard for corruption,[6] had been General Secretary of War On Want, an overseas aid charity. An able and dynamic organiser who had presided over a substantial increase in annual donations to the charity, Galloway had been criticised for the level of his expenses and some of the purposes for which he had claimed them. In 1987 he had been elected as Labour MP for Glasgow Hillhead and agreed to pay back some £1700 to the charity (he was cleared of any impropriety). When BBC Scotland ran a programme on the matter, Galloway called a press conference to rebut its allegations. Part of the repayment he had made concerned £525 for attendance at a 1985 World Marxist Review conference on the problems facing the Horn of Africa. The conference had been held on a Greek island. For some reason known only to him, Galloway thought that this trip could be the subject of journalists' questions, not just about the cost but about what happened there.

Therefore, to the amazement of the assembled hacks, when the question was raised, Galloway promptly told them that he had spent lots of time with people in Greece, many of whom were women. Then he gratuitously added: 'some of whom were known carnally to me. I actually had sexual intercourse with some of the people in Greece'. The actual number was two but the tabloids gleefully leapt on the story with 'MY SEX ORGY BY MP' and 'I BONKED FOR BRITAIN'. Galloway then announced that he had no intention of resigning over activities that happened before he was elected as an MP. Believing himself an 'extremely sad' man after the 'explosion of lurid headlines' he rushed off to console his very upset wife. He told reporters that the reason why he admitted to his behaviour in Greece was because 'I had said I would answer any questions. I could not lie'.

Geoffrey Dickens is a beefy eighteen-stone director of an engineering firm, who came to the Commons in late middle age as one of the Thatcher 'new boys' of 1979 as Conservative MP for Huddersfield West. He leapt from backbench obscurity in March 1981 when he decided to name a former senior diplomat who featured anonymously in a child pornography trial. The trial involved the activities of the Paedophile Information Exchange and included this former public servant who, police discovered, kept a collection of obscene material and explicit diaries. Dickens was interviewed by Sir Michael Havers, the Conservative Attorney-General who suggested that 'little would be achieved if the man's identity was revealed'. Immediately following this revelation, Dickens chose to call a press conference to call for the Attorney-General's resignation but astounded the assembled hacks by announcing his own intention to leave his wife of twenty-five years' standing and go off with a blond divorcee. He then asked the journalists to wait while he telephoned his wife and let her know this. He had met the divorcee, Mrs Maureen Knight, at the Café de Paris, Leicester Square where, for a £1.25 admission charge, afternoon dancers could waltz in the plush decorous atmosphere. 'A perfect gentleman and a very happy person', said the manageress about Dickens. Mr Dickens had left home for twenty-four hours six months earlier, a fact unnoticed by the press. Unfortunately Dickens unwisely drew the press's attention to another friendship with a second woman and this time Fleet Street quickly turned up a letter and poem – 'how am I to prove sincere, I really don't know', ran one line – with which to enliven the headlines. A protesting Dickens announced that this second *thé dansant* lady had misunderstood their relationship: 'I like to help people and I don't like disappointing them', he claimed. Two weeks later Dickens again had the press assembled to hear his decision to return home – they were invited to watch as he went off to telephone his wife the good news – to his wife and his favourite meal of onion soup, steak and salad with a bottle of beaujolais.

Despite the publicity given to Dickens's erratic private life, he was able to beat off the challenge of fifty-seven Tory hopefuls to win the nomination of an even safer Tory seat for the 1983 election after Huddersfield West disappeared with boundary reorganisation. He won the new seat of Littleborough and Saddleworth, a marginal Lancashire constituency, by a 5000-vote majority. Probably he was saved both by the farcical nature of his behaviour, and the almost painful desire to be honest in his own affairs. He was also probably wise to unveil the skeletons in his own cupboard before unveiling those of less savoury characters. In 1986 he was again using Parliamentary privilege to name a doctor and a vicar alleged to be sexually involved with children. Criticised by MPs for abusing Parliamentary privilege and for breaking the Parliamentary convention under which an MP does not take up the case of a constituent of another MP without first consulting him (Norman St John-Stevas's complaint), Dickens's actions struck a responsive chord with both the media and the public. His colleagues were less impressed, however, some of whom called him a 'nasty man' and asked rhetorically 'what about the woman from Sevenoaks?'. Dickens survived unmoved, if a little bloodied, and thereafter a target for the tabloids, as in the December 1987 story of 'Strip Show Glee of Porn Fight MP' about his apparent appreciation of a strippergram that arrived to celebrate the birthday of a business friend at a hotel.

'I'm no angel', Labour MP Ron Brown told journalists in 1988. Since his election for Leith in 1979 he had been criticised for visiting Afghanistan (and posing in front of a tank) after the Soviet invasion and visiting Libya. He had been arrested (but not charged) for lunging at Mrs Thatcher, suspended for five days from the Commons for calling Nicholas Fairbairn a liar and, later, for twenty days for sticking a slogan on the table in the Chamber. In April 1988 Ron Brown picked up and dropped the Mace during a debate in the Commons on the Poll Tax. Annoyed that this personal protest overshadowed their own efforts, and the potentially-embarrassing Tory backbench revolt, the Labour Front Bench sought to retrieve the situation with a public apology. Unfortunately, despite repeated promptings from the Labour deputy chief whip, Brown refused to read the 'personal statement' which, he claimed, was 'cobbled together' by them and the Speaker: 'I didn't write this rubbish'. Marched out by the whip and under criticism from his sponsors, the Amalgamated Union of Engineering Workers, for his childish stunt, he was suspended from the whip a month later: 'If that bauble or ornament is more important than all the struggle, there is something wrong with this party', said Brown.

Unfortunately for Brown, the day after his suspension he had to deny that 'because I drop the mace I also drop my trousers' in the great 'Naked MP and Girl in Commons' scare. It began with a naked MP being startled as he was taking a shower late one evening when a colleague entered the room with a female companion. The MP claimed they did not notice his state because they were 'preoccupied' as they entered a shower cubicle in the men-only room. Word spread and other MPs rushed to the room where Ron Brown allegedly emerged from the cubicle: 'the only thing that was visible was his mace', said Labour MP Bill O'Brien while another claimed that 'what I heard made my hair stand on end'. Brown denied everything for the Saturday press, but the Sunday tabloids were not to be denied. The *News of the World* announced that Brown was insisting his research assistant, Nonna Longden, had wandered into the room by mistake but he had not been there and nor was he having an affair with her: he even tried making jokes about his lack of sexual powers and insisted he was 'faithful to my wife in my own way'. Over at the *People* ('Romeo Ron MP for Sex') there were allegations that Brown had a 'string of sexy women' visiting his London flat where they 'paraded naked in front of the window with the paunchy politician'. The newspapers also claimed that the woman in the shower had cried out 'I want your baby'.

One week later both newspapers alleged that Longden was pregnant: the *News of the World* claimed Brown was the father; the *People* reported Mrs May Brown saying her husband had had a vasectomy: both agreed that Mrs Brown and Nonna Longden had had a bitter confrontation recently. Brown himself was sent for trial in August 1989 charged with stealing Ms Longden's jewelry and two pairs of her panties as well as causing £778 damage to her windows, mirrors, record player and pictures. But in October 1989, after his temporary expulsion from the Parliamentary Labour Party, the loss of AUEW's sponsorship and even censure from his own constituency party, he was reselected with 54% of the constituency ballot. 'It's a smear campaign', said Brown after the showers incident, 'perhaps some other MPs started the rumour to get their revenge on me'.

At the trial, in the Sussex town of Lewes in January, both sides agreed Brown arrived unexpectedly at Longden's Hastings flat one evening. Defence counsel alleged he was there to retrieve some keys, to stop her pestering him, and some sensitive tapes. He also claimed that the damage to the flat resulted from Longden's boyfriend's reaction to the sight of the panties she had put in Brown's pocket.

Prosecution counsel alleged that Brown had intended to persuade her to end her new relationship. Longden and the boyfriend left for the pub, rather than listen to Brown's 'slurred and incomprehensible conversation', but were followed by a wine bottle through a window. The police were called: they found Brown at the station and the flat somewhat damaged with a note from Brown saying 'love you but it will never happen again'.

After being told by the judge to forget Brown was an MP – 'he is a human being like the rest of us subject to all the limitations and frailties which beset the human race' – the jury found him guilty of causing criminal damage but acquitted him of theft. Although the judge praised Brown's 'distinguished record of public service' he condemned his 'disgraceful exhibition of uncontrolled bad temper' and fined him £1000 with over £3000 in compensation and costs. Brown celebrated his 'moral victory' with champagne. His constituency party was less impressed: two weeks later it passed a motion of no-confidence and asked him to resign.

There are those politicians, however, whose private conduct, or the conduct of those with whom they are associated, has been thought to be a matter of serious public concern. Such conduct moves beyond a one-day mention in the tabloids and becomes a longer-running, more serious issue that essentially focuses on the question – is this the sort of behaviour expected of an MP? They thus become cases of note because they not only show details of how such behaviour comes to public notice and of how both the public and the politician respond, but also because of their effect on the reputation or future career of the politician. Public censure, tarnished image, demotion, resignation or sudden retirement may be the outcome and thus provide guidance on what type of private conduct or qualities may or may not be suitable for a public figure.

# PART FOUR

## *SCANDALS – RESIGNATIONS AND TARNISHED REPUTATIONS*

# Chapter 9

## For Their Lordships' Pleasure: Lord Lambton and Earl Jellicoe

### An Old-Fashioned Tory

In 1973 Commander Bert Wickstead, head of the Metropolitan Police Serious Crimes Squad, was sitting with Lord Lambton in an office on the fifth floor of Scotland Yard. Accustomed to dealing with Soho vice and East End gangsters he was somewhat surprised when his Lordship stripped to reveal red flannel underwear – 'a little rare in this day and age', reflected the Commander.[1] Around the same time Jim Prior, Conservative MP and Leader of the House of Commons, was sitting in the historic Privy Council Office and listening to the wife of a nightclub owner regale him with details of his Lordship's relationship with a prostitute. 'I doubt if the room had ever witnessed a more bizarre yet intriguing story', said Prior.[2] Both men were learning that his Lordship's highly-individual approach to his private life was about to lead to his highly-publicised departure from public life.

Lord Lambton was then fifty-one. He was very rich, adding £100,000 a year from the 25,000 acres of farmland he owned in Durham and Northumberland to the personal family fortune that had been first accumulated by his coal mine-owning ancestors. In Durham he was a member of the county set, living in a seventeenth-century mansion, Biddick Hall, where he owned racehorses and was reputed to be one of the best shots in the country. In London he owned a house in St John's Wood and had a reputation as a 'man about town'. He wrote regularly for the press and could always be relied upon for independent if idiosyncratic opinions, particularly about his love of politics.

He had first been elected to Parliament in 1951 as Tory MP for Berwick-on-Tweed. He had served as a PPS to Selwyn Lloyd from 1955–57, resigning over Suez, and was a critic of Macmillan's during the Profumo affair. His was the old-fashioned brand of Tory politics that felt uncomfortable with the 'creeping socialism' of Macmillan's policies and with the later managerial style of the Heath Government. He was strong on patriotism, defence and constituency matters but equally prepared to argue for the rights of the individual or against the restrictions of censorship. Although never one of the party's inner circle he cared for the Party and was prepared to criticise the ways in which he felt it was being wrongly led (after the Profumo affair he wrote that the party had received a severe blow and the people hit the hardest were those who looked to it for truth and honesty). Additionally he had a languid charm and a sardonic wit behind the tinted glasses and haughty manner which adhered him to the party faithful and the Shire-archy that permeated the upper reaches of the Party organisation.

Certainly another Lord, Lord Carrington, thought enough of him to recommend him in 1970 for the position of Parliamentary Under-Secretary of State at the Ministry of Defence, where Carrington presided, with specific responsibility for the RAF. Able, intelligent, a good speaker, he performed his duties without any difficulty until an unemployed mini-cab driver saw his name on a cheque. Lambton had married Belinda Blew-Jones in 1942 after one week's engagement. They had six children but Lambton was not one to feel his individuality constrained by the marriage. In any case he was, by 1972, living his life as he wanted. Commander Wickstead noted: 'the remarkable feature of his London home was that it had been divided precisely into two halves. Lord Lambton's half was almost spartan in appearance, more befitting a bachelor than a married man. Lady Lambton's half, by contrast, was beautifully furnished and full of female fripperies.'[3] Lambton visited prostitutes who, he later told Chapman Pincher, he regarded as a part of the life of all manly men: 'I can't think what all the fuss is about, surely all men patronise whores.'[4]

One whore he patronised was Hanora Mary Russell, an attractive 25-year-old Irish woman who had graduated from nightclub hostess and escort agency employee to an exclusive high-class call-girl ring. The girls were handpicked; the clients could have access to them only by recommendation and personal introduction. Clients and girls were matched by taste, colour and specialities through the madam at a minimum cost of £50. While the service usually catered for visiting businessmen, its exclusivity and discretion attracted later allegations that it was used by the Foreign Office to ensure foreign politicians and businessmen were suitably entertained. Russell herself first met her clients, on average five a week, in their hotels but had then received them in her £40,000 flat in Marlborough House, Edgware Road, a short distance from St John's Wood.

Sometime in 1972 Lambton obtained the telephone number of the madam, the services of Russell and the services of 'other sexual partners whom she procured for him.' Starting off as Mr Lucas, Lambton soon made no pretence of his identity to the point of signing his own cheques for her fee. 'I voted for the Tories', Russell said later, 'because they are my best clients.' In November 1972 Russell suddenly married a mini-cab driver, Colin Levy, who allegedly had a criminal record, a predilection for drink and an inability to hold down a job. The relationship was doomed from the outset. After a few months Levy left on a business trip abroad but refused to tell his wife – now Norma Levy – where he was going or why. Norma Levy went to Scotland Yard in March 1973 and alleged that Levy was on a drugs-buying trip for a London gangster. In the course of her rambling interview she mentioned Lambton's name. Colin Levy was thoroughly searched on his return (no drugs were found) and, a few days later, he mentioned Lambton both as a client of his wife and a possible drug user.

Both the Levys had talked to Wickstead's Serious Crimes Squad at a fortuitous time. The SCS was then working on the Soho pornography and vice rackets. Now they had information on a possible underworld vice-ring for VIPs, a rumour that two newspapers, the *People* and the *News of the World*, picked up in their investigations of police corruption and Soho – the latter had already run a speculative story that police raids on Soho pornography shops had turned up a 'top people's sex ring.' The SCS had passed the Levys' story on to MI5, which was investigating potential security leaks by British politicians and officials using high-class prostitutes on European visits (one was apparently using his official car to visit a brothel). There were rumours of a German-British network (the ring Levy worked for had European connections) and of possible infiltration by East German-trained 'ravens', spies planted in European call-girl agencies for information-gathering and blackmail purposes. MI5 reported the information to the Home Office Minister Robert Carr, who told Prime Minister Edward Heath. Heath, not wanting to be caught out without knowing the facts – the plaintive and damaging claim by Macmillan when the Profumo story broke – ordered MI5 and SCS to co-operate in securing the evidence. During that time further information reached him from James Prior about Lambton's activities. The wife of the owner of the Eve nightclub had spoken to Norma Levy who was concerned that her relationship with Lambton was making him vulnerable to the possibility of blackmail. An 'old business acquaintance' of Prior's had visited the club and had been told this story which he passed on to Prior. Together with Robert Armstrong, Heath's Principal Private Secretary, Prior interviewed the owner's wife at the time. 10 Downing Street had learnt from the police that there were now photographs to confirm Norma Levy's unease.

## Photocall

After his unnerving conversations with the police, Colin Levy had decided he needed some evidence to substantiate the allegations, either as a form of protection, or, more likely, to sell to the press and disappear abroad on the proceeds. He and a friend scraped the silver backing off a mirror on a wardrobe door in Norma's bedroom. They hid behind it with a cine camera and a tape recorder, the microphone of which was embedded in a teddy bear's nose. With one of Lambton's cheques and some poor-quality pictures they went to the *News of the World* on 5 May in search of £30,000. The newspaper was loath to lose a good story for lack of publishable evidence, so they installed their own image-intensifying camera and high-quality listening equipment, from which Levy obtained a film of Lambton and two prostitutes – 'grainy, amateurish 1948 porn', one journalist called it – and a tape of conversations about drugs. For good measure the newspaper also had one of their own photographers take some still photographs of the bedroom activity. The newspaper then decided not to go ahead with the story but chose to return to Levy not only his own material but also the compromising photographs they had taken. The delighted Levy rushed round to the *People* on 17 May to offer them the material at an increased fee of £45,000. He got £750 in advance, with the promise of £5250 on publication, and went off to Spain with his wife two days later. The *People* turned the material over to the police.

## Two Lords Resign

Which was why on 21 May Lord Lambton was standing in his red flannel underwear in Scotland Yard. Confronted with the pictures of him lying on a bed with Norma Levy and a black nightclub hostess he was casually indifferent: 'she's a kind of prostitute . . . I liked her, but she played no important part in my life whatsoever.' When the police raised his repeated reference to drugs on the tape Lambton knew that he was in trouble – 'a rather confused and very worried man', said Wickstead. He insisted on stripping to prove he did not inject drugs and took the officers to his St John's Wood house to pull some cannabis resin and amphetamine tablets from a concealed cupboard in the skirting board. That night he wrote a letter of resignation, on personal and health grounds, which was immediately accepted by Heath – 'one of the most inexplicably glacial exchanges of published correspondence in recent years between a member of the Government and his Prime Minister', said an unsuspecting *Guardian*. They were rapidly enlightened the next day when Lambton issued a statement in which he admitted to a 'casual acquaintance' with a call-girl and one or two of her friends, behaviour he termed 'credulous stupidity.' He made the statement, he said, because 'if any unpleasant truth is covered up rumour multiplies and the innocent become involved.' All he asked was 'for the criticism to be instantaneous and not prolonged.' At the time the details of the *News of the World*'s involvement began to emerge, together with rumours of the involvement of other Ministers, as the police searched for Norma Levy, who had disappeared abroad with her husband.

Lambton then submitted himself to a TV grilling from Robin Day in which he admitted to dabbling in drugs although 'taking opium in China is different from taking it in Berwick-upon-Tweed.' He believed that in owning up to his conduct he had helped 'palliate the harm' although he said that 'I think that people sometimes like variety, I think it's as simple as that, and I think this impulse is understood by almost anybody.' He went on to argue that there should not be different standards for public figures in a 'relaxed society' or that people should be one sort of person for most of their lives and 'suddenly become an entirely different type of plaster saint.' As Robin Day finished, so the indefatigable Wickstead was arriving, clutching a summons for drug offences (Lambton was later fined £300). The same day, 24 May, Earl Jellicoe, Lord Privy Seal and Leader of the House of Lords, was tendering his resignation. Another true-blood Tory with inherited wealth – a town house in London's Onslow

Square and a Queen Anne manor house near Marlborough in Wiltshire – Jellicoe's first career as a Foreign Office diplomat had ended in divorce in 1956. Remarried, he began a second career as a Tory politician in the Lords. Unfortunately, as one of his associates put it, 'if he had a fault; it is because he wears his weakness on his sleeve. He is not flamboyant but he was a hedonist.'[5]

The hedonism took the form of hiring girls from two escort agencies advertised in the *Evening Standard*, taking them to dinner and then, occasionally, bedding them at his London home. Jellicoe, whose liaisons were discreet, sexually orthodox and carried on under an assumed name, had no links with the Levy ring but rumours reached the police from Soho informants. The police watched his movements and then reported their information to Heath. Asked about his knowledge of Lambton's activities and aware that other Ministerial names were the subject of gossip, Jellicoe admitted his transactions and offered to resign. Heath, unwilling to be put in a position where he could not deny the involvement of other Ministers in the scandal, quickly accepted it: 'your decision accords with the best traditions of public life', he wrote in response to Jellicoe's letter of resignation in which Jellicoe wrote that he 'had some casual affairs which, if published, would be the subject of criticism.'

## Orthodoxy And The Instruments of Blackmail

The speed of the resignation and the unloading of the stockpiled stories in Fleet Street quickly took the edge off the scandal. The *News of the World* ran a three-page story on 27 May, claiming a major rôle in bringing the story to light, before clashing with the *Daily Express*, which expressed concern that 'in this modern so-called permissive age a splendid member of parliament and junior minister had been cast into the wilderness . . . can we really afford to discard men of talent, wit and patriotism because their personal lives fall short of blameless perfection?' Nevertheless, despite press talk of further names, Heath was able to state categorically on 28 May that no further Ministers were involved. Heath, despite some Ministerial mutterings over his alacrity in accepting Jellicoe's resignation, was praised on all sides for his firmness, his openness and his immediate request to the Security Commission to look at the events leading to the resignations. Indeed some Ministers, seeing the Government's and Heath's popularity improve dramatically in the opinion polls, suggested that they needed a few more scandals.[6] His actions certainly brought to an abrupt end the House's and country's gift for, as the *Guardian* primly called it, 'moral outrage, smacking its horrified lips all the way to Fleet Street and beyond.'[7] Interestingly, John Grant, then a Labour MP, noted that Wilson had had a private session with Heath before his Commons statement and suggested 'it was essential Harold and the Labour Party generally should avoid seeking any political capital out of this Government's misfortune', an approach some of his colleagues saw as taking sympathy a bit too far, smacking 'unduly of the establishment old pals' act with MPs rallying around rather too readily to protect their own . . .'[8] On the other hand, when James Wellbeloved tried to raise security aspects in the House immediately after Jellicoe's resignation, he was faced by a walkout of both Labour and Tory MPs.

The Security Commission reported in July, emphasising that there had been no security leaks, no European callgirl networks and no reds in or under any beds. It insisted it would not express opinions on the moral aspects of the affair but only on the risk to security the Lordships' behaviour may have involved. 'Ordinary sexual intercourse' with a prostitute was not a real risk. If a criminal offence is involved the risk is greater. On the other hand public figures were at risk if their behaviour was 'punishable news' that could ruin their careers. What concerned the Commission was blackmailable behavior that could endanger security. In Jellicoe's case it believed that the risk of blackmail was so slight as to be 'inconceivable' and was sympathetic that his occasional discreet use of 'call girls' happened to come to light 'at the particular moment it did.' It did not see such liaisons in themselves as security risks and was almost congratulatory about Jellicoe's discretion and heterosexual orthodoxy but, as Geoffrey Marshall suggests, 'leaves it uncertain whether the Commission thought the behaviour acceptable only because it was unrevealed or whether they thought it, though inevitably revealed, permissable conduct for a politician . . .'⁹ The Commission was less enthusiastic about Lambton. Although it considered that compromising photographs and sexual practices that 'deviated from the normal' left him open to blackmail, the effectiveness of blackmail depended on a victim likely to betray his country. That, thought the Commission, was very unlikely with Lord Lambton. Its real concern was his use of cannabis which might lead him, 'without any conscious intention of doing so', to reveal classified information 'in a mood of irresponsibility.' Heath accepted the conclusions of the Commission and announced that Ministers would be reminded regularly of the standing instructions and guidance on security matters (the Commission did not think Ministers should be subject to positive vetting).

This latter point raises the question of who deals with Ministerial impropriety. The Press Council, asked to look at the actions of the press, severely censured the *News of the World* for handing back the material to Colin Levy but warned that those in sensitive public positions should not be protected from 'disclosure in the press in the public interest of activities other people might reasonably claim to be their private concern.' Nevertheless one MP, Winston Churchill, loudly complained of the grotesque journalism that allowed national newspapers to conspire with 'a pimp and prostitute to destroy a man's career in politics.' The *News of the World* had been the subject of increasing criticism for assisting Levy and taking the photographs but it defended its public-spiritedness in seeking to confirm the allegations and co-operating with the police. On the other hand the Security Commission was condemnatory of the newspaper handing back to its informants 'convincing evidence which they previously lacked' – 'instruments of blackmail' it termed those aspects of the evidence, and the newspaper admitted to the Press Council that they should not have returned them to Levy.

The Security Commission believed that, had Jellicoe remained in office, there would have been no security risk involved in his seeing confidential documents (his subsequent record of prosaic public service suggests his atonement was swift, if low-key). The responsibility for ensuring the security suitability of candidates for Ministerial office must therefore devolve upon the Prime Minister and upon the Chief Whip's ability to sniff out potential security risks. While an imperfect system, this allowed any Prime Minister and his or her senior colleagues 'to have regard to other political factors than those connected with the existence of security risk and to enforce whatever rules of behaviour and apply whatever sanctions they feel are appropriate to the Government's or the party's electoral image.'[10]

Certainly the Lambton and Jellicoe resignations happened at a time when newspapers were slowly unravelling the extent of Metropolitan police corruption. Sir Robert Mark had been appointed Commissioner in 1972 to clean up the Met, as press revelations revealed close links between Soho racketeers and senior officers and, tangentially, rumours of 'prominent' people patronising the former's vice-rings. As the *Sunday Times* suggested; 'it is the personal bad luck of Lords Lambton and Jellicoe . . . that their habits were uncovered in the context of a burgeoning public scandal which made discreet resignations impossible.' It pointed out that other Ministers involved in a potentially-scandalous relationship 'will resign without fuss, or continue in office because in some curious way, the chemistry of events has not ignited public attention.'[11]

# Chapter 10

## 'The Problem, Of Course, Is One of Money': The Friends of Reginald Maudling

### The Naive Crocodile

Maudling was quite frank about what he needed to maintain his well-developed taste for the good life: money. An MP has a Parliamentary income and a Parliamentary pension; a Minister gets an enhanced income but no enhanced pension. Although he remarked that his business interests did give him the opportunity to travel widely and thus increase 'the service I could render as a politician', it was clear that the real reason why he took on such interests was to accumulate capital in lieu of the pension rights to which he believed he was entitled. While he did not go into politics to make money he was quite happy to trade his political reputation for additional earnings. Politicians, he argued, 'cannot reasonably be expected to neglect their interest and those of their families.'[1] He joined the Real Estate Fund of America 'hoping to build up a little pot of money for my old age' and wrote to John Poulson that 'the account Baker sent to me set out very graphically the total cost to you of the Maudling family and their interests. It certainly is colossal.' While there were those, the *Economist* for one, who thought it was right for Ministers 'who felt obliged to go out to try to earn some money in a hurry after . . . ill-paid public service',[2] there were others who felt that judgement and integrity might be trampled in the rush. Wrote *The Times* on Maudling's resignation as Home Secretary in 1972: 'a leading political figure who goes into business puts the stamp of his reputation on those with whom he associates,

165

and he therefore owes a particular obligation to satisfy himself that he is dealing with sound business.'[3]

Nevertheless the balance of opinion was that Maudling's enthusiasm to get rich quickly clouded his better judgement and that he allowed himself to be persuaded to take up business interests because of the poor financial returns from a lifetime of political service. *The Times* wrote on his death in 1979:

> It is sad that imprudent business associations should have interrupted so promising a career . . . It is a cautionary tale for British parliamentarians whose ridiculously low salaries tempt them to listen to the blandishments of speculators. The contrast that stands out is between his naive and perhaps greedy mistakes in business and his thoughtful and steady prudence in politics.[4]

John Poulson was less forgiving. Maudling, he said later, was no more naive than a hungry crocodile. At the time he became involved with the three businessmen – Poulson, Jerry Hoffman and Eric Miller – he was probably earning over £20,000 a year, about four times a Ministerial salary. He was a member of Lloyds, a banker, a director of several companies, owner of a country house and a Regency home in Belgravia. But Maudling wanted more; he wanted capital, fringe benefits and something for his family. All three businessmen were to provide this and, in return, Maudling was not only prepared to lend his name to their schemes but also actively to promote them. It was a fine distinction as to who was exploiting whom. What brought his relations with three particularly rapacious businessmen into public notice were two issues. The first concerned the increasingly-controversial employment of politicians by business interests; the second concerned the widespread existence of corruption in local politics.

Lobbying, influence-peddling and MPs' business interests with Parliamentary relevance had occasionally exercised the Commons. Since it was the traditional view that being an MP was not a full-time job and because many MPs invariably had occupations before entering politics and were able to continue them while MPs, little attention was paid to MPs' business interests other than a convention that they should be declared when speaking on related matters in the House. Ministers, on the other hand, were expected not to have directorships or controlling shareholdings, not to accept gifts or services that would place the Minister 'under an obligation to a commercial undertaking', and not to become involved in any business activity where insider knowledge could be suspected. The governing principle was that no conflict should arise, or appear to arise, between private interests and public duties. The House had considered the role of paid spokesmen – it had dismissed the activities of freelance lobbyists and intermediaries as insignificant and doomed to failure. Nevertheless, during the Sixties there were politicians who were concerned that 'some MPs have failed to make clear their private rôles as businessmen and their public positions as Members of Parliament.'[5] While Parliament could hardly have expected to nursemaid MPs who chose to become involved in dubious business ventures – and these included insurance swindles and investment frauds – there was growing unease at the recruitment of MPs by firms seeking a sympathetic voice in the House or a pseudo-official endorsement of their activities: as Poulson was later to say – 'the only names that the foreigner knows are you people.'[6]

While it was clear that PR firms, overseas governments and big business were becoming increasingly keen to employ MPs, it took the combined activities of two Labour MPs in the late Sixties to force Parliament to act. First Margaret Mackay's emotional espousal of the Arab cause revealed that vast amounts of money were being made available. Some £250,000 was made available by Arab rulers following the Six Days War to counteract the widespread public support for Israel, money used to open cultural centres and fund trips for MPs and journalists. At the same time the *Sunday Times* was revealing the role of Labour MP Gordon Bagier as Parliamentary consultant to Maurice Fraser and Associates, the PR firm holding a contract to improve the image of the Greek Junta (see p. 180). Bagier was furious when he saw the report in the press, although his immediate denial then subsequent admission of a consultancy put him in 'a pretty awkward position'. The Labour Government was cynically tolerant and in any case the Government were chasing a warship deal with the Generals and did not want any further investigations for fear of hurting the Party. The Conservative Party's traditional indifference to reforms that might eat into their MPs' wallets did not, however, diminish the concern over MPs' business interests and it was a local government scandal that forced the Commons to take action.

In 1972 Reginald Maudling resigned as Home Secretary on the grounds that the Metropolitan Police Fraud Squad were beginning investigations into the bankrupt John Poulson, with whom he had had business dealings. John Poulson was an unqualified architect who exploited the Sixties' enthusiasm for public sector and local government redevelopment by surrounding himself with a highly-competent, hardworked staff and an umbrella of companies that offered an all-inclusive range of architectural, engineering and consultancy services. He used his political, social and freemasonry contacts to win contracts and bought key individuals by using the resources of his firm to provide them with fringe benefits – holidays, accommodation, mortgages and so on. Blinded by his 'inherent sense of Christian charity' and his 'natural generosity' he was later to claim that these acts of kindness were symptomatic of his wish to use his 'large and sophisticated' organisation to offset some of the malaise he saw destroying 'our once glittering reputation abroad.' His success, he believed, attracted malevolence and sucked him into political intrigue. After all, he considered he was an honest man 'who made it a strict practice in any organisation to fire anybody who behaved dishonestly, took bribes or was guilty of immorality.'

Poulson's break into the British big-time came with the recruitment of T. Dan Smith, former leader of Newcastle City Council, whose disillusion at the lack of material rewards at local level persuaded him to try his hand at PR work. Between them Smith and Poulson sought out and hired as consultants the most influential members of councils in the North of England. By the mid-Sixties they were heavily engaged in 'municipal farming' – the science of intensely cultivating each and every facet of a council's leadership for the largest possible cash crop – an activity facilitated by one-party domination, the intricate world of local political networks, an enfeebled local press and inadequate means of official scrutiny. Poulson was not alone in doing this. Dundee, Merseyside, Birmingham and London also suffered similar depradations; the level of corruption in South Wales was even more overt, systematic and deliberate than that organised by Poulson who, even though he was believed by his competitors to have 'a stranglehold' on the North-East, was only one of several firms 'farming' in the area. What brought Poulson his notoriety was his decision to chase overseas contracts and to hire MPs to front his companies for this.[7]

## Value For Money

Construction Promotions was set up by Poulson through his wife in 1964 on the advice of Herbert Butcher, MP, and Leslie Pollard, a civil engineer, both of whom were enthusiastic proponents of the lucrative overseas market. Butcher, the tax-expert who had developed the interrelated package of companies that formed the Poulson empire, was also a well-connected businessman-politician. He proposed Albert Roberts as a consultant for CP to assist in winning a harbour contract to Portuguese Angola. Roberts, with his established Portuguese and Spanish Government contacts, was able to introduce Poulson to the right people. Although Poulson only won the harbour contract he felt the four-years' payments of £11,000 to Roberts was worthwhile, something he did not believe of his second Parliamentary recruit, John Cordle (see also p. 182). A militant Old Testament Christian and right-wing Tory, Cordle already had overseas business interests. Like Albert Roberts and Herbert Butcher, he was an active member of the Inter-Parliamentary Union and used the same firm of solicitors as Butcher and Poulson – Joynson-Hicks, the firm that was later to act as the London solicitors to the Real Estate Fund of America. Cordle was signed up as a consultant and enthusiastically began promoting CP in West Africa. Unfortunately his airport-hopping produced no contracts and Cordle wrote a lengthy defensive letter to Poulson spelling out his efforts, including taking part in a Commons debate 'largely for the benefit of Construction Promotion', and ending by saying that the payment he had so far received 'is uncomplimentary to myself'.

In 1966 Herbert Butcher, CP's chairman, died. Poulson tried to replace him with Sir Bernard Kenyon, Clerk to West Riding County Council, while he was still employed by the Council. Realising that Kenyon had neither the time or the contacts to do the job effectively Poulson asked Roberts for another name. Roberts came up with Reginald Maudling.

Maudling was one of the Commons intake of 1950. By 1955 he was a Cabinet Minister and Privy Councillor; by 1964, when the Conservatives lost office, he was Chancellor of the Exchequer. He was the epitome of the Party's centrist tendency where he 'represented the new middle class that the Tories had to win over. He espoused all the solid middle class values. He was strong on the work ethic, on rewards commensurate with effort. His political credo was of the pragmatic rather than dogmatic kind.'[8] In 1965 he lost the fight for leadership of the Party to Ted Heath and, embittered and suffering withdrawal symptoms from the drop of £5000 in his annual income, turned to business to sustain his and his family's upwardly-mobile lifestyle. He knew what was expected: 'after all, when a public figure becomes a director or chairman of a company it is presumably because his name and influence will be valuable.' Within months he snapped up non-executive directorships with Dunlops, AEI and SIH, crowning them with an executive directorship at Kleinwort Benson, the merchant bankers, who were keen to revive their reputation after investing in the Rolls-Razor debacle and to 'have on tap the knowledge and contacts made by a former Cabinet Minister.'[9] The £18,000, together with his shares and membership of Lloyds, was clearly not enough because, in the next four years, he also accepted consultancies and directorships with three less reputable organisations. In 1965 the socially-ambitious Eric Miller, who used the resources of his Peachey Property Corporation to win friends (see p. 247) as Poulson used his to influence them, offered Maudling a directorship. Anxious to avoid paying more income tax and to protect his two houses from the proposed capital gains tax, he offered himself as a consultant, through his own firm of RBM & E Maudling, on 'a wide field of public and international affairs, tax matters and economic prediction.' He traded his £5000 a year fee for a deal in which Peachey bought the freehold of his country house from his wife – Maudling held a lease on the property from her – and paid to repair and improve it. The deal effectively gave Maudling years of salary in advance, without any tax loss, and was of no commercial advantage to Peachey.

In 1966 he signed up with Poulson, who provided a substantial covenant to Maudling's wife's pet charity, an East Grinstead theatre, a job for his son and the chance to buy shares in Poulson companies. Maudling believed the covenant to be an unsubtle inducement to join the company; Poulson said Maudling accepted the job offer with alacrity but wanted the benefits to be in a form that did not incur tax. Brought in as chairman of CP, he was rapidly switched to International Technical and Construction Services, Poulson's new international front that was to search out hospital contracts, and for whom Maudling began a series of Mediterranean and Middle East forays to charm the Sheikhs and, in particular, persuade the Maltese Government to give Poulson a hospital contract on the island of Gozo. A charming talker and convivial host, he could open doors but could never raise private capital for Poulson's clients' projects. In Gozo, however, where British Government funds were involved, his influence helped win the contract and ensure Poulson was paid.

In the midst of these trips, Lord Brentford of Joynson-Hicks proposed Maudling's name for the Board of REFA, the offshore investment vehicle of Jerry Hoffman that promised massive tax-free profits on international property speculation. Once more, Maudling rapidly agreed, again waiving a fee in return for 250,000 shares in REFA's holding company. His function was to join a coterie of well-known public figures fronting REFA and intended to attract bank funds. Again enthusiastic in banging on doors he persuaded two foreign banks, solely on the basis of his involvement in REFA, to invest money in what was an international swindle: Hoffman's operators were running an interlocking network of companies intended to buy properties worldwide. Using investors' money they paid the deposit price while charging themselves commissions and fees on the basis of the full purchase price. This spread out investors' funds and inflated the apparent extent of the company's activities while making Hoffman and his colleagues rather rich.


## Public Attention And The Poulson Collapse

By the end of the Sixties Maudling too was rather rich on paper but, in 1970, the Conservatives were returned to power and Maudling again took up Ministerial office. Fortunately he had resigned from REFA in 1969 following adverse media criticism of Hoffman. He gave as his reason for resigning the approaching General Election but failed to mention that at least two British journalists had warned him of Hoffman's legal difficulties in the USA.[10] He later denied any involvement in the activities of REFA and claimed he never attended any board meetings. In 1970 he resigned his Peachey consultancy and chairmanship of ITCS. In 1970 the first articles on Poulson appeared in *Private Eye* and the *Bradford Telegraph and Argus*, the *Eye* noting that the latter's revelations 'have been studiously ignored by the national press, much to the relief of leading

172

politicians of all parties.' Poulson, however, was in deep trouble, over-extending his organisation, front-loading his costs against large contracts that never materialised and forgetting to pay the taxman – a contrast to the meticulous and annotated paperwork he kept on payments to his politician-consultants. That contrast coincided in Wakefield County Court in 1972 at his bankruptcy hearing, as Muir Hunter, QC, used the paperwork to reveal where all the money went. This in turn attracted the attention of the Metropolitan Fraud Squad. Maudling, Home Secretary and thus constitutionally responsible for the Metropolitan Police, resigned. He argued that his only connection with Poulson was 'a covenant in favour of a charitable appeal which had my support. I do not regard this as a matter either for criticism or for investigation.' Nevertheless since there were matters 'not relating to me that do require investigation' he believed he should resign 'solely because of my connection' with the police. He complained stridently at the mention of his name in the bankruptcy hearings. The disingenuousness was blatant. The £8000-a-year covenant was only part of Maudling's indebtedness to business partners; his house was still owned by Peachey, he left Hoffman with a testimonial that REFA was an admirable concept that 'can have a great future' and he kept his REFA shares for a further twelve months in the futile hope of realising his little pot of gold. More amazingly, he later made it plain that, if he had held any other post than that of Home Secretary, he would not have resigned from ITCS. He was lucky. Despite articles that suggested Maudling was tardy in disinvesting himself from REFA, despite knowing Hoffman was a crook, he resigned grudgingly from ITCS, aware that his role in Poulson was unlikely to attract further attention until the police inquiries were completed. Those were restricted to the 'jurisdiction', (that is, inside the UK), with the attention focused on T. Dan Smith's 'army of paid lieutenants' of councillors and public sector officials who later paraded through the courts.

Interest in MPs' business interests increased dramatically with the steady flow of information about those MPs who were employed by Poulson. It reached a climax with the allegations by T. Dan Smith that he had paid £250 to the Labour Leader of the House, Ted Short, a payment that Short (who said it was reimbursement of expenses for official business) had asked be kept confidential, Joe Ashton's public allegations of MPs for hire and Brian Walden's £25,000 five-year contract with the National Association of Bookmakers.

In 1974 the incoming Labour Government tried to patch up Parliament's tarnished image by forcing through new requirements on disclosure of financial interests, together with a compulsory register and an attendant Select Committee to draw up categories of entries and regularly publish it. 500 MPs crammed the House for the debate and, despite mutterings of constitutionality and panic, supported the bipartisan belief that something needed to be done. Said Tory MP Jim Prior 'we are not crooks and we want it to be seen that we are not crooks.' On the other hand more worldly MPs were aware that Parliament was faced with a peaking public attention cycle. Brian Walden argued that, 'if my experience of life is any guide, there is nothing so disappointing to the prurient as a revelation. Once they actually know what is going on, their interest in it will subside rapidly. The suspicions will go to lusher pastures where someone is trying to conceal something . . .'[11]

He was right. The new Select Committee later reported arrangements for entries in the Register to an emptier and less interested House which decided to leave the definition of a 'relevant' financial interest and the amount of detail to be entered up to Members' discretion. Worse, the Select Committee did not propose any action against Members who refused to make any return for the Register, including 'nil' entries, and delayed publication of the Register until 1980, thus nullifying any practical effect of the 1974 Resolutions.

Indeed, the House even managed to avoid any debate

on the 1976 Report of the Royal Commission on Standards of Conduct in Public Life while successive Governments stonewalled any implementation of its wide-ranging if modest recommendations. The Labour Government even tried to duck out of the issue of those MPs who had had dealings with Poulson. In October 1976 the Attorney-General announced the end of further criminal inquiries. The *Observer* immediately raised the spectre of certain MPs who might thus avoid prosecution, prompting MPs to demand that Prime Minister James Callaghan act. Hiding behind a bland admission of an ignorance of proper procedures and past precedents, Callaghan argued for a committee to look at future practice. Given the Government's failure either to respond to the 1976 report of the Royal Commission on Standards of Conduct in Public Life or to ensure the effective implementation of the 1974 Resolutions, this breathtaking sidestep brought down a barrage of criticism that forced a retraction within twenty-four hours with the establishment of another Select Committee. This Committee looked at several MPs whose names, incorrectly or otherwise, were linked to Poulson and investigated three – Maudling, Cordle, and Roberts – in detail. Despite its lack of investigative capabilities and the problem of determining what were the conventions on disclosure of interests prior to 1974, the Committee reported that all three had failed to declare their interests at appropriate times. Cordle was considered to have committed a 'contempt' for advocacy for money while the other two were merely castigated for imprudence in not declaring an interest; Maudling was further rebuked for his lack of frankness in his letter of resignation in 1972. Cordle, already doomed by his self-justifying letter to Poulson, chose to resign to avoid, as he put it, an 'acrimonious and divisive' debate on the Committee's Report and may well have been 'persuaded' to go because his Party were concerned at the effect his staying to fight might have had on Maudling's position.

With Cordle out of the way, Roberts responded to the tone of the debate by apologising for 'some ways in which I have transgressed in shallow waters.' Maudling was much less contrite, arguing that 'the general nature of my business relations' with Mr Poulson should not be a matter for discussion in the House in any way and bitterly criticising the Committee for saying his resignation letter lacked frankness. This bald disingenuousness was not challenged in the House. This was despite the fact that Maudling failed to make his promised 'startling' revelations about the Committee's conduct but owed a lot to Maudling's long-held belief that he was victim of left-wing journalists (he accused Paul Foot and his 'usual gang of Granada-type people' in 1974 of a concerted plot against him). Indeed, with Heath calling him an honourable man and the Speaker allowing him to remain in the House to face his critics personally, he was able to watch his reputation emerge publicly unscathed but politically damaged as the House voted to 'take note' of the Committee's Report.

Thus the Commons never had an opportunity to learn of a report by the DPP's leading counsel that alleged that Cordle, if he had been anything other than an MP, could be prosecuted on various criminal charges. In the case of Maudling, whom the Select Committee seemed to feel had behaved as if he had let the side down rather than been guilty of more serious offences, neither the House nor the Committee asked for or learnt of alleged company offences listed by a Department of Trade Inspector, which included illicitly obtaining money, perjury, larceny and publishing false accounts.[12] Maudling, as with many MPs, was attracted by the money and the flexible, often representational, rôles they were asked to play. They never checked the rules, whether through ignorance, indifference or deceit, or because of a Parliamentary tradition of not questioning a colleague's private interests, and never thought to consult their Party Whips or Leader. Yet they failed to understand that, as politicians, the conflict of interests between their Parliamentary duties and their business interests – whom they represent – must of necessity exist, whatever their own view of what they are doing. Maudling survived because of the failure to take into account all the officially-available information on his activities, on the 'gentleman' ethic of the House and on the strength of his parliamentary reputation: 'Who is to guarantee', he later wrote in his autobiography, 'that the Home Secretary will exercise his judgement with responsibility and discretion? I fear, having thought about it a great deal, that there is no guarantee of an absolute character, only the personal standing of the Home Secretary and the estimate that the House of Commons has formed of his integrity and his judgement.'[13]

# Chapter 11

## *Not Even a Minnow: John Cordle, MP*

John Cordle, Tory MP for Bournemouth since 1959, was convinced that there had been a 'collapse of moral Christian principles' in Britain. He himself was 'an outspoken believer in evangelism, morality and the highest possible standards in public life'.[1] Aside from his main formal Parliamentary duty as chairman of the Anglo-Libyan Parliamentary Committee, he was an assiduous businessman, collector of public positions and of wives. For the first, he owned the family linen and cotton manufacturing firm, was a broker in Lloyds, chaired a further five firms, and was director of another three. As a public-spirited citizen, as well as his directorship of the *Church of England Newspaper*, he had been or was a member of a Commission on Evangelism, a director of the Church Society and a member of the West African Committee of the Conservative Commonwealth and Overseas Council. Of wives he had three, the last being a 30-year-old Finnish woman whom he married in 1976 when he was sixty-four.

He was forthright on moral issues, despite the odd unfortunate hiccup in his private life (paying his first wife for not libelling him in her autobiography and evicting his second wife's mother from his home), and comfortably off, almost well-off, from his membership of Lloyds and his business interests, which focused on the export trade and West Africa. He was, however, always on the lookout for means to further those interests and, in particular, capitalise on his extensive contacts in West Africa – an activity that other MPs had also not been slow in pursuing elsewhere.

There had been much concern during the 1960s over the number of foreign governments keen to influence

British MPs with visits and (sometimes) payments, such as East Germany, Nigeria, Israel, the Central Africa Federation. MPs from both Labour and Conservative parties worked partly as consultants, partly as representatives. Sometimes right-wing Conservatives worked for communist regimes; sometimes Labour MPs worked for right-wing regimes.

One early voice of concern was that of Francis Noel-Baker MP. He wrote: '. . . the growth of so-called "public relations" in all its aspects, and of the power of the pressure groups, means that Members of Parliament have themselves become more attractive allies for business interests than they have been in the past . . . Whereas in the past these various interests and their representatives were usually well-known and identified themselves openly, in the new "grey zone" that is growing up the interests are often not known and declared. The existing convention in the House of Commons seems inadequate to meet this situation'.[2]

Francis Noel-Baker's concern was underlined by a number of media stories which suggested that the existing requirements on disclosure did not go far enough in revealing MPs' links with those seeking to push their views before Parliament or the extent of funding available to achieve the latter's objectives. One particular case emphasised the issues involved.

In October 1968 the *Sunday Times* published the secret report of a firm of lobbyists – Maurice Fraser Associates – to their clients, the Greek military government. The report was intended to retain the contract from the government to create a favourable climate of opinion abroad. In the report the firm claimed to pay a British MP working behind the scenes to influence other MPs. The MP allegedly involved – Gordon Bagier, a right-wing Labour MP – denied the relationship, although he had visited Greece as a guest of the Greek government. In March 1969, *This Week*, a commercial TV programme, published a programme that named Bagier as working for the firm. Bagier then admitted he had been a consultant (he was the only consultant) to the firm which only had one contract (with the Greek government). He had resigned from the firm in October 1968 and denied he had worked as a lobbyist.

Such activities were not unusual. As Richard Crossman, then a Minister in the Labour government, noted at the time: 'for years everyone had known that this kind of thing goes on. As well as the Greek government there are the Israeli and East German governments, which both systematically dole out free holidays to MPs and some-times quite a lot of pocket money too'. Crossman was keen for a Parliamentary inquiry to look at the rôle of PR firms in Parliament and the Bagier case particularly annoyed Prime Minister Harold Wilson, who wanted an inquiry into specific cases. More pragmatic Ministers such as James Callaghan and Richard Marsh believed that an inquiry could concentrate on Labour MPs and this 'could damage the Government'.

On 26 March 1969, the Prime Minister announced an inquiry into MPs who had 'some paid connection with an outside interest . . . involved with matters which are the concern of Parliament and Government'. He also said the inquiry would look at public relations firms working for 'an overseas Government, or an overseas political interest'.

There was a two-hour debate on the establishment of the inquiry. Two features were noteworthy. The Leader of the Opposition asked the Prime Minister to make it clear that there was nothing improper about any Member having an outside interest. The Prime Minister agreed. He also announced a membership comprising very senior MPs, nearly all of whom had business interests and were Privy Councillors. This, the 1969 Select Committee on Members' Interests (Declarations), spent much of its time looking at the form of a new declaration. When the issue of public relations firms arose, the Committee was uncer-tain how to identify their connections with MPs and how to register both them and their use of foreign visits – 'the biggest pourboire that can be given to MPs', as Andrew Roth put it.

The Committee was, however, concerned about the activities of such firms, particularly if these led to MPs becoming paid spokesmen on behalf of outside interests rather than their more traditional use as advisers on Parliamentary matters to them. It did not see anything wrong in MPs speaking in the public interest on matters in which they had a continuing financial interest, such as farmers, but strongly objected to MPs as paid advocates – paid as a mouthpiece for other people's interests. While the recommendation for a clear disclosure of interest was intended to deal with the former category, the Committee decided that MPs should not act as paid spokesmen in the House. The short 'code of conduct' which incorporated its recommendations reflected its faith in the 'traditional practices of the House' rather than 'cumbrous inquisitional machinery'.[3] It also reflected both the Committee's and the House's lack of enthusiasm for reform. The report was not debated in the House or acted upon by the Labour government before the 1970 General Election, and it was subsequently abandoned by the incoming Conservative government.

In the meantime, however, John Cordle, MP, had met John Poulson, architect. Born in 1910 Poulson had set up an architectural practice in 1932, in Pontefract. By hard work, competitive rates and good staff he had managed to carve out a lucrative business by the late 1950s with all the trappings of success – use of a private plane, lavish hospitality and a permanent suite at a top London hotel. Two further developments, however, cemented his success. First, one of his longstanding friends, Sir Herbert Butcher, Tory MP and tax expert, had suggested, (as Poulson told the bankruptcy hearings later), that 'a professional man unfortunately has too high a taxation in relation to other businesses, and that a service company was the answer'. He thought up Ropergate Services, a firm that could provide several building services so that Poulson could progress beyond being someone's architect to pursuing his own building contracts. This business development saved tax, allowed the accumulation of funds, and, as an all-in-one organization covering surveying and engineering as well as architectural services, permitted Poulson to achieve savings when seeking work by offering both a composite estimate as well as continuity on the site. This was a particular boon to smaller councils who did not employ their professional or technical staff. This development led to his joining a large building firm to chase the increasing number of local government contracts in the late 1950s and early 1960s. This led in turn to Poulson meeting T. Dan Smith, the dynamic Labour leader of Newcastle who was keen to leave the world of politics for that of public relations. Persuading Poulson that he knew the people who could influence the award of contracts, Smith set up a series of PR firms, funded by Poulson with over £155,000 during the Sixties, to employ key councillors and council officials.

As his practice grew, so Poulson's thoughts turned to overseas markets and to the employment of British MPs; as Cordle himself once said: 'the British statesman is never without a platform when he visits another country'. Cordle was approached in 1963 to work for Poulson's Construction Promotion in West Africa providing that, as Poulson said, 'there is nothing in a representation arrangement on your part which is repugnant to your other businesses and your parliamentary duties'. The offer was a £500-a-year retainer together with a contribution to expenses. It was gratefully received and by March 1965 Cordle was writing to Poulson, setting out his efforts country by country and noting the use of his official positions to further Construction Promotion's interests.

More seriously, Cordle began speaking in Parliament about the need for more government aid and for that aid to go to British contractors. Indeed when pressing for a formal contract with Construction Promotion and an enhanced payment, he wrote to Poulson that 'it was largely for the benefit of Construction Promotion that I took part in a debate in the House of Commons on The Gambia, and pressed for HMG to award constructional contracts to British firms'. When the new contract was agreed in April he again wrote that 'over the past fifteen months I have done what was asked of me, and to the best of my ability. I shall continue with renewed vigour knowing I am in your hands and under your watchful eye'.

Cordle was a man of his word. All his contacts, he said

later, were placed at the disposal of Construction Promotion and he organised 'a number of luncheon and dinner meetings in England with a view to promoting the interests of the firm'. Unfortunately little came of Cordle's efforts and by the end of 1967 Poulson wanted to end the arrangement – 'all he got me to do was support him. I am too soft' – but, contractually, he was required to employ him until 1970 at a total cost of £5678 over the six years. By this time, however, Poulson was bankrupt. Front-loading his costs, he never achieved the subsequent flow of contracts to cover them. In 1972 at the bankruptcy hearings in Wakefield, the counsel for the creditors clinically trawled Poulson's meticulous and voluminous files to find out what had happened to the money. The names of councillors, officials, civil servants and MPs tumbled out as the media began to investigate the full extent of Poulson's bribery and corruption. That investigation was galvanised by the involvement of Reginald Maudling, former Conservative Home Secretary and one-time possible party leader (see chapter X). For Cordle, however, Poulson's remarks at the hearings were dismissive: 'I consider I was conned'.

By 1976 the massive Poulson inquiry had resulted in several convictions, changes to the rules of disclosure of financial interests in the House of Commons, the establishment of a Register of Interests, and two official inquiries. The major inquiry of the two, the Royal Commission on Standards of Conduct in Public Life, stated in 1976 that Parliament did not have the necessary investigatory powers and sanctions to deal with MPs involved in bribery.

In October 1976 the Labour Government Attorney-General announced that 'there were not sufficient grounds to merit' further prosecutions of politicians and officials who had been paid by Poulson. Expecting this announcement, the *Observer* newspaper alleged that three MPs (Reginald Maudling, Albert Roberts and John Cordle) could escape the possibility of prosecution for receiving money from Poulson. It especially pointed to Cordle and quoted the judge (who chaired the Royal Commission on Standards of Conduct in Public Life) as saying Cordle's payment 'was one of the more flagrant cases of corruption he had encountered in his 30 years on the Bench'. The new Leader of the Liberal Party, David Steel, then asked Labour Prime Minister James Callaghan to clarify the position of MPs accused of receiving money. The Prime Minister wanted an inquiry to focus 'on the practice for the future rather than to re-run the past'. This meant he did not want an inquiry into the three MPs. He claimed the position was obscure, that he was neither a constitutional historian nor a lawyer and that he preferred an inquiry to focus on procedure rather than specific allegations and warned against 'vindictiveness'. The next day the Prime Minister decided, because of the public interest and media attention to the *Observer*'s allegations, to hold an inquiry. He proposed a Select Committee, supported by the Leaders of the Conservative and Liberal Parties.

The Committee interviewed four MPs, Poulson and Dan Smith, relying for the bulk of its evidence on the contents of Poulson's files. It took oral evidence, later published, and, in the case of John Cordle, decided he was 'guilty' of not declaring an interest and, on the basis of an old Parliamentary rule, 'guilty' of pressing Poulson's interests in a Parliamentary debate for reward. Of the other MPs, a payment to Ted Short, a Labour MP, by Dan Smith had nothing to do with Poulson and the Committee therefore decided there was no need to make any further comment. The Committee felt, however, that the other two MPs – Albert Roberts and Reginald Maudling – had not acted as MPs could be expected to act in terms of declaring their financial interests where relevant.

The Report was published on 15 July 1977. Maudling stated he would 'contest the evidence published by the Committee'. Cordle called the committee unfair in not providing him with any opportunity to rebut its criticism of him. By 21 July rumours were circulating that Conservative MPs intended to allow Labour MPs to vote for Cordle's expulsion. On 22 July Cordle resigned after trying to get support among his colleagues. It is possible that Cordle was 'stampeded into resignation' to allow senior Conservative MPs to rally support for Maudling who promised 'a series of startling revelations' in the debate. In the event Cordle turned up to the debate, friendless and emotional, apparently having given up his intention of using 'every proper means in my power' to persuade the House to reject the Committee's criticism. Wanting, he said, to protect the House's good name from acrimony, he was resigning despite his clear conscience. In the subsequent debate Maudling resisted the findings of the Committee, was called an 'honourable man' by former Tory Prime Minister Edward Heath and, surprisingly, was allowed to remain during the discussions. Albert Roberts objected to being considered with Maudling and Cordle because he had not known what standards he had been expected to obey and because he had only 'transgressed in the shallow waters'. Both MPs were given the benefit of the doubt and the Committee's conclusions relating to them were simply noted. During the debate one Tory MP spoke up for Cordle, defending his reputation and suggesting he had resigned because he was not popular and lacked friends. He alone spoke up for the man described by Poulson as 'not even a minnow' in terms of his importance to Poulson's organisation.

# Chapter 12

## *The Disappearing Minister: John Stonehouse*

*In The Laundry Room*

How is it that the merest hint of scandal, based on the flimsiest of evidence and propagated by obviously maladjusted or twisted men, can erase a lifetime of constructive endeavour motivated by the highest ideals', mused John Stonehouse in April 1975 in the laundry room of Number 7, 840 Toorak Road in Melbourne, Australia.

At 4.05 pm on 20 November 1974 John Stonehouse, Labour MP, ex-Minister, businessman and alleged Czech spy, walked out of the Fountainbleu Hotel in a pair of shorts and disappeared along the Miami seafront. 'He is dead', said his wife Barbara; 'he is not running away from anything', said Phillip Gray, his personal assistant; 'he has been destroyed by the Mafia', said Labour MP William Molloy, his loyal former Parliamentary Secretary. Nothing could have been further from the truth. Picking up a false passport, cash and clothes at a prearranged location, he had flown to San Francisco to stay a night in a suite at the Fairmont Hotel (and a bored evening in a topless go-go bar) followed by four nights in the Sheraton-Waikiki Hotel in Hawaii. From there he undertook a Melbourne-Copenhagen-Melbourne excursion during which he had the feeling 'many warped people were dancing on his grave' as he read the newspaper reports of his disappearance. He rented a £20-a-week City Centre Flats apartment in Flinders Street before the Victoria State police arrested him on Christmas Eve, 1974, on a passport offence (he had been under surveillance for a possible bank fraud after setting up accounts in two different banks under two

187

assumed names; Markham and Mildoon). Stonehouse told the police he wanted to start a new life there, away from the pressures on him.

## The Rise of the Achiever

Stonehouse was an ambitious achiever born into a working-class socialist world. His mother was a President of Southampton Co-operative Society and his father a union official. Stonehouse grew up in a political atmosphere of meetings, fund-raising events and the espousal of left-wing causes. Leaving school at sixteen he went to work as a clerk in Southampton Council's Probation Department before joining the RAF during the war and subsequently going, on an ex-serviceman's grant, to the LSE, where he also met his future wife. There he chaired the Labour Society and became active in the International Socialist Student Movement before being selected at the age of twenty-three as Labour candidate for Twickenham, London. Losing there in 1950 and again at Burton in 1951 he took his wife and two children off to Africa to work for the African Co-operative Movement. Two years later he returned to England (he had to fly the land, said Dick Crossman, because of the 'stink' of the Co-op's collapse) and got elected to the Co-op Board of Management, where his management style attracted an 'orchestrated campaign of vilification' but, in 1957, he beat off the challenge of Ray Gunter to become the Labour MP for Wednesbury (now Walsall North). After the 1964 Labour victory, he rapidly climbed the Ministerial ladder to become Minister for Technology in 1967–8 and hence to become a Privy Counsellor and Postmaster-General in 1968. He was energetic, hardworking, ambitious and increasingly mistrusted by his colleagues. Over a pay dispute with post office workers Stonehouse managed to alienate his Cabinet colleagues as well as appear to shift the blame for the dispute on to them. Castle was livid, Jenkins wanted to get rid of him, and Crossman described him as a 'violent, fierce, implacable, unscrupulous young man . . . a kind of dangerous crook, overwhelmingly ambitious but above all untrustworthy . . . he stood loyally by the Government but in a most skilful way, letting it be seen that he thought the whole thing was a disaster and that he was a hero being forced to do what was wrongheaded.'[1]

## The Businessman

When Labour lost the 1970 General Election Stonehouse chose to supplement his salary by establishing his business career. He took a consultancy with the UK computer firm ICL but most of his efforts were directed to setting up his own firms so that he had 'enough to live reasonably comfortably, to afford to travel and to have the peace of mind to devote myself to political work';[2] he still had ambitions to become Prime Minister one day. Connoisseurs of Claret Ltd was set up in March 1970, trying to sell wine by mail order. Its buying policy was erratic – 'the work of either a madman or a person who just talks so big', said a colleague – and never made a profit. It folded in 1975 with a £48,000 deficit. Export Promotion and Consultancy Services Ltd was set up in March 1970 as an export consultancy service and did a modest amount of trading before becoming landlord to the British Bangladeshi Trust and part of the money-go-round to support BBT. It collapsed in 1975 owing some £241,533. Global Imex Ltd was set up in January 1972 to promote exports. Unlike EPCS it had other shareholders – it was headed by an ex-Lonrho executive – and acted as an agent to businesses with interests in Bangladesh and Africa. Its turnover never exceeded £90,000; its projected deals – cement to Iran and Nigeria, and Racal electronic equipment to North Yemen – collapsed because of political reversals, business competition and lack of available capital. Around the three main companies floated a host of subsidiaries which did little or nothing until the BBT debacle unfolded. All, however, had banking and overdraft facilities which, the DTI report later indicated, were regarded by Mr Stonehouse as his own and he drew freely on them as he wished: 'we should emphasise that this attitude did not develop only at a stage in the story when he was in the process of creating his aliases and preparing for his disappearance; he juggled monies from one company to another, sometimes into and out of his own pocket, from a much earlier stage.'[3]

In 1971 the internecine conflict between West and East Pakistan exploded into bloody civil war. Stonehouse went out to report for War on Want and Oxfam, returning committed to the Bangladeshi cause, for which he raised funds and sought political support. When a Bangladeshi proposed a bank for migrants in Britain, Stonehouse was keen to seek Bank of England approval and other institutional assistance to set up the British Bangladeshi Trust. He cobbled together financial support from such disparate groups as Banque Belge, GKN, Trust House Forte and the Crown Agents, printed his prospectus, acquired a building in 27 Dover Street (the landlord of which was EPCS, and the interior of which was revamped by Mrs Stonehouse), recruited staff and then toured the country to elicit subscriptions for shares. Unfortunately, according to Stonehouse, 'certain opponents of our plans had travelled the country before me, spreading rumours and the meetings were mostly poorly supported.'[4] Then more critics emerged, this time in the form of Anthony Mascherenas and Richard Milner of the *Sunday Times*. Their article, published one week before the subscriptions opened, was, to him, damning. The tentative official and business interest would evaporate in the face of what he perceived to be biased and ill-informed criticism. The 'vicious knocking job' of the *Sunday Times* was the push that forced Stonehouse to defend his integrity and pride and support BBT totally. As the Inspectors noted: 'he regarded the article as a challenge from an unjustly powerful enemy and he resolved to join battle and fight to the apparent death. His sense of proportion lost, his judgement distorted and his bitterness increasing with each sign of adversity, he abandoned the rules, repeatedly and with ingenuity broke the law, and destroyed his own idealism . . .'[5] To others the article simply drew attention to the somewhat cavalier tactics used by BBT, such as using the names of two nationalised Bangladesh banks and a Bank of England official without permission but with the imputation of their official support.

The launch attracted £15,000 from Bangladeshis and was only saved by Stonehouse borrowing from banks and using personal and company funds to boost applications for shares. He got his companies to open accounts there and use its facilities but, as he himself melodramatically proclaimed; 'I had saved the day but in the process I had shackled myself to the wheels of a chariot; and as the wheels turned the spikes dug into me, slowly draining me of blood, and preparing me for a final sacrifice at a Roman Circus.' Stonehouse felt the bank was at least alive and his companies were operating successfully. But in the background, Stonehouse used his companies, nominee companies and employees to bolster the poor subscriptions for shares. At the first meeting of BBT on 30 November 1972 with Stonehouse in the chair, applications for loans and overdraft facilities to Stonehouse and Stonehouse companies of £215,000 were approved as fast as it took to read out the list. £140,000 of that money was drawn upon within two weeks to pay off the overdrafts of his companies which had been used to finance the shares applications for BBT. Most of the overdrafts were on Stonehouse's personal guarantee and the money-go-round was seen by Stonehouse as 'a necessary and not very serious evil' until the shares were bought up. They weren't, the advances remained unpaid and Stonehouse became 'enmeshed in his own web, which grew more tenacious as he struggled to escape from it.' The struggle largely involved concealing the Stonehouse interest in supporting the shares – which pulled in employees, relatives, friends of relatives, window-dressing the accounts to make the company look profitable, inflating balance sheets, temporarily 'settling' loans. The 1973 accounts failed to show that in the first year 26 per cent of BBT's total outstanding loans were to directors and their companies and that Stonehouse, his firms and family had received loans of £545,895 during the year with £145,604 still owed at the end of the year; 'the responsibility for this disgraceful state of affairs lies with the directors and the professional advisers', said the DTI inspectors. Worse,

191

the apparent clearance of loans was done more with sleight of hand than cash: 'the various objectionable loans had merely been shunted around, thinly disguised or replaced by others equally objectionable.'

When BBT appeared financially sound, on paper at least, it tried to expand its activities and take the first steps to becoming a real bank rather than an institutional money lender. In December 1973 it got its Section 123 Certificate (which under the 1967 Companies Act deemed it to be suitable for carrying on the business of banking), had a rights issue (half bought up by Stonehouse and his firms) and issued an unaudited interim statement of account, all of which appeared to show BBT growing while it was in fact collapsing. In order to continue the flow of funds to the Stonehouse companies and other firms who had borrowed to buy into BBT, Stonehouse used friends and his daughter's friends to buy BBT shares from those firms, using BBT money to repay them, and recycling loans through 'middlemen' firms 'all under the direction and immediate supervision of Mr Stonehouse himself.'

Unfortunately the Middle East War and the rise in oil prices depressed the stock market just at the moment Stonehouse chose to try and use BBT for dabbling in it. Faced with – for once – the caution of his colleagues ('a most imprudent transaction' said one) shares were bought through BBT subsidiaries but, showing a marked reluctance to sell (he claimed he knew the chairmen of the companies in which he bought the shares), the gamble was 'singularly unsuccessful.' Borrowing some £74,000 at the start of 1974 from BBT and Global (he was buying at the margin – paying a deposit and hoping to sell at a higher price before paying the balance) he invested some £285,000, not the least because he anticipated that a Tory win in the 1974 General Election would turn the market round. The Tories lost, Labour won (Stonehouse was not offered a Cabinet seat) the market continued its slide and the investments flopped. Stonehouse tried to conceal the losses from appearing in the 1974 Accounts but by this time the auditors smelt a rat. Following the collapse of London and County Securities there was a credit squeeze on other secondary banks and it was assumed that BBT would have problems and the collectability of outstanding loans would be important. Despite Stonehouse's desperate attempts to secure unqualified Accounts the auditors, particularly one of the partners, steadily penetrated 'what was, by then, a jungle dense with improprieties' with interconnected loans to Stonehouse companies and back again involving some £757,000 or 56% of BBT's total lending.

In addition to manipulating the affairs of BBT and its subsidiaries, Stonehouse was juggling the money through company accounts and his sixteen personal bank accounts; between March 1970 and December 1974 some £1.3 million 'tramped' through them. During this time he was drawing about £76,000-a-year from hidden companies, had personal overdraft facilities up to some £284,000 as well as claiming his expenses and his Parliamentary salary. Certainly he appeared to have achieved a degree of material success with a London town house, a Wiltshire country home, a constituency flat and two rented London flats.

In January 1973, however, the Companies Investigation Branch of the DTI hove into view followed, amid the rumble of 'petty intrigue and scandal-mongering', by the Fraud Squad's Detective Inspector Grant, a note-taking constable, and an official caution. Stonehouse found himself being investigated for possible fraud as a result of the newsletter circulated to Bangladeshis to persuade them to invest in BBT. The investigation was only called off when Stonehouse appealed to the Bangladeshi High Commissioner for help.

Stonehouse himself soon constructed his version of the truth. The investigation was triggered off by his public prominence, the shadow of which would destroy his business interests and political career. He believed that no one wanted to help him, preferring to stand to one side and let the investigations take their due course. It was unjust persecution – a 'psychological enigma' – exacting an intolerable, crucifying pressure on him. The case was dropped but the damage was done. Stonehouse made one last effort to salvage the BBT disaster: he subsumed it into a new organisation, the London Capital Group, in April

1974. As he felt he had cleared that hurdle, the Czech spy story surfaced. The Czech defector Josef Frolik had been debriefed by the Americans who informed the British Secret Service that he claimed contact with a senior Labour Minister. In 1969 Stonehouse met Harold Wilson, Michael Halls (his PPS) and an MI5 officer in a sitting room in 10 Downing Street. He was informed that he had been named by Frolik (the allegation being that Stonehouse had been entrapped by sexual blackmail). Stonehouse emphatically denied the allegation and, after the Secret Service had told Wilson that there was no evidence to substantiate Frolik's allegations, Wilson took no further action. There was, however, some marginal corroborative evidence. Stonehouse had been to Czechoslovakia, Wednesbury was twinned with Kladno and he had lunched on several occasions with Czech diplomats. Certainly on more than one occasion he met Robert Husak who was deputy chief of Czech intelligence in London. The story lay buried until 1974 when Josef Frolik published his autobiography, which alleged Stonehouse was one of three contacts (another Labour MP, Will Owen, admitted in 1970 he received Czech money for information) and added a dramatic aspect to the impending collapse of his business career. Stonehouse felt stunned and wounded: 'the miasma of suspicion was suffocating', he claimed, 'no one in authority even talked frankly to me to help dispel it, and I could not grasp it myself.'[6] He tried for bigger deals for his various companies, the last itself full of intrigue and mystery. Nigeria in the early Seventies was undergoing a building boom with cement highly-prized as an import. Stonehouse's plans for the 'deal to end all deals' – cement bought in bulk from Romania and sold at nearly double the cost in Nigeria – collapsed with the failure of one partner to come up with the funds in time and the unfortunate death of another while inspecting suitable transport.[7] Whatever the reasons for the failure of this deal – there was, following his disappearance, fanciful talk that the Mafia were trying to run a massive swindle or that international currency fraudsters had liquidated him for refusing to use BBT as a conduit – Stonehouse decided enough was enough. He chose the 'psychiatric suicide' of himself and the emergence of another personality, which he planned by obtaining passports of two deceased constituents and siphoning money overseas from his firms. He had a trial run to Miami where he secreted clothes and documents before returning to London. In the chilly atmosphere of 27 Dover Street Stonehouse realised that it was time to go: letters from his brokers asking for settlement of his personal share-dealing losses heralded the second Miami trip.

After his transglobal peregrinations he settled for Australia where, following his arrest, he entertained a stream of personal and official visitors as he awaited the outcome of the extradition proceedings on charges relating to his companies in England.

## The Public Exorcism of John Stonehouse

In January 1975 the House of Commons had set up a Select Committee to consider Stonehouse's position as an MP. It invited him to return to England and appear before them. Stonehouse was not fooled by any invitation at that time to return to England. He wrote back that it 'would be extremely dangerous to his psychiatric health' to do so. Since the Committee was concerned for his health, and there was no precedent for expelling or otherwise punishing an MP on the grounds of absence, the Committee chose not to take any action at that time. It did, however, indicate it would act if his constituency continued not to be represented.

Stonehouse's subsequent action was to write an extraordinary letter to the Swedish Prime Minister Olaf Palme in March 1975 appealing to his 'well-known humanitarian outlook'. Stonehouse alleged he had suffered a mental breakdown as a result of the 'frustration of my idealism in a hostile political and business world' and a 'most vicious campaign of persecution by the British press.' He said he intended to renounce his seat and his citizenship and apply for a Swedish passport. He was unsuccessful, as he was when he applied in April for a Mauritian passport and later when he wrote off to Botswana, Zambia, Tanzania, Kenya, Bangladesh and Canada.

The advent of criminal charges and extradition proceedings prompted the Select Committee to give him one month to attend the House, resign or face expulsion: the Committee felt it 'irreconcilable with membership of the House for a Member of Parliament, when charged with serious criminal offences, not to submit himself to the processes of justice established by Parliament.'[8] Since Stonehouse had been under the misapprehension that the Committee's first 'do-nothing' report reflected sympathy, understanding and objectivity for him on the part of his colleagues, this hardening of attitudes sparked off another unusual letter. This accused the press of a most brutal and dishonest vilification and of creating a 'miasma of suspicion' that was being exploited by the police for their own 'sinister reasons.' Claiming he was on the way to recovery Stonehouse subjected the Committee's chairman and the Prime Minister (and the Queen) to a flurry of letters and cables to forestall any recommendation to expel him. It did not alter the Committee's decision to recommend expulsion but, before this could be debated in the House, Stonehouse returned to an embarrassed Parliament and a constituency party which had already selected his successor. Stonehouse made a personal statement in the House in October 1975: he attributed his destruction to events beyond his control and claimed he was suffocated by the anguish of lost ideals. He then occupied the months up to his trial sniping at his colleagues, being ordered out of the House by the Speaker and then giving the country 'the fresh air of frankness' by deciding to represent the English National Party in Parliament – 'the renaissance of England begins today', announced ENP chairman Dr Frank Hansford-Miller – and voting against Labour. He resigned as an MP in August 1976 on his being convicted of various offences at the end of his Old Bailey trial, which had begun with Stonehouse, a 25p red rose in his buttonhold (he objected to the price) and a flag of St George in hand, announcing he would conduct his own defence, defeat the politically-rigged charges against him and expose the national sickness that had led to his prosecution.

The charges were actually rather prosaic – relating to misuse of credit cards, forgery, false pretences, theft and fraud. Beside him in the dock was his secretary, 29-year-old Sheila Buckley, who was charged with stealing the proceeds of cheques and conspiracy to defraud. Stonehouse decided to defend himself because he saw the trial as politically-motivated and because he wanted to give the jury all the facts as he saw them – 'besides being jurymen they are representatives of the nation as a whole.'

The Crown's case was that Stonehouse, facing ruin, disgrace and bankruptcy over the failure of his various businesses – he owed banks and credit card companies some £250,000 – decided to fake his own suicide, take money from sources still open to him, provide some £125,000 through short-term insurance policies for his wife and then begin a new life in a new country with his secretary. The Crown sought to show he planned all this systematically. As Stonehouse he guaranteed loans to his companies so that he could draw out some £200,000 and run up large overdrafts through twenty-four separate accounts in seventeen banks. Then he went to a Walsall hospital saying he had funds for widows whose husbands had died recently. Furnished with the names of Joseph Markham and Donald Mildoon he visited their widows and, on the information they provided, applied for passports in their names. As Markham, the late 42-year-old foundry worker who had never been abroad, he established a residence in a London hotel and set up a post box business address. As Markham he was inoculated, and obtained visas and an American Express Card. As Markham he made arrangements for his flights and shifted some £12,000 abroad for his new life.

After clashes with the judge and a time in the cells to cool off, Stonehouse argued that the Crown had fitted many of the pieces of the jigsaw together but in not doing so correctly had created a misleading impression of what he had done and why. With shouts, whispers and tears he explained how he used his parallel personalities to relieve the pressure before they took control of him – a 'bizarre, extraordinary and incredible' story, he called it.

In contrast to the lengthy and discursive time Stonehouse spent on his political and business career, Sheila Buckley's defence lasted one hour. Defence counsel argued that she had a 'very personal and intimate relationship' with Stonehouse but was not party to the frauds or the disappearance. The Crown's prosecuting counsel was less sympathetic: she was a shrewd and tough operator who was infatuated with Stonehouse and was involved with cooking the books. Buckley, the daughter of a South London butcher, became Stonehouse's secretary in 1968 when he was Minister of Technology. 'It is not a crime when a pretty girl falls in love with a married man', said her defence, in describing the beginning of her affair with Stonehouse, following the collapse of her marriage in 1971 and divorce in 1973 on the grounds of her husband's adultery. She became a director of some of his companies – 'I did not realise what was happening' she claimed. She stayed in his rented London flat in Petty France from 1971 to October 1974 after which Stonehouse moved her to a Hampstead hotel – Highfield House – where she was booked in as his wife.

In his summing-up Mr Justice Eveleigh stressed that everyone is assumed sane and accountable for his actions unless the contrary is proved; Buckley and Stonehouse should be found guilty if the jury agreed that they were aware of what they were doing. The jury evidently agreed; forewoman Beryl Darbyshire announced they found them both guilty of most charges – they were acquitted of the joint charge of conspiracy to defraud EPCS, one of Stonehouse's companies. Stonehouse was sentenced to seven years' imprisonment (he received several concurrent sentences totalling over twenty-three years) while Buckley was given a two years' suspended sentence. The judge made a criminal bankruptcy order against the two after telling Stonehouse: 'you did not simply decide to disappear because you were oppressed by business burdens. You decided to do so in comfort, and it is clear to me that self-interest has been well to the fore. You aimed to get rich quickly. You falsely accuse other people of cant, hypocrisy and humbug when you must have known all the time that your defence was an embodiment of all those three.' As to his business dealings, the judge told him: 'you were not an unlucky business man escaping from undeserved financial problems, it all arose from your own initial devious behaviour, whatever its object may be.'

In prison, Prisoner 333093 lost his appeal to the Lords, quit the House, resigned the Privy Council, suffered a heart attack and had his and Sheila's financial indebtedness spelt out – he had some £816,000 in liabilities and £137,185 assets (including £115,000 in Zurich) – before the curtain was rung down in 1977 with the publication of the DTI report on the Stonehouse group of companies by a barrister, Michael Sherrard, and an accountant, Ian Davison. Their report was unequivocal; the companies were 'saturated with offences, irregularities and improprieties of one kind or another'. The chief perpetrator was Stonehouse, who was 'concerned in the conception, execution and attempted concealment of almost all the irregular schemes' and who was 'propelled into crime by his pride'. His staff and associates 'held Mr Stonehouse in awe and great respect. He treated them well, took them for walks along the corridors of power and enabled them to rub shoulders with men and women of considerable eminence who were themselves impressed by his charm, confidence and seeming integrity. Mr Stonehouse was, as events have shown, a sophisticated and skilful confidence trickster. His pleasant manner and fluency, as well as his apparent grasp of affairs, were the most potent weapon in his armoury'.[9] The inspectors pinned the blame on Stonehouse as the architect of the falsification of records, the misrepresentations and the illegalities designed 'to avoid his own actual or potential criminal and civil liabilities for them . . . for Mr Stonehouse truth was a moving target'. As to his nervous breakdown, the DTI report concluded that his 'lapses of memory were too selective to be involuntary and we came to realise that his apparent inability to recollect even cursory detail of wrongdoing tended to be confined to those areas of maximum danger to himself.'[10]

Certainly Chief Superintendent Ken Etheridge, the Fraud Squad officer in charge of the Stonehouse inquiry, saw him as a man who 'sanely manipulates people and situations, ready to use even his own family, to leave his loyal wife grieving, and to involve his unquestioning daughter and her friends.'[11] Nevertheless John Stonehouse, who died in 1988, refused to the end to admit he was to blame: 'The trouble with people back home is that they are looking for a logical reason. They don't realise my state of mind before I left England. I had come to the end of my tether. Business associates were blackmailing me to get their own way. Economic environment was playing havoc with my companies. Everything was wrong. You have no idea how I felt. In the end I just wanted to get away and become a plain human being again. All right, so it wasn't a normal thing to do. I wasn't in a normal state of mind.'[12]

# Chapter 13

## Slag Heaps, Kitchen Cabinets and The World of Harold Wilson

### Loyalty and The Man

The key to understanding the various rows and controversies that clouded the last years of Harold Wilson's Premiership, and the first few years of his return to the backbenches, lies in the twin tracks of his ambition and his insecurity. The first pushed him into 10 Downing Street while the second strongly influenced his choice of those with whom he surrounded himself. In 1966 Dick Crossman wrote: 'his main aim is to stay in office. That's the real thing and for that purpose he will use almost any trick or gimmick if only he can do it.'[1] In 1967 Christopher Mayhew told Sandy Gall of ITN that Wilson is 'extremely clever intellectually, but he has no profound principles at all. Getting there is all he cares about.'[2] 'His success, indeed his entire career', wrote Bernard Levin, 'cannot be understood without understanding the intensity of his ambition to become, and having become, to remain Prime Minister, together with an ability to disguise from himself almost (though not quite) entirely the strength of that ambition and the extent to which he has been willing to go in its pursuit . . .'[3]

His anti-Gaitskell campaign and drive for the Party leadership in the 1950s was a series of bruising conflicts, plots and recriminations that left Wilson unsure of his political power-base and keenly aware of the need to create coalitions and support out of individuals and groups of very different political persuasions and temperaments. At the same time he was also aware that while he had to manipulate and massage his support, leading from the front also meant looking over his shoulder to make sure his supporters were following him. As a result he became a politician who prized personal loyalty very highly. In 1964 Wilson was, in the public's eyes, the undisputed leader of the Labour Party and self-proclaimed harbinger of the new technological era. Within the party, however, he was also leading a contentious and often combative group of politicians: 'I am', he believed, 'running a Bolshevik Revolution with a Tsarist Shadow Cabinet', staffed by 'bitterly hostile and suspicious, miserable creatures.' On the other hand, Crossman suggested that, organisationally, Wilson was not prepared to devolve responsibility or control; 'he is a general without any chief of staff and indeed without any structure of command . . . he hasn't even got a secretarial staff to answer his letters but above all he has no right-hand man to plan his political strategy and to put up suggestions to him. Therefore he is in a weak position inside his hostile Shadow Cabinet, despite his overwhelming strength in the country.'[4]

Instead Wilson built up his own personal retinue and, later, funding, from where he could play the national leader free from the vagaries of party politics and ungrateful colleagues. 'When Wilson became Leader, most Labour MPs accepted the fact, some with deep reluctance. On becoming Ministers, a very few tried strenuously to influence him in the direction they wanted a Labour Government to move. This was largely a doomed effort: whether Left, Right or Centre, few felt in communication with the Prime Minister . . . More and more he seemed influenced by his cronies – the 'Kitchen Cabinet' whom he trusted. It wasn't evident that he trusted many people.'[5] As James Margach suggested:

to understand this picture it is necessary to identify Wilson as the loneliest of all the Prime Ministers, a man bedevilled by a great sense of insecurity. He had no friends as the rest of us know personal and family friends and so, in his solitude, his political entourage assumed a greater importance in his life than would otherwise have been necessary. It was this over-dependence upon an odd assortment of acolytes – his 'Kitchen Cabinet' – which prevented his becoming a Prime Minister of substance.[6]

Those who consistently and uncritically supported him were rewarded with loyalty: those who did not were regarded with suspicion: his two greatest confidantes were George Wigg and Marcia Williams. Wigg was Wilson's closest colleague at the onset of his career because, according to Wigg: 'I knew Wilson well enough to understand the need for somebody near him who would speak fearlessly and would hold up a mirror from time to time. He did not want a crony. He wanted a colleague and trusted friend linking him with the outside world with which all Prime Ministers inevitably lose touch'.[7] As Castle quoted Crossman: 'he thought Wigg had a disastrous influence on Harold, seeking intrigue everywhere and knowing everything that was going on.'[8] Wigg himself was equally scathing about his up-and-coming successor. 'The increasing disquiet', said George Wigg in 1967, 'I felt in No 10 was shared by many. It became all too clear that civil servants and ministerial colleagues had a formidable competitor for the Prime Minister's ear in Mrs Williams. Unfortunately her growing influence was not in my view always exercised with wisdom or discretion . . .'

Nevertheless Wigg soon lost to Williams, who provided the organisational buffer and political loyalty that Wilson wanted or needed. The relationship was politically, not sexually, symbiotic: 'she met', said Joe Haines, 'for a great many years a deep craving within him: for someone else to whom politics was meat and drink and the very air that was breathed; someone who, at her best, had a political mind capable of testing and matching his . . . someone who was prepared to devote all her time to Harold Wilson's service . . .'[9] Once Wilson was Party Leader, Williams took over his secretarial and *alter ego* role. She 'satisfied for Harold Wilson the need of such a deeply insecure and enormously ambitious man for a woman obsessively devoted to realising his ambitions; in turn Williams could come late to official functions, could keep him waiting at airports, nag him in front of managers, use his chauffeurs, his doctor, his lawyer, crowd his office with her relatives and "borrow" his helicopter'.[10] Wilson was very touchy about any misinterpretation of his relationship with Williams: two libel suits in 1964 soon emphasised how touchy. George Thomas, a Cardiff Labour MP, tells of a teatime conversation with Percy Holman, Labour MP for Bethnal Green.

> Holman asked me if I had ever seen Wilson's wife, commenting that it was strange that she was never with him. Sensing hostility to Wilson, I said that I knew Mrs Wilson well and asked him what he was driving at. There was no reply. The truth was, I had never met Mary Wilson but I felt angry at the low-level campaign of some of Wilson's opponents who were spreading rumours about his private secretary, Marcia Williams . . .[11]

Yet he himself was only too ready to become involved in her private life. When Fleet Street got their hands on Williams's affair with Walter Terry, by whom she had two children, 'Wilson's sense of persecution was fed to the point of uncontrollable fury' and 'his lawyers moved in with threats of injunctions.'[12] When John Allen had a brief affair with Williams in 1965 he backed out of a marriage plan as he was sent out to Swaziland to prepare a report on African development. On his way he allegedly received a note initialled by Wilson to the effect that he 'should sort out his problems while he was away. The decision he arrived at would make a difference to his employment on his return.'[13] The influence of those around Wilson increased during the politically-turbulent years up to his defeat in 1970 and consolidated thereafter, thereby creating a bunker mentality that was described by James Margach as 'not a meeting of great minds to keep the Prime Minister in touch with new thinking, and inspire his administration. The reality is that, with its rapidly changing composition, they lived in a world of cops and robbers, conspiracies, ploys and intrigues. It was the worst conceivable world for Harold Wilson, a man always addicted to the conspiracy theory of politics'.[14]

## The Land Deals Affair

Wilson's attempts to be free from party constraints were achieved in the early years in Opposition when his office was funded privately both from his own and his supporters' efforts when the Party had, as Williams put it, 'neither the funds nor, I fear, the will to help him . . . this chaotic situation was exacerbated by something impossible to mention – or admit – at the time: the tacit antagonism that existed between Transport House and Westminster.' Neither were his relations with his colleagues improved: 'after a while, their increased and involuntary leisure bore unexpected fruit: old quarrels resurfaced, intrigue flourished, there was a hatching of plots and counterplots to forward this or that political ambition.'[15] Williams was determined to protect Wilson from the reorganisation and dislocation that electoral defeat had caused. In that she was helped by the nature of the funding of his private office, a story that broke in February 1977 with the *Daily Mail* headline: 'Wilson had a Secret Fund'. In June 1970 Wilson was out of 10 Downing Street. At that time there was no funding for the Leader of the Opposition other than £6000 a year from Transport House, enough for two secretaries but not for Marcia Williams (who was then paid for by Wilson personally) or Joe Haines who had given up his Fleet Street job to work as Wilson's Press Officer. Part of the financial problem was resolved by Wilson's £224,000 book contract with the *Sunday Times* which, using existing taxation provisions for selling the documents on which the book is written as a 'unique' asset, paid for Grange Farm in Great Missenden and a London base. The surplus, together with US lecture-tour fees, only partly paid for Wilson's private Office.[16] Interestingly, Joe Haines thought the book paid for all the costs of the Office. In fact part of the costs came from a Trust set up in 1970. It was chaired by Lord Wilfred Brown, a longtime industrialist who had been created a

Life Peer in 1964 and served as a junior Minister at the Board of Trade between 1965–70. It was, he said later, 'low-profile. We did not want the Labour Party to know about it because they would have wanted to get their fingers on it. It was for Harold Wilson as Opposition Leader. If it had gone through Transport House, we could not have been sure it would have got to him'.[17] At this time Wilson and Transport House did not get on too well. Williams claimed that Transport House resented 'any attempt by the "glamour" side to take funds away from Party Headquarters'.[18]

Assisting Brown were Samuel Fisher, Rudy Sternberg, Arnold Goodman and Arich Handler. Before it was wound up in 1974, up to ten individuals were claimed to be paying £2000 each to pay for Wilson's secretarial and research assistance. Such were the relations within the Labour Party that Williams – she called herself one of his 'political advisers' by then – and Wilson nearly decided to run the 1974 campaign presidential-style, by appealing to the electorate over the heads of the politicians and Transport House where, 'within the PLP and the metropolis there were individuals and groups whose attitudes towards him shaded from a vague disenchantment to outright hostility . . .'[19]

Once installed back in 10 Downing Street in 1974, as head of Wilson's Political Office, Williams determined not to function under all the traumas of the previous Labour administrations. Having known Wilson for as long as she did, she determined to act as gatekeeper and go-between with 'only the good of the leader of the Party at heart' with no thought of 'her own political good or advancement.' Thus positioned she could, or the office could, 'advise, describing what they know of the current political climate and of the likely reaction among their network of contacts to any Prime Ministerial decision. In turn, the Prime Minister can bounce ideas off a dedicated and disinterested man or woman who has an obvious strong interest in public affairs.'[20] Others in the Office, particularly Joe Haines, were less enthusiastic. Wrote Haines: 'respect and importance were what she wanted. Recognition that she was out of the ordinary. Well, she *was* out of the ordinary. But like the rest of us, she was in the end only an appendage of the Prime Minister, because he was the Prime Minister. She confused power with respectability; influence with admiration.'[21]

The core of the Office revolved around the Marcia Williams connection. While Williams's father tramped the Buckinghamshire countryside to find Wilson a house her elder sister, Peggy Field, left her job at Hendon Technical College in 1969 to work as a secretary at 10 Downing Street while the brother Tony moved from being Wilson's volunteer-driver and golf companion to being his office manager for eighteen months from 1971. In him 'Harold had the sort of friend with whom he could chat and talk, knowing that not one word would be transmitted under any circumstances to any outside person, not even his own family.'[22] The place, according to George Wigg, became progressively filled with Marcia's relatives and friends. 'I would go in to see the Prime Minister and find Marcia, her brother, her sister, her boyfriend. The place was like a bloody railway station.'[23] With Williams in control 'people who could not take the tensions or who were frightened of her, as many were and still are today, simply left. In their place came others who could, and also members of her family . . . she wanted her gang', says one observer, 'she put Tony [her brother] on the golf course, Peggy [her sister] to type the letters.'[24] Joe Haines was scathing about the demands this connection made and on the status Williams expected and 'which was always so important to her.' There were rows over expenses, the use of office staff to get a visa for a Filipino servant, the informal contacts with Israeli politicians, the 'desire to be associated with show business folk' and the help for the family, such as 'her insistence that the Prime Minister should send a letter of introduction on behalf of her brother to the Prime Minister of Saudi Arabia to coincide with a visit Tony Field was making to the Middle East [the then Foreign and Commonwealth Secretary was asked to deliver the letter while he was in Saudi Arabia]'.[25]

Field was a graduate geologist who had spent a number of years in the Middle East working for the Iraqi Petroleum Company. On his return he worked as a quarry manager for the Bath and Portland Cement company. He left in 1967 after the company did not act on his advice to buy a slag heap and quarry near Wigan.[26] He set up his own company, J. Taylor's Slag Ltd, after buying the 29.83 acre site in Ince-in-Makerfield himself from John Taylor, friend and slag merchant, for £27,281. Slag, or aggregate, is a common base for roads and buildings and Field sold it for local motorways, road networks in Skelmersdale New Town and Fiddler's Ferry Power Station in Widnes. The one million ton site was worked both by Field (the slag had a sale value of up to 40p a ton) and by subcontractors (to whom Field sold it at 5p per ton). He also bought Ardite Ltd, which owned a gritstone quarry in the Parbold area, with a £50,000 loan from the Industrial and Commercial Finance Corporation which took a 20 per cent stake in the firm. Field used his other firm to work the quarry. Although Field wanted to keep the slag heap site under family control ICFC insisted it was used as collateral for the loan. This included the option to turn part of the loan, £12,500, into a shareholding in J. Taylor's Slag Ltd. Field and his mother were directors of JTS, Field and Marcia Williams directors of Ardite. The idea was to give them a return that would provide a steady income, and in the case of Marcia, to establish a pension fund. She herself was later to claim that she was 'a backroom girl', a private person with no means of redress, doing mostly routine and boring work without any interest in the 'corridors of power' side of political life. She was overworked ('no completely free holiday' over eighteen years) and underpaid ('bearing in mind both my education and secretarial qualifications and my duties'). The money was to be invested to provide a pension and it was Tory Party policy that transformed land values – which they had not expected. She pointed out that both businesses and trade unions did things involving land and property 'not entirely consistent with party principles' and no-one asked them to stop or resign – 'I shall not . . . there is no reason why I should. My conscience is clear'.

Although the slag business started well – a pre-tax profit of £16,000 on a £153,000 turnover – the gritstone was less than successful. By 1971 JTS had an accumulated deficit of £32,579.[27] Field was already considering the potential of the slag heap site for redevelopment once it was levelled. In 1971 Ince Council granted planning permission for the site to be used as an industrial estate and paid for a £180,000 access road that also touched on adjoining land. In that year Ardite was sold off and of the outstanding £13,400 debt to ICFC, £12,500 was converted into a 20 per cent stake in JTS. In 1973 Field, still needing to pay off the loan, began to prepare a package of land, including his own, for a suitable industrial site to be offered to developers. Two of those interested – Ronald Milhench and Victor Harper – turned out to be unfortunate choices. Ronald Milhench was a successful insurance broker who decided to get into the Seventies property boom with backing from Cripps Warburg, a new London merchant bank. Victor Harper was a Birmingham businessman whose affairs were being studied by the local Official Receiver. Harper acted as a go-between for the sale of the slag heap site at £10,000 an acre (the net proceeds were over £200,000) in February 1973. In March Field joined an Isle of Man-based developer, James Moore-Clague, who was also developing a site in Kirkby,[28] to buy a four-acre site next to the slag site from an engineering firm for £13,324 and to sell to Milhench for £10,000 an acre. This deal also went through because the Field family then put up £103,000 from the sale of the two sites to pay the £135,000 asking price for a third, related deal of a further sixty-one adjoining acres. That final sale, for which planning permission was also obtained, was not completed, although a buyer had already been found for the whole ninety-five acres, because of Milhench's arrest for forging a letter with Wilson's signature to help him with his own sales pitch. Field's statement in April 1974, made at the time to explain his actions, as Wilson was defending reclamation, was a straightforward account of someone who realised that packaging sites with planning permission was more lucrative than selling slag. While the family made little if any profit because of the failure of the final deal, there was potential profit even with the previous trading losses on the slag operation. He quoted £85,000 net profit on the slag-heap site and £25,000 net profit on the remaining sixty-five acres. Since ICFC received £40,500 for its 20 per cent stake in JTS then that would suggest a £202,500 value on the slag-heap site, but a substantial part of that was used to purchase the other sites and therefore not included in any net profit figure. Similarly Milhench's merchant bankers were supposed to have paid out £341,000 for the slag-heap site and the further four acres adjoining it. Milhench himself claimed that he was intending to spend a total of £950,000 for the whole ninety-five acres.

Milhench's enthusiasm to play the 'Wilson connection' to attract buyers also attracted those with an eye to another type of speculation. An associate of Milhench rang the *Guardian* with some well-informed details of the deals, the key to which was the incorrect but explosive claim that 'Marcia Williams was investing money in speculative land deals on behalf of Harold Wilson'.[29] Checking many of the details as accurate, the *Guardian* were dissuaded from publishing after 10 Downing Street confirmed Wilson was not involved (there is some confusion as to whether the *Guardian* rang Number 10 or whether they rang the newspaper). The informant, however, had also telephoned the *Daily Mail* who quickly learnt of 'a letter' from Wilson himself. It obtained a copy and sat on it – it was the Milhench forgery – as the ubiquitous Lord Goodman persuaded the newspaper's owner that publication, while not in itself unacceptable, might be taken as an electioneering smear that could have widespread adverse consequences for the press.

Labour won the General Election in February 1974. Aware of the interest in Milhench following the inquest into his wife's death by drowning after a car-crash with him at the wheel, the *Daily Mail* chose to publish the land deals story: 'The Case of Ronald Milhench and his £950,000 Land Deals.' The story invoked no reaction until a disgruntled Birmingham estate agent telephoned Chapman Pincher on the *Daily Express* with another story. In 1972 Harper had an option on forty acres of land at Jerrings Hill Farm on the edge of the Birmingham green belt. Unable to find out about decisions on planning applications for the land he wrote to Field at Wilson's office in the House of Commons. Field was on holiday in the Scilly Isles at the time, so an office secretary sent off a letter headed 'From the Rt Hon Harold Wilson, MP' to the Council asking for the information: it was signed 'pp H. A. Field.' The Council's reply to Harper began: 'I have had passed to me by the Rt Hon Harold Wilson MP, the enquiry you made of him for advice regarding possible planning permission . . .'[30]

Thanks to the Fleet Street courtesy of exchanging copies shortly before publication, the *Daily Mail* decided to publish the forged letter on the same day, not forgetting to leave in the quote in which Wilson allegedly wrote to Milhench that 'Tony and I feel sure you are quite capable of carrying our Ince-in-Makerfield deal through with efficiency and discretion'. The stories provoked a Parliamentary furore, particularly when Wilson chose to defend the motives of those involved. Wiser political counsel urged caution. Haines and Bernard Donoughue, a political adviser, warned Wilson that his intended statement to the House 'invites disaster. You will inevitably involve yourself in the transactions which . . . are not your concern.'[31] Wilson paid no heed and stood up in the House on 4 April 1974 to announce when provoked by a Tory MP that 'my honourable friends from Durham know the difference between property speculation and land reclamation . . . This is not a laughing matter. My honourable friends know that if one buys land on which there is a slag heap 120 ft high and it costs £100,000 to remove that slag, that is not land speculation in the sense that we condemn it. It is land reclamation'.[32]

That stunned his party into silence. As Labour MP Maureen Colquhoun put it: 'We didn't just feel bloody, most of us. We felt let down, all our hopes and ideals, crushed. It destroyed us as Socialists. The idea that we, the Labour Party, were determined to end land speculation for individual gain had actually, if it was to be believed, been undermined by close friends of our Prime Minister . . . many of us, particularly those new MPs (new not only to politics but the way the press handled political stories) were driven to despair.'[33]

The press and Tory Opposition were delighted that

Wilson had given them the chance 'to harry him on various statements he had made in defence of the Fields in the hope of being able to accuse him of misleading the House [and] why he had defended the Fields so vigorously at what looked like personal political risk'.[34] The refusal to back away from the story only served to draw attention to it. Wilson and Williams rapidly issued writs while the press found that the other people were using the Wilson name in vain. On 14 April the *Sunday Times* found his name on documents sent to a potential buyer by Milhench. Some days earlier the *Daily Mail* had picked up the *Daily Express*'s story about correspondence from No. 10 to the local council finding it was now incorporated into the promotional material of Townfield Homes, who had bought Harper's option on Jerrings Hall Farm, with its reference to the council's reply 'in response to an inquiry made on behalf of the Option Holder by the Rt Hon. Harold Wilson MP concerning the possibilities of future development of this site,'[35]

A few days later the *Sunday Times* turned up a document issued by Milhench's company which had contracted to buy the ninety-five acres but was still looking for a purchaser. The document, which claimed Field, JTS and Moore-Clague's firm were the vendors, also listed the 'Walmsley Family Trust (trustee: Harold Wilson)' as a reference for the former owners of the land.[36] This, like the 'letter from Wilson' Milhench claimed he possessed, was a forgery. Milhench later went to prison for three years.

In the meantime Wilson was livid and his later statements in September that year confirmed his views of what the press were up to: 'my colleagues and I throughout this summer have received many warnings . . . about the assiduous and dedicated work going on to prepare stories held back, ready for issue as the election nears its climax. Cohorts of distinguished journalists have been combing obscure parts of the country with a mandate to find anything, true or fabricated, to use against the Labour Party.' He said later that he believed that the aim was to spread allegations, 'however vague, however hidden, of corruption at worst, dubious standards at best.' Wilson believed that 'his personal staff, anyone connected with him, anyone even thought to be connected with him, ran – and runs – a constant risk of his or her private life being raked over.' Wilson was constructing a global onslaught by the media against himself and the Labour Party. Yet he tended to forget that his Office persuaded the *Guardian* not to run the Land Deals Story at first, that Lord Goodman did the same for the *Daily Mail* (whose first publication of the story sank without trace in any case), and that the *Mail* and *Express*, once each was aware the other had part of the story, were engaged in a circulation battle to stay in front with the story. Even if there was a plot, and there was little evidence there was (Wilson later toned down his claim that editors were ordering 'distinguished journalists' to uncover hostile stories in 1974), Wilson did much to fuel the furore by not heeding his advisors who wanted him to issue 'an immediate statement frankly admitting his embarrassment over the affair, acknowledging the points of public interest raised and reiterating his disapproval of profits from any sort of land development – however socially worthy.'[37]

Instead Wilson stood up in the House in 1974, ready to defend his staff and armed with a list of detailed facts: 'While I have always drawn a distinction in my public speeches before and during the election between property development and land speculation . . . one cannot compare the kind of land speculation with the particular kind of operation involved here . . . There is no justification whatever in the attempts that have been made to sensationalise the affair and no reason why any member of my own staff should forfeit the trust I place in them.'[38]

By not disassociating himself from what had happened Wilson put himself on the defensive, appearing to use his public position to try and justify the private activities of private staff and thus giving his opponents the opportunity to create a political controversy that need never have happened and which certainly diminished his status as a political leader and Prime Minister.

Thus Wilson's statement became justification, loyalty overtook prudence and those involved were back in the public eye, with Marcia Williams receiving the most press attention. She was besieged for days by reporters, as they camped outside her central London mews house and her modern four-bedroomed Bucks house ('my cottage' as she called it). *Private Eye* then broke the story of Williams's two children by Walter Terry, then political correspondent of the *Daily Mail* and subsequently the *Daily Express*. Wilson then chose to crown the whole episode in July 1974 by putting his secretary into the Lords as Lady Falkender. According to Marcia Williams, Harold Wilson had already suggested in 1970 she take a more active part in political and Parliamentary life. After the 1974 Election they agreed that any such part – involving a seat in the Lords – should take place on his Resignation List. The slag heap affair precipitated the decision, Wilson feeling that her 'contribution and work was being buried under a sea of irrelevant comment.'[39] Others were more concerned; Haines reported that 'everyone in the office was chilled by the prospect . . . we were all sunk in gloom at what we knew would be the reaction both in the press and the party.'[40]

# Chapter 14
## *The Trials of Jeremy Thorpe*

### *A shaggy dog story*

The *News of the World* usually titillates its Sunday readers at breakfast time with lurid front page stories of sin and crime involving household names. Curious, therefore, that in December 1975 it should raise the case of a murdered Great Dane on a Somerset road and the apparent reluctance of the authorities to talk about its death. Curiouser still, was the suggestion that the demise of the unfortunate animal was materially linked to MPs 'on whose support the continuation in office of the Government depends'. For, while the dog did not appear to be an active supporter of any particular party or to have shown much interest in the continued survival of the then Labour Government, its weeping owner could claim some personal knowledge of someone who could have such an interest – and he was Jeremy Thorpe, MP. For the distraught Great Dane owner was to claim that the shooting of his dog had been a preliminary to his own murder, a murder intended to silence his allegations of a sexual relationship with Thorpe, to protect the Liberal leader's political career. In the event it led to Thorpe's indictment for conspiracy to murder and one of the most dramatic political scandals of the century.

### *Jeremy's Tale*

The central character in the scandal was a skilful and ambitious politician with a streak of ruthlessness and a well-developed sense of showmanship. In February 1974, after a four-year period of Tory rule that had been less than successful dealing with the economy and militant trade unionism, the General Election had left the Tory Government unable to command an overall majority in the House of Commons without the support of Liberal MPs. The Conservatives proposed a coalition deal, including the offer of Ministerial posts (Thorpe was pencilled in for Foreign Secretary). Thorpe's speed in reaching Downing Street for consultation left him no time to canvass his party, which flatly refused to consider co-operating with the Tories. The Labour Party took office as Thorpe warned his party 'not to shrink from the possibility of sharing power'. For fifteen years he had kept faith with a minority political party that had finally come close to attaining real power and a real rôle for its leader. He was not prepared to give up that opportunity willingly.

That single-mindedness was part of Thorpe's public make-up, dynamic, principled but with a well-developed sense of the art of the possible. Son of a barrister and former Tory MP, he was brought up in a comfortable upper middle-class environment and educated at Eton and Oxford. After work as a barrister and a television journalist he won the North Devon constituency as a Liberal in 1959 at the age of thirty. Another Liberal parliamentary candidate, and later MP, in Devon was Peter Bessell, a congregationalist lay preacher who campaigned in a Cadillac and pursued a variety of business schemes.[1] Bessell introduced Thorpe to some of them, starting Thorpe on a series of directorships that led in 1971 to an appointment as a non-executive director of London and County Securities, a merchant bank. Despite rumblings of idealist discontent, particularly among Young Liberals, he had ruthlessly stamped his organisational mark and personal style of leadership on the Party. One meeting was described by a party member as 'one of the nastiest I've ever sat through' and party staff would face the full brunt of his ridicule and sarcasm when minor errors upset the public image of the efficient and progressive third party – 'I nearly go out of my mind', Thorpe used to say about such errors. He himself actively pursued a central public rôle for himself as he 'began to be much in evidence at royal banquets, City dinners, diplomatic functions and parties at Number Ten where he established contacts with Wilson's entourage, and in particular with his powerful personal and political secretary, Marcia Williams.'[2]

By 1973 he was a Privy Councillor, confirmed leader of his Party, a national figure, with a comfortable lifestyle funded by several modestly-paid directorships. He had survived the deeply-felt shock of his first wife's death in a car crash and married Marion, Countess of Harewood. His political future was riding high on a general revival of the Party's fortunes, particularly at local level. Only one setback had occurred: London and County, amidst the secondary bank boom of the early 1970s, had overreached itself and run into increasing debt; after trying to conceal this by some nifty, if illegal, creative accounting, it collapsed owing £50 million. Thorpe had previously been embarrassed by revelations of the excessive interest charged on second mortgages by a London and County associate company. In January 1976 he had to take a public lecture from DTI investigators in their Report on the bank's collapse about the inadvised practice of leading politicians taking paid directorships (in Thorpe's case £5000 a year, a car and share options) in companies whose affairs they were ill-equipped to understand.

They reminded him presciently that 'his reputation is not only his most marketable, but also his most vulnerable commodity'.[3] He weathered the crisis, apologising for not paying sufficient attention to the company's affairs. Since the Report exonerated him from involvement in the nefarious actions of some of the other directors, his apology reflected the sort of honesty, said Liberal Party Chief Whip Cyril Smith later, that 'would satisfy public concern and allow him to escape without too much damage to his reputation.'[4] On the day the DTI Report appeared, however, Bob Carvel of the *Evening Standard* rang Smith for his comments on another story. What, he asked, were Cyril Smith's comments on the Barnstaple courtroom outburst by a Norman Scott?

Norman Josiffe (or Scott, as he later called himself) was a good-looking young man with underlying psychological problems stemming from his upbringing and his bisexuality, which were increasingly reflected in bouts of personal insecurity and highly-charged emotional intensity. A love of horses took him to a Chipping Norton riding stables where he met the 31-year-old Thorpe, who offered a helping hand if ever he was in trouble. After treatment at an Oxfordshire clinic, a couple of drug overdoses and an increasingly-complex private life Josiffe decided to take up the offer. According to Josiffe – and repeatedly denied by Thorpe – Thorpe then whisked him off to Thorpe's mother's house for sex with the infamous tube of vaseline, the start of a four-year relationship.

Certainly Thorpe felt a personal responsibility for Josiffe; he arranged accommodation and work for him and told the police he was 'more or less a guardian' to him when they were inquiring about a coat stolen from the clinic. Certainly he felt affectionate towards him, he was writing to 'My dear Norman', nicknaming him 'Bunnies' (because he looked like a startled rabbit) and professing that 'I miss you'. After a few months, however, when Josiffe thought he was in love with Thorpe, Thorpe was distinctly offhand. Believing himself used and spurned Josiffe took himself off on a peripatetic and confused journey around various parts of the country, through short-lived jobs and personal crises. All the time, however, he never lost sight of the Thorpe connection. Indeed, he increasingly blamed his troubles on Thorpe's cavalier treatment of him and was prepared to talk about it. Thus the police had information on the alleged relationship when, in 1962, Josiffe, working in London was heard to threaten to kill Thorpe and was visited by police officers who took him to Chelsea police station. There, he talked of his 'homosexual relations' with Thorpe. The police kept a statement and two letters. Scott told his employers about Thorpe in 1965 and, in the same year, wrote to Thorpe's mother repeating allegations about the relationship and urging her to intercede with her son because he 'was desperate'.

When his mother passed on the letter Thorpe turned for help to Peter Bessell, now a fellow Liberal MP and a man whose sexual and business exploits clearly impressed on Thorpe that he, as a man of the world, could confidently and discreetly deal with Josiffe's indiscriminate outbursts. Bessell went to see Josiffe who appeared apologetic and wanted 'so much to forget the past'. Bessell also went to see George Thomas and Sir Frank Soskice, both Home Office ministers, and the latter appeared to suggest that, although Josiffe's allegations were known about, Thorpe was unlikely to be investigated (the alleged homosexual relationship took place before the repeal of the law that made such relationships a criminal offence).

Unfortunately Josiffe had another emotional crisis which required hospital treatment; he then decided to acquire the surname Scott and began looking for money, insurance cards, a passport and a visa in order to plan a new life. Bessell, who had been told by Soskice to keep Scott away from Thorpe and not to allow him to get a hold over him, put Scott on a retainer and provided money for a new career in modelling. Scott then married; while it ended his career it also reduced his demands on Bessell. Unfortunately the marriage was short-lived and Scott was in difficulties again. There was talk of a contested divorce and the possibility of a court case involving Thorpe's name. Then there were difficulties at the local DHSS office over Scott's lack of documents when he wanted to claim maternity benefit for his now-pregnant wife. One of Scott's perennial complaints was that Thorpe had retained his insurance card since the days he was helping him find work. That particular crisis faded when Scott left the West Country for North Wales but he was still talking about Thorpe. To Scott, Thorpe's continued (and to Scott, malign) influence was now the main reason why he could not shake off the events of the past and settle down to live a normal life. There were those who listened to the distraught young man and believed that he had a genuine grievance.

One immediate consequence of Scott's volubility was that, in 1971, one of those concerned about Scott's state of mind contacted Liberal MP Emlyn Hooson about a 'leading member of the Liberal Party' who had ruined this young man's life. She wanted Hooson to help this leading member keep his word (paying Scott's expenses to settle in Wales) and thus preserve the honour of the Party. Hooson and David Steel, the Party's Chief Whip, assumed that Bessell – by this time in constant financial trouble and in the USA after a string of ill-concealed affairs with his secretaries – was the problem. Hooson and Steel interviewed Scott. Scott handed them some letters that showed he was receiving retainers from Peter Bessell and told them of his interview with the police (which Scott was now pretending had followed his arrest at the Commons in 1965 where he claimed he was armed with a gun). Hooson spoke to Bessell, who confirmed the payments and then tracked down the officer who interviewed Scott in 1962 and who now confirmed an interview had taken place. Hooson confronted Thorpe, who denied any relationship and warned Hooson that 'if he pursued the matter he would see to it that his legal career was ruined.'[5] Hooson persisted and won the promise of an internal party inquiry to be headed by Lord Byers. Thorpe was furious that Hooson had contacted the officer and complained to the Home Secretary, the Conservative MP Reginald Maudling. 'The first lesson in politics is that no one can be as disloyal as one's own colleagues', he wrote at the time. Thorpe himself sought the help of Maudling and John Waldron, the Metropolitan Commissioner of Police, when writing a letter for Byers' inquiry. Thorpe asked Waldron if the 'gun' incident had taken place and if the police had any psychiatric reports on Scott. He then asked for their comments on his letter for Byers in which he argued that the proper authorities for any inquiry into Scott's allegations were the police. He described how the Home Secretary had told him, Thorpe, that Scott had gone to the police himself, had been interviewed by the police who 'didn't really know why he had gone to see them' and that 'there was nothing which called for action on their part.' The letter also referred to his asking Waldron about 'the background' to the police interview – the alleged 1965 gun incident of which Waldron had told him there was no record and which 'one might safely conclude . . . had never happened'.

By this tactic the letter, posited on a non-existent incident, appeared to suggest to any reader that Scott had been making wild allegations, that the police had dutifully talked to him but had found no evidence of any criminal behaviour on the part of Thorpe and that Thorpe could indeed be the victim of someone else's fantasies. The letter avoided any reference to the 1962 interview with the police, the statement and the letters they retained and any explanation as to why Scott had been so upset as to make the threats that he did. 'The whole exercise', wrote Peter Chippindale and David Leigh, 'was based upon the proposition – flawlessly understood by Thorpe – that under the rules of the game as played a well-connected politician could deploy in his own cause a selective access to official records which could not be checked by others.'[6] As Thorpe ended the letter: 'as far as I am concerned, apart from the possibility of periodic and neurotic eruptions, this tiresome matter is closed. I know this is your view.' Maudling had noted: 'thank you for showing me your letter to Frank Byers. I have shown it to the Commissioner. Neither of us see any reason to disagree.'

The submission of the letter to the inquiry, together with Maudling's note, ended the Party's inquiry in Thorpe's favour and remained firm evidence of an official vindication of his name until his 1978 Old Bailey trial when the defence counsel appeared to suggest that Thorpe had 'expressly' asked the Commissioner and Maudling to investigate Scott's allegations. In the end both defence and prosecution counsel agreed a formal statement that no request was made of either. All Thorpe had done was to ask questions about the non-existent gun incident and as to whether the Home Office possessed any psychiatric reports on Scott, to which the answer had been that there was no evidence of either on the files. 'The truth', said *Sunday Times* journalists later, 'is that

Thorpe used both Maudling and Waldron to protect his reputation in front of his own party members by presenting an incomplete account of his relationship with Scott. By endorsing this account they were helping to give him a clean bill of health.'[7] As Peter Taylor, the prosecution counsel, told the jury at the trial, the tactic in sending a letter whose contents were approved by two senior public figures 'looked very businesslike, frank, forthcoming and very impressive' but it did not deal with the issues under investigation by the party inquiry. Thorpe had not asked the authorities to investigate Scott's allegations. 'This is important', said Taylor, 'because it gives some insight into the way Thorpe works. I am sorry to have to put it this way but it comes to this – trying to fix the record.'

Someone else who felt fixed was Scott. Reacting to the hostile tenor and conclusions of the Party inquiry, feeling browbeaten, colluded against and suspected of blackmail, he threatened to take his tale to the media.

### Enter a red herring with a time-fuse

Scott's complaints reached the *Daily Mirror*, who passed it to a freelance reporter, Gordon Winter. Winter coaxed the story out of a suspicious and highly-strung Scott who alleged: 'I was deeply in love with Jeremy for three years. We were inseparable and I thought our idyllic friendship would last forever. But he discarded me like a cheap tart . . .'[8] Winter hawked the story round the *People* and the *Sunday Mirror* without success but the rumours were now percolating into Fleet Street and, through an ex-intelligence contact of Winter's, reached MI5. Knowledge of Thorpe's alleged sexual proclivities had been circulating around Secret Service and police circles from the early Sixties. MI5 had already investigated Thorpe in 1960 when he was a candidate for best man for the wedding of Princess Margaret. Their inquiries to Devon's Chief Constable at the time elicited the allegation that it was 'fairly common knowledge in Devon' that Thorpe might have homosexual tendencies.[9] Following the experience of the Profumo affair, and Denning's subsequent comments (see

222

pp. 95–6), MI5 kept the information to itself and did not pass it on to Heath when he was considering Thorpe for a Ministerial appointment in the proposed coalition. It is doubtful if Thorpe knew that either Winter's or the earlier information was in the hands of MI5 but, in any case, the official vindication of his reputation by Maudling was as close to an official clean bill of health as was possible, and unlikely to be contradicted. Nevertheless, Winter had one further, undisclosed contact for his story – the South African Bureau of State Security (BOSS). Winter was later to claim that he was a BOSS agent and had, on BOSS's orders, delayed publication of Scott's allegations in order to achieve a much greater impact at a later date.

## The scandal unfolds; press interest

Meanwhile two events were to take the story dramatically onto the fringes of the public arena. First, Andrew Newton was arrested in late 1975 on charges of possession of a firearm with intent to endanger life following the shooting of Scott's dog. Due for trial in March 1976 he enlivened pre-trial press interest with gratuitous comments – such as 'I think it is wrong for Mr Thorpe to be dragged through the mud by men of straw' – when his offence was supposedly related to his blackmail by Scott over a nude photograph of himself in a compromising position. Second, in January 1976, Scott was in court in Barnstaple on charges of defrauding the DHSS. From there, press reports were being filed that Scott was alleging he was being hounded because he once had a sexual relationship with Thorpe. Until Scott's court outburst, the press, or those parts of it that were aware of the allegations, had been remarkably cautious. When the *Daily Mirror* first heard of the story it was aware that 'there would certainly be libel problems and possibly political pressures'[10] which was why it was given to Gordon Winter to follow up. When he completed his inquiries he took them to the *People* who put his report in a safe. In 1974 some workmen refurbishing Bessell's old London office in Pall Mall found some letters and photographs;

one of the former was Scott's 1965 letter to Thorpe's mother. They handed them to the *Sunday Mirror* whose owner, Lord Jacobsen, 'decided that since the letters hinted at blackmail, and had come into the hands of the *Mirror* in dubious circumstances they should be returned to Thorpe, who was a personal friend.'[11]

Even after Scott's Barnstaple courtroom outburst in 1976 (over £58), however, the media had no firm evidence to indicate any involvement between Thorpe and Scott although their inquiries were beginning to unravel the activities of two of his closest associates; Peter Bessell and businessman David Holmes, who had been best man at Thorpe's first wedding and had been appointed a deputy treasurer of the Party by Thorpe. From the outset, therefore, the media tended to be favourably disposed towards Thorpe. The *Sunday Times*, an indefatigable defender of Thorpe, had published Thorpe's views on Scott's allegations as 'this tissue of . . . elaborately woven mendacity and malice' and argued that any relationship that may have existed was 'essentially trivial.' Other newspapers were equally helpful; the *Daily Express* was alleging Bessell had deserted his wife and left a trail of debts in his flight from the USA, where he had gone to live following the collapse of his political and business life in Britain. The *News of the World* was frontpaging Scott as weird, bizarre, devious and 'living in a world of almost fantasy.' In the *Sunday Times* John Whale accused Fleet Street of an obsession with sex under the guise of puritanism, triggered by specific stimuli – sex, the hint of cover-ups, the circulation battles, the presence of exotic elements such as the California-based Bessell. He argued that Fleet Street was motivated by disclosure which it tried to justify on moral grounds, thus encouraging 'one another in a restrictive estimate of national moral attitudes' which, indeed, 'need not have much to do with public opinion at large.'[12] In March, believing Thorpe to be the victim of a 'vicious smear campaign', the *Sunday Times* itself attacked Scott as a habitual liar, Winter as a relentless seeker after discreditable gossip and Bessell as a credulous man with a capacity for exaggeration, all in sharp contrast to Thorpe

– 'a man whose word has proved reliable throughout a long career in public life.'[13]

## The Facade Cracks

In March 1976 Newton was sentenced to two years' imprisonment. During the trial it was announced that the police had made extensive inquiries but had found no connection between Newton and 'any member of the Liberal Party'; Scott had come out of the case as, counsel suggested, 'a spiteful blackmailer, eaten with hatred'. The press had that month, however, uncovered the payments to Scott by Bessell and payments by Holmes to obtain some documents from a doctor who had been treating Scott, but both had made it plain that they had acted on their own initiative to keep Scott quiet over embarrassing revelations about Bessell's private life. Despite continued media attention, Thorpe felt confident enough to tell Parliamentary colleagues that he would ride the storm because he had the three most important people on his side – 'Harold Wilson, Lord Goodman, and MI5'. He had, however, lost the support of David Steel who had been told by Nadir Dinshaw, a friend of Thorpe, about the payment of monies intended for party purposes to Holmes. Thorpe had also neglected to ensure the loyalty of his less exalted supporters, particularly Bessell. Bessell was annoyed by the *Sunday Times* article in March which used information fed in by Thorpe. Thorpe had done much to help Bessell's increasingly-disastrous business ventures (he was prepared to 'stake his life' on his support of Bessell's efforts to coax money from a major donor to Party funds) and, when he wanted a favour, Bessell gladly obliged. The favour was the pretence that he, Bessell, and Holmes were involved in buying Scott's silence to protect Bessell from Scott's attempts to blackmail him. The apparent details of this were included in a letter from Bessell saying Scott was blackmailing him. The letter was to be held for use in the Newton trial so that, if Scott began talking about Thorpe, he could be accused of lying and perjury. The letter was for lawyer-to-lawyer consumption only; media references to its circulation in Westminster and the slighting comments about him in the *Sunday Times* caused him rapidly to distance himself from Thorpe. Bessell's payments to Scott and his meeting in January 1976 with David Holmes to concoct the letter were predicated on a loyalty to Thorpe. Bessell expected that loyalty to be reciprocated – he valued his 'credibility' – and the article prompted him to change his mind. In a *Daily Mail* interview in early May he was denying that he was at risk and claiming that he had been shielding Thorpe's reputation on the grounds that he assumed Scott posed a serious threat to it; 'I Told Lies to Protect Thorpe.'

The *Sunday Times* scurried after Thorpe for his views. Together with his lawyer, Lord Goodman, Thorpe offered the newspaper two letters, including the 'Bunnies' letter with its postscript 'I miss you', together with a six-point denial of the relationship, the retainers and any involvement in the shooting of Scott's dog. Thorpe's intention was to clear the air, and pre-empt any further allegations by Scott and adverse speculation of Bessell's angry recantation. It had the opposite effect. The *Sunday Times* had been prepared to trim its sails in what it said about Thorpe. When Thorpe and his solicitor Lord Goodman decided to publish the 'Bunnies' letter through the *Sunday Times*, Goodman asked that it was not presented in 'a blatantly hostile way.' Journalist Bruce Page wanted to couch the presentation within the context of Thorpe's homosexual tendencies which the editor Harold Evans rejected, less on libel grounds than because he was 'concerned whether the paragraph threatened the undertaking he had given in their private meeting to Thorpe and Goodman'. The 'tendencies' context was not used; nor was the private meeting made known to the newspaper's staff at the time.[14]

Despite the *Sunday Times*'s assertion that 'assumptions about Thorpe have been a threat to him, as much as the confusion of moral attitudes to sexual behaviour and especially, an inability to distinguish between an accusation of private eccentricity and accusations of public dishonesty'[15] its middle-class readership must have been rather bemused wondering what 'I miss you' meant. It also provided the basis for even more speculation about the importance with which Thorpe was apparently treating the matter. Indeed Thorpe's position was worsened by fellow MP Richard Wainwright asking on radio when Thorpe was going to issue a writ against Scott for defamation. Thorpe decided to resign on 10 May 1976. In his letter of resignation (discussed with Steel) he blamed the press for turning a series of allegations into a sustained witch hunt and blamed Wainwright for publicly challenging his credibility: 'no man can effectively lead a party if the greater part of his time has to be devoted to answering allegations as they arise and countering continuing plots and intrigues', he complained.

## The scandal unfolds; party reaction

If Thorpe was less than generous to his Party then he had only himself to blame; his Party had been ill-prepared for the shock of Scott's outburst in the Barnstaple court. In March 1976, analysing Thorpe's political difficulties with his Party, journalist Simon Hoggart suggested that, instead of becoming Foreign Minister in a Conservative-Liberal coalition government, Thorpe 'seems to be condemned to a quiet and perhaps humdrum life in the legal profession. Things could be worse.'[16] How much worse was yet to unfold. Thorpe's resignation in May 1976 was firmly placed at the door of the Liberal Party and Fleet Street newspapers. George Thomas, Speaker of the House of Commons, was to say later: 'My feeling has always been that Jeremy Thorpe was destroyed by his parliamentary colleagues as much as by the press campaigns against him. The Liberal MPs behaved very badly by showing disloyalty just when their leader needed it most. Jeremy had been in dire trouble for a long time and had a right to expect far greater loyalty from those around him than he received. In fact he had more friends outside the Liberal Party than inside.'[17]

Yet the Byers inquiry had been hostile to Scott (Byers made Scott cry: 'like a jilted girl', said Hooson) and those involved had assumed the allegations against Thorpe to be groundless. Furthermore Cyril Smith, the Party's Chief Whip, knew little of the Scott business – 'my hot head', Thorpe called him – and was ill-prepared for the barrage of questions that the media flung at him as they gradually pieced together Bessell's efforts to keep Scott quiet and then David Holmes's attempts to buy up Scott's letters for the same reason. Two incidents spelt out his quandary.

When he asked Thorpe about a meeting with Labour Prime Minister Harold Wilson during the mounting press interest in early 1976, Thorpe tried to make a secret of it by claiming that 'we were talking on Privy Council terms' (that is, in confidence). When pressed he said: 'it will be pushed on to South Africa'. 'What the hell does that mean', demanded Smith. 'The PM believes that there are South African influences at work', snapped Thorpe. 'It was obvious', said Smith later, 'from his tone that no further information would be forthcoming'. Later Smith had to ask Thorpe if he knew who this David Holmes was that the press were talking about. Thorpe, Smith said, snapped angrily 'of course I bloody well do'. It is hardly surprising that the luckless Liberal Party should be caught between ignorance of and concern over the nature of the allegations. Emlyn Hooson's summary of a February 1976 party meeting summed up the dilemma:

> it would be an appalling injustice and condemnation of our democratic society if Jeremy were to resign merely because the party is embarrassed by allegations which were untrue . . . on the other hand, if there was a sound basis of truth in the allegations, Jeremy Thorpe owes it to the party . . . not to lumber us with the stark choice between apparent disloyalty and engagement in a kind of cover-up . . .

With that meeting portrayed as a kangaroo court – although it accepted Thorpe's word that the allegations were untrue – and with Smith's resignation as Chief Whip ('there are things going on I know nothing about', he said) the Liberal Party looked equivocal in its support, but then it had little information on which to assess its position and a natural tendency to look first to the interests of the Party. As Simon Hoggart had already noted: 'The Norman Scott affair certainly brought matters to a head but it is a total mistake to imagine that it is the only reason for Thorpe's hazardous position. A more popular and politically successful leader would have weathered such a difficulty triumphantly; instead he was faced with supporters who were already trying to get rid of him'.[18]

The Party had been caught unawares by the Scott allegations but Thorpe had not sought Party support and, indeed, had discouraged full disclosure. The Party, or at least certain members of it, felt unsettled at Thorpe's tactics. It was prepared to defend him in the presence of untrue, if embarrassing, allegations; it was less enthusiastic if Thorpe was not demonstrating 'good judgement and the discretion to be entrusted with high responsibilities.' That it felt that Thorpe was not demonstrating them was evident from its internal deliberations (the press talked of Thorpe being 'gored' and 'assassinated' by his colleagues and their treatment of him as a star-chamber or kangaroo-court response).

Yet Thorpe's apparently high-handed behaviour reflected both his predilection for leading from the front and his Party's increasing unease with that form of leadership. The Liberal Party's revival in national terms – for which Thorpe had been largely responsible – and its 'community politics' success – for which he was not – was seen as something for which Thorpe's continuation as leader was not essential. Indeed the Party was somewhat disillusioned over a leadership that had yet to develop positive policies – 'anyone voting Liberal could scarcely have had the faintest idea of what he was voting for', said one commentator in 1976. Between February and October 1974, it had also failed to capitalise electorally on its major national asset, the showmanship and personal style of its leader. Faced with the possibility of coalition, the Party and the Leader had different objectives and principles in mind and ultimately blew away the possibility of political office. After that, each was suspicious of the other's intentions, and, when Thorpe ran into the Scott allegations, the one stood by as the other fell deeper into

229

trouble. Yet Thorpe had felt it unnecessary to rely on the Party when he believed he had a stronger ally to help him: Labour Prime Minister Harold Wilson.

## Wilson and the South African Connection

In March 1976 Wilson got up in the Commons and announced that 'I have no doubt that there is strong South African participation in recent activities relating to the Leader of the Liberal Party based on massive reserves of business money and private agents of various kinds and qualities.' In May, Wilson told a Parliamentary Press Gallery lunch that 'what we have seen in recent years has been the work of an underground and well-heeled organisation which did not scruple to use any weapon against the British politicians and parties of whom they disapproved'. These statements, based on flimsy evidence, had two consequences. As a helpful red herring it gave the media an added incentive to pursue the Scott story. If the homosexual allegations were untrue, an equally-attractive tale of international intrigue and a BOSS-inspired smear campaign was worth pursuing. It also kept the scandal on the boil. The red herring had its genesis partly in the activities of Gordon Winter and partly in a 1976 extortion trial.

In 1975 a *Time Out* advert called for 'men and women, race and age immaterial, needed for a group of adventurers being formed abroad'. The adventurers were being recruited by Faoud Kamil, an illicit diamond-smuggling investigator, who believed that his former employers, the Anglo American Corporation, owed him money for his work in breaking up smuggling rings. In 1972 Kamil had hijacked a plane that he thought, wrongly, was carrying the son-in-law of the Corporation's boss, Harry Oppenheimer. Kamil spent some time in a Malawi prison as a result but, on his release, recruited his adventurers to continue his efforts to obtain his money. The 'adventurers' were soon arrested in London for demanding money with menaces. One of the defendants, a convicted pornography dealer, alleged that he had seen in Kamil's possession

Corporation documents relating to bribery payments and to plans to destabilise the Liberal Party. This allegation, without any documentary proof, he passed on to Peter Hain, the Young Liberal activist. Hain told Thorpe and Thorpe told Harold Wilson. The first result was the Commons speech; it was a welcome lifebelt for Thorpe who argued: 'I had no reason to disbelieve this coming from so authoritative a source'. The second was the sight of Fleet Street hurtling down 'some strange cul-de-sacs peopled by an assortment of fantastists and frauds'.

There was, of course, evidence that BOSS was operating against opponents of apartheid in Britain; Peter Hain had been arrested on a patently-unlikely bank robbery charge; the Anti-Apartheid Movement was at the receiving end of a disinformation forgery, the Club of Ten was advertising South Africa as the anti-communist bulwark in Africa, and a draft book by the Club's former campaign manager was allegedly stolen from Harold Wilson's home.

Though the media had little hard evidence to go on it amply filled the gap with a few more red herrings. Thus the *Guardian* ignominiously fell for a pack of lies involving BOSS, the South African Embassy, a pornographic film of a Liberal MP and the confession of a plausible 20-year-old youth, Andrew Thorne. Thorne had already been shown the door by the *News of the World* ('he's a dangerous, deceitful rattlesnake. Gave him the heave ho', wrote the reporter that interviewed him). Thorne had then told the *Guardian* ('it's read by snobs and Ministers', he said by way of explanation) that the South African Embassy was willing to talk to him about the film which he claimed depicted a Liberal MP committing acts of gross indecency with young boys in a barn in Surrey. The *Guardian* reported that it had a direct link between the Embassy and an attempt to discredit an MP. It didn't; Andrew Thorne did not have such a film, he admitted later to *The People*. The *Guardian*'s publication of an Embassy recording of an interview between Thorne, a *Guardian* journalist (who revealed his identity at the end of the interview to a total lack of interest) and an Embassy official was an embarrassing non-event. On the other hand, there was some concern as to why a South African diplomat should be interested in obtaining a pornography film for 'personal reasons' and, shortly afterwards, the official was recalled by the South African Government. The *Guardian* went down fighting – 'we strive to print facts' – under the sanctimonious onslaught of the *People* ('unsavoury role') and the *News of the World* ('investigations revealed serious doubts about the man's credibility'). At the same time BBC News carried an exclusive interview with a 'Colonel' Fred Cheeseman alleging BOSS involvement. It was a hoax.

For the reporters, Barrie Penrose and Roger Courtiour, it was a salutory lesson in checking the details of a story. Their interest, however, had led to a call for a meeting with Wilson over the South African angle. Wilson believed himself the target of a major destabilisation campaign by dissident MI5 officers and BOSS. He hyped up the rest of the press by specifically excluding them from the assistance he was giving Pencourt (as they called themselves), by playing secrecy games ('I see myself as the big fat spider in the corner of the room,' Wilson told them) and by hinting to the Director General of the BBC that he, Wilson, would provide material for a massive documentary exposé involving break-ins, CIA involvement, rogue MI5 agents and BOSS smears.

Nevertheless, the BBC, like other parts of the media, took only a few months to realise that the loose allegations by Wilson did not then match up to an organised conspiracy and, like Pencourt, realised that the relationship between Scott and Thorpe was a more fruitful line of investigation.[19] Unfortunately the BBC got cold feet. The Penrose and Courtiour inquiries were moving away from the vague and often unsubstantiated South African theme to the Scott story which alarmed the BBC hierarchy; 'you're like puppy dogs who keep bringing back sticks. The sticks always seem to have some connection with Thorpe', said one. When the BBC offered the two journalists contracts that made 'South African interest' the focus of their research and gave it exclusive control over their material the two journalists pulled out. Said their boss later: 'even if our information all turned out to be true, it set an organisation like the BBC so many problems. The overwhelming reaction was one of intense worry, either way. It involved too many difficult factors. The truth isn't necessarily the overwhelming consideration'.[20] The then Director-General of the BBC was more blunt: 'the story seemed to be turning into a kind of semi-criminal investigation and I thought that for the BBC to be financing airtrips for two people to California and South Africa on what was going to be a police investigation anyway seemed to me to be an unjustified use of public money. I was not interested in pushing Jeremy Thorpe further down the hole.'[21]

## The Pencourt File

After Wilson sold Penrose and Courtiour his belief in 'anti-democratic agencies in South Africa . . . threatening democratic societies like Britain', they went to work with alacrity on a story offering fascinating and fantastic allegations; Winter's intelligence links, CIA and BOSS involvement, private armies, MI5 destabilisation, and an alleged coup d'etat. More importantly, however, they worked back from the Scott angle of the story and found that it led less down the Wilsonian route than to an equally strange tale of how Andrew Newton acquired his unaccustomed role as a canine hitman. One of David Holmes's business interests concerned carpets (he obtained cheap carpets for the Party HQ). John Le Mesurier ran a carpet discount firm in Port Talbot. One of his friends was a fruit machine supplier, George Deakin. One of *his* friends – David Miller – did printing work for him and Le Mesurier and Miller knew an airline pilot who liked taking risks and showing off. Thus the stuff of conspiracy was born.

Holmes said he had a 'blackmail problem' and friend asked friend until Newton was hired to frighten off the blackmailer. Thus was born the tale of one shot dog and one imprisoned Newton. Before his trial Newton was promised £5000 by Holmes; on his release in April 1977 Le Mesurier paid it over. In October £3000 came from the *Evening News*, for Newton's claim that 'I was hired to kill

233

Scott' and that he had accepted £5000 from a top Liberal supporter – 'it was a contract to murder.' The police were called in to look at the allegations, their inquiries converging with, and facilitated by, Pencourt's contacts with Bessell in California. The new Liberal leader David Steel complained of 'total dismay that we are going to have to go through this again' and Wilson was protesting that 'I had no idea that one of the outcomes of the investigation would be an alleged murder plot involving Liberals'. The South Wales connection took on greater significance as Peter Bessell talked of a Mr X suggesting that David Holmes be instructed to kill Scott.[22] Thorpe unfortunately chose to hold a press conference to argue there was not 'a scrap of evidence' to link him to any plot and that his 'close, even affectionate' friendship with Scott was non-sexual, only to be faced with BBC reporter Ken Graves's question: 'Have you ever had a homosexual relationship?' While that was quickly stamped on – 'if you do not know why it is improper and indecent to put such a question to a public man, you ought not to be here', snapped Thorpe's solicitor – sex was also re-established on the agenda.

By the end of that year the South Wales names were published in *The People* (they paid Miller £8000 for photographs of the pay-off to Newton and for taped conversations with Le Mesurier). The *Daily Mirror* ran a lengthy inquiry suggesting that various individuals used 'go-it-alone methods' to shield Jeremy Thorpe, an Establishment figure with 'powerful allies' from 1962 onwards. It argued that the protection involved the police, Liberal Party supporters and politicians who were unified by their perceptions of the 'best interests of Jeremy Thorpe, the Liberal Party and political stability in this country.' Even the loyal *Sunday Times* ran the South Wales link arguing that, amid the five attempts by Scott to air his allegations and three attempts to silence him, 'the possibility remains that we are dealing with a case of attempted political murder.'[23] Which only left one part of the affair unrevealed: where was the money coming from to pay for incriminating letters, for retainers and for hitmen?

The Liberal Party, without the support of large organisations like industrial concerns or the union movement,
was poor. The high-profile political presence Thorpe
adopted for himself and the Party, and the cost of trying
to build up a professional secretariat, required money the
Party did not have. Thorpe was very keen to find a
handful of large benefactors rather than to continue relying on erratic personal contributions from the Party membership. He met Jack Hayward, a British businessman
with Bahamian interests, through an appeal to save Lundy
Island for the nation. Thorpe and Bessell quickly persuaded him to save the Liberal Party. Hayward's contributions, unknown to him, went into several Party
accounts, some of which Thorpe personally – and jeal-
ously – guarded in terms of who had authorised access
and what the money was used for. When the Party
President Lord Beaumont suggested auditing one of them
Thorpe warned him: 'if you bring that up I will tear you
into little shreds'.[24] Thorpe believed that the money was
being paid to him personally, to be used as he directed.

In one 1974 letter to Hayward, Thorpe was soliciting
money for his election expenses and asking that part be
paid into a Party account and part to Nadir Dinshaw, a
Jersey-based business friend of Thorpe. Thorpe's argument was supposedly based on election expenditure law
which limits an individual MP's constituency expenses
but makes no requirement for general election expenses.
Dinshaw sent his money to Holmes. Nearly a year later
Thorpe was asking for the same arrangement on the same
grounds (thus a total of £57,000 went to the Party; £20,000
to Dinshaw); the second, equal, payment to Dinshaw also
went on to Holmes. When Dinshaw saw the reports of
Holmes's payment to obtain papers from Scott's doctor he
was less than happy, even more so when Thorpe asked
him to cover up to whom the money went and then
threatened him if he told the truth; 'it will be curtains for
me and you will be asked to move on'. Thorpe was also
to ask Hayward to threaten to sue Bessell for money
owing if he returned to England. Both men refused. No

newspaper – the *Sunday Times* had the first details of the money-go-round – was able to publish the results of their inquiries because, as the final pieces of the jigsaw were being fitted together by the media, so the police had concluded their investigations. In August 1978 Thorpe was charged with David Holmes, George Deakin and John Le Mesurier with conspiracy to murder. Thorpe was additionally charged with 'incitement to murder'. All had refused to co-operate in police inquiries. Exasperated police officers leaked Thorpe's 'ditto' interview (he indicated that he had nothing to say at the start of the questioning and met every question with 'ditto') which appeared in *Private Eye*.

The committal hearings in Somerset in November 1978 were intended to demonstrate to the courts that there was sufficient evidence for the case to go to trial. Such hearings hear only prosecution evidence, for whom the witnesses were Bessell, Hayward, Dinshaw, Newton and Scott. They also allow defence cross-examination to challenge that evidence which in turn often reveals defence tactics in how they intend to treat the witnesses. Newton and Scott were attacked as unreliable and weak personalities; Bessell was to be a liar, a schemer and with a vested interest in securing a conviction (the *Sunday Telegraph* had signed him up for post-trial articles whose contents and news-value would obviously vary according to the verdict, and the newspaper had therefore indicated two prices depending on the outcome). Nevertheless the court believed there was a case to answer. The media attention at the hearings was enormous and the decision by Deakin's counsel to allow reporting restrictions to be lifted ensured the fullest coverage. It also produced an instantaneous book that retailed the details of the hearings.[25]

Despite this reversal, and the fact that 'he was isolated from the party leadership whom he regarded as hostile, and contemptuous of the press whom he blamed for his misfortunes',[26] Thorpe refused to leave the public stage. After his arrest he had turned up at the annual Party Conference, much to David Steel's concern, and in April the following year he had accepted his constituency party's enthusiastic renomination of himself as Liberal candidate for the forthcoming General Election.

On 3 May 1979 Thorpe lost his seat to a Conservative, with his previously-safe majority of 7000 being turned into a 8473 vote defeat. On 8 May he was seated in the Old Bailey as Scott began his long exposition of his alleged relationship with Thorpe. Nothing was spared, the vaseline, the pillow-biting and the fondling. Bessell's tale concerned Thorpe's alleged decision to 'get rid' of Scott – 'It's no worse than shooting a sick dog' – as Scott staggered from one emotional outburst to another. The South Wales connection provided the conspiracy in action and the £20,000 the money to pay for its operation. The defence strategy portrayed Bessell as a fraud with an elastic definition of the truth and a predilection for invention. Both he and Newton, also accused of trickery and deceit, were shown to have a financial interest in the prosecution of Thorpe from past or future newspaper payments. Scott's character was also denigrated, the defence deflecting the sexual relationship by announcing that, when Scott went to see Thorpe in the House of Commons, he knew 'Mr Thorpe had homosexual tendencies' (this was used later by the judge to suggest that Scott had found some incriminating letters from Thorpe to the owner of the riding stables where he worked and may have intended to blackmail him). Only Deakin went into the witness box; the others announced they would not be giving evidence on their own behalf. This meant that, not only would there be no defence witnesses, but they would not be available for cross-examination.

The defence counsel summing-up re-emphasized the unreliability and unprincipled nature of some of the prosecution witnesses – Bessell was Judas Iscariot, Scott was a liar and a scrounger, Newton a moral amputee – and argued that while there was a strong suggestion of a conspiracy to frighten there was none to kill. Indeed the Bessell-Newton evidence was denounced as 'so tainted with doubt and so comprehensively incredible' that it could not be relied upon. Mr Justice Cantley found a certain degree of favour with the defence counsel. He was highly critical of newspaper contracts with witnesses (offers to witnesses who have low moral standards), dismissive of Bessell (a humbug) and Newton (a chump), scathing about Scott (a hysterically warped personality, a crook, an accomplished liar). As the judge impartially suggested of Scott: 'He is a fraud. He is a sponger. He is a whiner. He is a parasite. But, of course, he could still be telling the truth. It is a question of belief . . . He is a spineless, neurotic character addicted to hysteria and self advertisement rushing to others for help whenever he felt it would do any good.'

As to the money which defence counsel had claimed was being solicited and used for illegal election costs, the judge told the jury that obtaining money by deception was no proof of conspiracy to murder and that there had been no evidence to suggest the latter. Indeed the judge, in his more orthodox comments, took time to explain what 'conspiracy' was and the difference between 'to murder' and 'to frighten'. In either case he thought Newton's efforts amateurish and futile – furthermore he cast doubt on whether there was any prior agreement to murder Scott or whether the gun was used as an on-the-spot decision to frighten or kill Scott (of a witness's claim that Le Mesurier was heard talking of a shooting, the judge suggested the talk was 'very dangerous, but very foolish, nothing more'.) For the jury 'reasonable doubt' was crucial. They lacked corroborated evidence about the threats, had no positive evidence to show where the £20,000 went or where Newton's £5000 came from, and no positive evidence of a conspiracy to kill. The defendants were acquitted.

Amid the sound of hastily-rewritten copy and shredded TV film the aftermath of the trial reflected a confusion over the verdict; if they were acquitted, what had actually happened? While most did not go so far as did the Vicar of Bratton Fleming, Devon, in holding a thanksgiving service for Thorpe, some believed, as the *Daily Star* did, that he had emerged as a 'statesman' of stature, courage, vision and truth. Others hoped, like his defence solicitor, that he would be allowed to rebuild his life 'in the shadows'.[27] But there were those who were less than happy with the circumstances of the acquittals. Auberon

Waugh's admirable dissection of the trial and the behaviour of the judge was followed by Bessell's autobiography in which he agonised over his decision to end an eighteen-year Establishment cover-up and 'grass' on someone he felt to be as 'ruthless as the rogue elephant, trampling all before him in the cause of self-preservation'[28] and, two years later, Thorpe's closest friend David Holmes confirmed the sceptics' view. In return for a 'substantial fee' to charity, Holmes told the *News of the World* that Thorpe was the inspiration behind the attempts to silence Scott. In a statement that closely paralleled Bessell's earlier account, Holmes alleged that, when retainers and efforts to get him a job clearly weren't going to silence Scott, Thorpe became obsessed with the threat Scott posed to his political career; giving 'Jeremy a sense of permanent persecution and a feeling that he would never be safe with that man around.'[29] Holmes claimed the plan to frighten Scott (killing was a knee-jerk reaction that he believed Thorpe could and would not sustain in reality), to buy the letters and to pay off Newton was done 'after discussion with Jeremy, and with his authorisation'. Interestingly, Holmes's argument for speaking to the newspaper concerned his perception of Thorpe's character and his ability to manipulate the actions of others to protect his own position. As with Bessell's recanting over what he saw as Thorpe's betrayal, so Holmes's road to Damascus was during the trial, when Thorpe's counsel suggested that Holmes may have been acting without Thorpe's knowledge. After Thorpe himself had thanked Holmes for keeping his name 'out of it all' and suggesting 'you must agree that there doesn't seem much point in both of us going down', Holmes realised in court that he might go down 'with someone else standing on my shoulders'.

For many the scandal was rooted in 'the stamp of one defect', his alleged homosexuality, which led to his 'slow but inevitable destruction because the public is unsure how to react to deviance in public figures that is freely available to the rest of society'. This in turn was made worse by what Cyril Smith called 'some undeniably damning machinations by members of the Liberal Party, from its very centre, to its ultimate lunatic fringe'. For others, however, the impact of the scandal lay less in the sexual aspects than in the capacity of the Establishment and its agencies to contain a long-running allegation – and an insider's ability to rely on or utilise that capacity – until the relentless pressure from Scott pushed the issue into public attention, where Thorpe was increasingly defending himself on two fronts, sex and the cover-up, which sustained media and public interest until he was shown to be, if neither a liar nor homosexual, then one willing to use the system and other people in the furtherance of his political ambition and the protection of his public reputation.

# Chapter 15

## 1976: Harold Wilson's Resignation and his Resignation Honours List

### An Opportunity To Do A Job Of Work

In 1964 Harold Wilson announced the end of hereditary titles and the exclusive use of life peerages and knighthoods, tenable only for the lifetime of the recipient and awarded solely for merit. In the next three years he underlined his reforms by deciding to discontinue honours for political service and to reduce the numbers of automatic awards for senior civil servants. His final effort, to take away the legislative rights of hereditary peers, floundered in the press of government business at the end of the Sixties and, with it, Wilson's enthusiam for future reforms.[1] Thereafter the names began to reflect Wilsonian loyalists and 'star dust' recipients from the world of sport and entertainment. While these latter tended to reflect Wilson's long-held belief that honours should go to those who were 'less stuffy, more original and more representative of the kind of people who made Britain tick', his views on what constituted merit changed substantially. In 1964 he had wanted to see: 'A Britain whose motivation is not private profit and the aggrandisement of personal fortunes . . . but national effort and national purpose – a responsible Britain based on public service, not a commercialised society where everything has its price . . . nothing so perverts our national life as Conservative attempts to identify the British standard of independence, ingenuity, and venture with the self-interest of the share-pushers, take-over bidders, land and property speculators . . .' He also wanted at that time to create life peers who had 'something of importance to say, in the national forum which the House of Lords provides; not a reward for past services but an opportunity to do a job of work'.[2]

What the 1976 Resignation Honours List did was to focus attention on Wilson's public stance and private inclinations. There was a predictable public row – 'frankly distressing' said the *Guardian*, 'such farce' said *The Times* – as over a hundred Labour MPs signed a motion disassociating themselves from the List. The row was further exacerbated by two members of the three-member Political Honours Scrutiny Committee publicly expressing their astonishment that their reservations over 'at least half the list' were ignored: 'we were, in fact, faced with a *fait accompli* which we had no power to upset', said Lady Summerskill. Many of the controversial recipients, such as Lew Grade, Bernard Delfont, Joe Kagan, Max Rayne, George Weidenfeld, John Vaisey, James Hanson, James Goldsmith, Sigmund Sternberg (the last three knighted by Wilson), kept quiet as both Wilson and Williams vigorously defended the appointments. Wilson's defence for Grade and Delfont was that they entertained 'real' people and others were rewarded because Britain's survival depended on 'a really tough almost piratical enterprise in foreign trade'.[3] Williams claimed that the critics were snobbish and anti-semitic, calling their complaints a 'sanctimonious protest by the unimaginative half of the Establishment'.

## Some Friends of Harold Wilson

Certainly there seemed to have been a Jewish-East/West-businessman nexus that Wilson valued. Williams claimed it was due to Wilson's view of the state of Israel as 'a unique and extraordinary milestone in the history of the western world'.[4] Roth sees it rather as developing from his predilection for Jewish businessmen who fitted better his image of support for 'producers of wealth', and whose loyalty and personal kindness he valued. Conversely, however, he suggests that such businessmen 'have always felt very vulnerable and therefore very sensitive to the advantages of having a highly-placed "protector" sympathetic to their interests and problems.'[5] Indeed, while at the Board of Trade, he met many of the energetic export businessmen he was later to call friends, who were often involved in the East-West trade from their own connections, which Wilson believed would ease relations between the ideologically-divergent systems. There was Harry Kissin, a commodity trader of Russian origins (a Life Peer in 1974), Emmanuel Kaye (knighted in 1974), Frank Schon (on whose payroll Wilson was for five years; a Life Peer in 1976) and the Meyers, for whom Wilson also worked as a consultant.

Other businessmen-friends were supporters of his 1970 Office Fund, a story broken in 1977 by the *Daily Mail* and thus adding to the furore surrounding the List. As well as the chairman of the Fund, Wilfred Brown (a Life Peer in 1964) it included Arnold Goodman, who became a Life Peer in 1965 and Samuel Fisher, who was a former Labour Mayor of Camden, vice-chairman of the London Diamond Bourse, and a senior member of the Board of Deputies of British Jews. He was made a Life Peer in 1974. There was Rudi Sternberg who, in 1975, became Lord Plurenden. Sternberg was a German-born button-maker who won monopoly trading rights with East Germany in 1953. His Dominion Export Company employed British MPs as consultants, such as Will Owen, the left-wing Labour MP, who had admitted in 1970 receiving £2300 from Czech intelligence, and right-wing Terence Clarke, who headed Voice and Vision, the PR firm hired to save the Central African Federation through R. Sternberg and Co Ltd. Other contributors were George Weidenfeld, Wilson's publisher (a life peer in 1976) and Joseph Kagan.

It was alleged, about some of the names honoured in 1976, and earlier, that there appeared to be 'a degree of personal croneyism, reaching back to the beginning of Wilson's political career, which has encouraged the honouring of men who often (but of course, not always) have no convincing record of public or political service.'[6] It was clear that the businessmen honoured had links with Wilson from his days at the Board of Trade (such as Lord Schon – by whom he was also employed as a consultant,

Sir Emmanuel Kaye, Lord Kissin, Lord Brayley), from his support of export efforts (Lord Kagan, Lord Plurenden) or from business support of his political activities (Sir Eric Miller, Sir Sigmund Sternberg). As the *Sunday Times* put it, the group of business entrepreneurs 'have two things in common: many were refugees from Europe, usually before or during the last war, and many have a link with Wilson which goes back to his days as President of the Board of Trade . . .' [7] One further factor was their support of Israel. Wilson had long been an admirer of Israel – his son once worked on a kibbutz – and pro-Arab critics complained that the pro-Israeli supporters who 'enjoyed easy access' to Wilson did so 'not only as members of the Parliamentary Labour Party, the Labour Friends of Israel, the Jewish Board of Deputies and Paole Zion, but as his ministers, legal advisors, publishers, employers, press officers and friends.'[8] Certainly there is the question of how many of those Wilson honoured since 1964 did 'perform' a job of work in the Lords. The *Sunday Times* looked at the voting record of Wilson's Lords between 1974–76 on fifty-three important divisions when Labour was defeated. Of ninety-eight peers appointed during his terms as party leader only thirty-six were regular supporters (voting in over 50% of the divisions); twenty-four voted fewer than ten times and nine never voted at all.

## That Fragrant List

Bernard Donoughue claimed later: 'odd people, with a lot of money but few socialist credentials, made approaches through the political side and some of these appeared in Mr Wilson's curious resignation honours list. Some were fortunately removed from the List at the last moment following advice from the Home Office and the Inland Revenue.'[9]

Explanations for each individual honour are hard to come by. The furore over the 'lavender-coloured' list, the alleged leak of names before publication of the List, only served to create a series of controversies as to why certain people had been picked. The greatest row was reserved for James Goldsmith's knighthood, for services to export and ecology; his brother was a noted campaigner on environmental issues. There were rumours that he had intended to appoint Williams to the board of Cavenham Foods Ltd, (claimed by Haines, denied by Williams). Goldsmith believed it was to show support for his rescue of the finance and property firm of Slater Walker. The press thought the reference to 'ecology' was an allusion to Goldsmith's criminal libel action against *Private Eye* – the award being for the eradication of vermin.

If Wilson's choice of the energetic entrepreneur who later moved the locus of his business activities abroad, whose self-confessed convoluted personal life titillated the tabloids and whose obsession with communist infiltration cost him an expensive magazine, was somewhat controversial, the public criticism of the other recipients underlined what the *Daily Telegraph* gleefully portrayed as 'the Wilsonian rogues' gallery' when it drew attention to the contrast between the honours bestowed on people 'who could not be said to be in the direct line of descent from Keir Hardie' and the fact that Wilson had founded 'much of his career on abusive chatter' about such people.[10] That he should be attacked through his own earlier statements was underlined by close inspection of three of those honoured but whose falls from grace came back to tarnish the Wilson image. After the Land Deals Affair Wilson's personal staff were, according to Joe Haines, 'on continuous watch for the warnings of an election scandal story – of which we had been hearing for several months – to bear their fruit.'[11] The strongest rumours concerned Wilson's stolen tax papers but, in the event, it was to be one of Wilson's ennobled business friends who was to be the potential source of embarrassment and precede the Resignation affair by two years.


## The Invisible Peer

Desmond Brayley was one of the inside circle, friend of Samuel Fisher, Bob Mellish, George Wigg and Barbara Castle (although neither of the latter two managed to mention him in their autobiographies). Wigg got him the post of Parliamentary Under-Secretary of State for the Army, a surprising and not very successful appointment between March and September 1974. In 1946 Brayley had become a sales representative for the Phoenix Glass Company in Bristol. He was successful and the firm's owner lent Brayley the money to buy his house and shares in the company before promoting him to the Board. In 1961 a finance group moved Brayley from Phoenix into its major supplier and later owner, Canning Town Glass Works, where he re-arranged its product market and pushed up the company's turnover and profits. By then he began to live well – a Rolls-Royce, a Bentley, racehorses, a large yacht moored in Malta at a cost of £1000 a week, a London penthouse flat, a country home and (an early luxury) a car telephone. In 1964 he gave 50,000 shares to the Labour Party, its only industrial investment. In 1970 he became a knight in Wilson's resignation honours list (the first one) and a life peer in 1973. He had begun to make friends in Labour circles to the extent that Labour politicians used his yacht and Wilson his London flat after the 1970 election defeat.

In April 1974 Arthur Bell, the Scottish whisky distillers, paid £1.5m for Canning Glass (it made whisky bottles), just as Brayley was about to move into his short-lived post as a Goverment Minister. Brayley's personal share was a reputed £500,000. Bell then decided to take a close look at the books and, as a result of what they found, outside accountants and a QC were called in. In September the press picked up the first signs of the impending row from Canning Glass's annual report which suggested that profits were 'understated' because of sums outstanding from its directors. Initially £16,515 was asked for from Brayley but the accountants' report, leaked to the *Daily Mail*, listed a series of 'items of discussion' totalling a further £197,105. These concerned £30,000 commission paid to Brayley over eight years; £40,000 for expenses, including a £2000 Jamaica trip for two; a payment by the company of £8500 for his own Rolls Royce which was allegedly worth £3000; £109,415 paid to Brayley by one of Canning's transport subsidiaries and payments of commission to haulage

246

companies in which Brayley's friends and relatives had shares. Brayley's solicitors claimed that he had explanations for all the sums but the report had prompted the DTI to take a closer look. This provoked the banner headlines: 'Wilson and the Brayley Affair' and 'Minister Asked Where Did £197,000 Go'.

With the second 1974 General Election pending there was no chance that Brayley could be left in office. Lord Brayley may have been 'bewildered and shattered' by the speed with which he was unceremoniously ushered out of office – the grounds were that Brayley could not remain in office when another Minister, Peter Shore at the Department of Trade, had decided to order a DTI inquiry into the company (he handed the report to the DPP in March 1975) – but there was no alternative if he was not to be made an election issue. Newspapers made the political link – that Brayley was 'a spectacular example of the involvement of Labour Ministers in the kind of financial activities they condemn in others'[12] – but his resignation effectively ended their interest. Nevertheless there were some raised eyebrows at the Ministerial Office, and the peerage, for a man whose enthusiasm for predatory capitalism rested uneasily with the Wilsonian public image. It was a contrast that was to become even more marked by the revelations that Brayley's alleged depradations were nothing compared to two others who claimed Wilson as a friend.

## The Friends of Eric Miller

In 1977, on the Jewish Day of Atonement, Sir Eric Miller shot himself in the rear patio garden of his South Kensington home with a Walther automatic pistol. Two weeks earlier, businessman John Brown had taken over as managing director of Peachey Property Corporation Ltd at the request of Lord Mais who had taken control of the company from Miller after the April annual meeting.

Born in 1926 in the East End, Miller worked in an estate agency before qualifying as a surveyor and becoming involved in the post-1945 property boom. Bomb damage, neglect, demand for private accommodation and rent restrictions put a premium on the limited stock of properties that had protected tenants who were bought out and the properties then sold for a profit. He joined Peachey Properties; by 1967 he was its chairman and managing director. Installed in Flat 67 of the Park West complex near Marble Arch which Peachey bought in 1961 for £3 million, he built the Peachey empire into London's largest residential property owner. The rewards were many and varied; two Ferraris, a Range Rover and the private London taxi, a £500,000 London home, jetset travel. Ella Fitzgerald, Oscar Peterson and the Count Basie Orchestra were flown over to entertain at his daughter's wedding at the Dorchester Hotel. In 1973 he spent a reputed £250,000 flying a jetload of friends, including Lord Mais, Douglas Bader, Harold Lever MP and DCS John Groves to Israel for his son's bar mitzvah. When he charged the company £56,000 for a three-week yacht charter the auditors' clerk nearly fell through the floor; the thought the company had bought one at that price.

Unfortunately Miller 'had an insatiable curiosity to mix with the successful in all walks of life' and, bankrolled by the company's funds, he set out to do just that. He contributed to a number of Jewish and RAF charities. He bailed out Fulham Football Club as well as making a loan to its former chairman, Tommy Trinder. Through Marcia Williams he met and became a friend of Harold Wilson; readiness to help the Labour cause at the drop of a hat became a Transport House legend.[13] He lent Wilson the company helicopter for the 1974 General Election and escorted Marcia to Annabel's, a top London nightclub. Through the Labour Party Secretary Ron Hayward he became Honorary Treasurer of the Socialist International and hosted receptions for foreign dignitaries at the company-owned Churchill Hotel; the organisation occupied Peachey property rent-free.

His political links, however, went wider. He employed Reginald and Martin Maudling, the former taking his fee in the form of Peachey buying the family home, repairing and maintaining it, and renting it back at a low rent of £2-per-week – an unusual but commensurate recompense, said the later DTI Report, that excused Maudling from paying too much tax. The company's legal advisers were Lewis Silkin and Partners, the family firm of Labour Minister John Silkin. Maurice Orbach, when Labour MP for Stockport South, challenged a rent increase when Peachey took over the blocks of flats in which he lived in Eton College Rd, Hampstead, in 1958. As a result Miller kept the rent low, so low that by 1977 Orbach was paying £500 a year on a flat whose services cost £489 a year – 'less than a fair rent', as the MP put it. As the director of the Trades Advisory Council of which Miller became Honorary Chairman in 1970, Orbach also had use of a Peachey car. Albert Murray, the former Labour MP for Gravesend, who joined the Wilson circle as political office manager in 1973, received fees as a political consultant and a £10,000 bridging loan. 'A perfectly clear arrangement, straightforward and aboveboard', said Murray; 'it is not customary practice for major property companies to provide loans for private individuals', suggested the *Sunday Times*.[14]

But then not much of what Miller did was customary practice. Boardroom discontent surfaced in 1976 over Miller's financial withdrawals from the company. By the next year the company ousted Miller and slapped in claims for repayments of £282,000, including the £10,000 he spent on the racehorse Princely Chief, the £42,000 spent on an emerald and diamond necklace and the £130,000 Miller kept in a Keyser Ullman account for what he claimed was a 'European venture which was not forthcoming' (there was the small matter of a forged letter Miller used to back up the claim and forestall its repayment).

If there was 'a possible way into something prestigious, he would have his cheque book out in his sleep', said a friend. Before the 1977 annual shareholders meeting in April Miller paid back £177,671 together with £50,000 for an 'unspecified' asset and £80,000 allegedly used to buy his daughter a flat. At the meeting questions were raised about free Park West flats for footballers and a lost £200,000 deposit on a custom-built Mystere jet. There was also some concern expressed about why his fellow Board members and auditors (whose qualification of the accounts, particularly over the missing £282,000, led to the crisis) were apparently unaware of its financial malpractices. In 1977 Edmund Dell, Labour's Trade Minister, ordered a DTI inquiry which gave some of the answers.

Essentially Miller used the funds of Peachey Property to enhance his social standing. He moved money around to balance the books; the £130,000 in KU was to reduce the overdraft on the KU loan he had previously used to pay back Peachey for earlier loans. The money from the resale of the Asprey necklace went the same way. Some £70,000 disappeared into a Gibraltar-based bank owned by financier Judah Binstock. One of Miller's contacts was DCS John Groves of C11, the Metropolitan Police's Criminal Intelligence Branch. In October 1979 he was acquitted of corruptly accepting Miller's hospitality but found guilty of passing on secret information about Binstock. Binstock began his varied business career dealing in shares in a company – the Victoria Sporting Club – that employed a Labour MP as a consultant and had Mafia connections. C11 had details of international exchange control deals, Binstock's speciality, and Miller wanted information on Binstock with whom he was planning property deals in Europe (Binstock was then residing in Spain, away from the British police who were anxious to interview him about currency offences). The Report also revealed that Miller was simply taking cash out of the company – £188,700 allocated for introductory commissions went directly to himself – or using its funds for personal entertainment. This included a £4300 bill for Labour Party banquets, the £3304 worth of champagne for Harold's resignation party, and the £1280 worth of filing cabinets for Downing Street. Wilson was described in the DTI report as a 'personal though not close' friend. The Labour Party and the Socialist International received nearly £13,000 of Churchill Hotel entertainment. Miller paid eight visits to No. 10 between 1974–76 as well as paying for the filing cabinets and champagne party in 1976. Orbach received a £1465 birthday party at the Churchill in 1976.

But, as Adam Raphael points out: 'what is important about the Miller affair is not the misdeeds of the one individual but the climate of political and commercial morality in which he operated.' [15] Miller surrounded himself with consultants and a wide circle of friends, widened further by his donations, paid for by the company. Generous, ambitious and insecure, he used the resources of the company – the flats, the Churchill Hotel, the account at Asprey's, the slush funds – indiscriminately. In 1974–75 the company was paying £15,000 in car hire, £58,000 in helicopter costs, £32,000 on travel, £19,000 on entertainment, £136,000 on Churchill Hotel functions, £10,000 on gifts, £19,000 on Asprey presents and £3600 in ties to sustain Miller's extravagance and favours. In ten years his travel and entertainment bill came to £305,129. He used, said the Report[16], 'the Company as his private bank' and was able to avoid criticism or control because the Peachey Board was, by and large, weak, 'unduly compliant, uncritical and gullible'. He was guilty of 'numerous misappropriations of Company funds. To cover his misdeeds he told lies freely, fabricated false documents, and caused others to fabricate and utter false documents.' He used Company money recklessly so much so that his net income was quite insufficient to cover even the repayments to cover acknowledged expenses: 'effectively, therefore, he had a substantial negative disposable income,' said the Report.

## The Pint-Sized Peer

In March 1978 the Customs and Excise arrived on the premises of Kagan Textiles, looking for evidence of a major tax swindle by the Yorkshire-based manufacturer of Gannex raincoats, Peer of the Realm, Joe Kagan. Son of a Jewish Lithuanian mill-owner who saw Britain as having a more secure future than any country under either Russian or German rule, Kagan experienced at first hand the oppression of both regimes. Surviving the ideological intransigence of the former through his cheek, and racist brutality of the latter by being fit enough to be given a work certificate, he and his wife fled to Bucharest in 1945. There, a judicious and rewarding mix of working the black market and making himself indispensable to British officials he was able to secure a visa that took him to Britain in 1946. Kagan began working for his father in Leeds but set up on his own first as a garage-owner and then in 1951 as a blanket manufacturer – Elland Blankets Weavers. In 1952 he invented a means to bond together nylon and wool which resulted in the warm and waterproof Gannex raincoat. He was assiduous in cultivating publicity for the raincoat – sold at first to police forces – by putting them on the backs of the rich and famous; he employed a public relations consultant to ensure that his Gannex-clothed stars frequently appeared in the press. His most successful coup was to have Prince Philip clothe himself and his family in the raincoat, a useful piece of publicity consolidated by loans of cars and a directorship to certain Buckingham Palace officials.

He became a friend of Harold Wilson, another Gannex enthusiast whether raining or not, before Wilson's election to 10 Downing Street in 1964. Although he did not join the party until 1968 he was already part of the Wilson entourage, where one of his major functions was to act as nursemaid to Marcia Williams's problems. He was involved in trying to persuade John Scholefield Allan to stick to his 'misguided' offer of marriage to Williams in 1965. He rented a car for her and arranged for staff to deal with minor domestic problems. In 1967 his firm paid the deposit and he personally guaranteed the mortgage for an eighty-year lease on 20 Albany Court for her. Three years later he bought the flat from her for £15,000 – £3500 more than the purchase price.[17] In 1976 he was made a Life Peer.

Kagan Textiles was financially healthy but it was tightly controlled by Kagan, a man described by a colleague as 'overwhelmingly selfish' and who ensured that, according to another Wilsonian peer who knew him, the company never paid a dividend. Kagan on the other hand had a Lakeland home, a London flat, an eighteenth-century manor house near Halifax and a large detached house near Huddersfield. In 1971 the chairman of the bankrupt cotton-weaving firm, Charles Crabtree, was advised to seek Kagan's help by a Labour MP anxious to save the jobs of one of his constituency's largest employers. With

£40,000 of his own money and a further government grant of £47,000, Kagan bought up the company, which made denim, just at the time the Sixties material was coming back into fashion. Rather than pay the tax due on the increasing sales Kagan devised a scheme to export the bulk of Crabtree Denim's output (as the company was now called) as substandard material with a sale value at 10p a metre or less. In Europe it was sold for up to £1.25 a metre but the paperwork reflected an income based on the 10p value; the surplus was skimmed through an untraceable front set up by Kagan – Denim Continental SA – and deposited in a personal Swiss bank account. By the time of his arrest some £546,645 had been deposited. In 1975 he embarked on his second fraud, involving the highly-prized indigo dye for denim produced by ICI, Britain's sole manufacturer. Despite arrangements that the purchase of the dye was for company use and not for resale, the labels on the drums were doctored and the drums put on the market. Demand by brokers was so great that they willingly fell in line with Kagan's insistence that payments be made through accounts in Antwerp, from where Kagan transferred the money – some £189,730 – to Zurich. For both operations false records were prepared under Kagan's guidance but Swiss customs' curiosity about the role of Denim Continental, and thus its liability for Swiss tax, began the trail of inquiry that finally led thirty detectives and customs officials to make a series of raids on Kagan's homes and factories: 'I do not know of anything we should fear', said the managing director of Kagan Textiles, adding that the activities of Crabtree Denim were part of 'normal trade arrangements.'

At the end of 1978 warrants for the arrest of Kagan, his wife, and some of his business colleagues were issued; they alleged conspiracy to defraud the public revenue and to falsify records. Kagan was safely ensconced in Israel with his twenty-year-old secretary but pressure from the authorities forced him to flee to the Costa del Sol. In April 1980 he arrived in Paris, supposedly to meet the authorities under a flag of truce but in reality to ensure he could be prosecuted only for 'the comparatively small part of the offences', as the trial judge said later. He was arrested on charges of theft and false accounting relating to the dye swindle. Despite arguing that he was the victim of speaking out on the iniquities of the tax system and of his friendship with Wilson, he was extradited to England. In October the trial began, with prosecution counsel retelling the story of the denim fraud, but Kagan's appearance in the dock to plead guilty to the theft and accounting offences meant that he could, under the terms of the extradition treaty with France, only be proceeded against in relation to those offences. Accordingly the prosecution dropped the other charges against his co-conspirators – 'the mountains of justice have been in labour and it seems to me that they have produced a mere mouse', said Mr Justice Jupp later. His defence argued he was 'not just of good character but a man upon whom richly-deserved honours had been showered' and that the money in Switzerland was used to help Jewish refugees reach Israel. Unfortunately the judge was not convinced, accusing Kagan of disregarding all legal and moral restraints and weaving a tangled web of deceit. He then sentenced Kagan to ten months' imprisonment and £135,000 in fines and costs (later reduced to £86,000); the total liability to him and his firms ran to £1.1 million.

Stripped of his knighthood – but not his peerage – while in prison, Kagan's lifestyle came under close media scrutiny. The *News of the World* devoted a whole page to 'The Amazing Sexploits Of The Runaway Tycoon'[18] which alleged how wealth, power and a silver tongue 'enabled him to get and dominate his numerous girlfriends and mistresses'; 'my little peer had a king-sized appetite as a lover', gushed one. 'The point of these stories', said the *Sunday Times* later 'is not that Kagan had outrageous sexual manners; it is that Harold Wilson allowed such a man to become too close to him, and eventually recommended him for a peerage.'[19] Unfortunately, as with his 'Kitchen Cabinet', Wilson liked to be surrounded by the loyal and the politically unthreatening. Trading his loyalty for theirs, his apparent public endorsement of their links with him, without any checks as to their own essential qualities, left him wide open to allegations of incompetence or naivety. There were those, however, who saw something worse in some of the friendships and others who looked there for the reasons of his sudden departure from office in 1976.

## The Wilson Resignation: Did He Go Or Was He Pushed?

Kagan was thus to become involved in the final question about the 1976 Honours List: why did Harold Wilson resign? When the *Pencourt File* (see chapter xx) was bought by the *Observer* for serialisation, the newspaper ran a front-page story in July 1977 – 'Wilson: Why I lost my faith in MI5' – beginning 'what Sir Harold saw as a constant whispering campaign against himself, his personal entourage and Labour Ministers led the former Prime Minister to doubt the competence and loyalty of MI5.'[20]

With his successor Jim Callaghan avoiding calls for an official inquiry into the Honours system and with the Thorpe affair turning from a BOSS-manipulated international conspiracy to more prosaic allegations of a home-grown murder plot, Wilson then began backtracking. The 'disaffected faction' was small, probably all retired, and the Security Services, as Callaghan claimed, were 'at present properly conducted.' Therefore, suggested Wilson, 'this unfortunate matter can now be laid to rest.' Only Pincher referred to it again, in 1978, when he wrote that 'the undermining activities which Wilson complained of were not only genuine but far more menacing than he revealed. Certain officers inside MI5, assisted by others who had retired from the service, were actually trying to bring the Labour Government down . . .'[21] Pincher was by then making contact with the major source who was to resurrect the plot some nine years later, Peter Wright, a senior MI5 figure whose book *Spycatcher* was to cause the Thatcher Government all kinds of embarrassment as it tried to stop publication on the grounds of confidentiality. Almost as an aside in the book, Wright mentioned MI5's interest in Harold Wilson and it was these allegations that attracted media attention. What was uncovered was MI5's steady putting together of a dossier on Wilson that detailed those alleged grounds on which MI5 thought his public position may have been jeopardised or compromised by the Russians.

First there was his involvement with the Soviet bloc, beginning with East-West trade in the 1950s, and their possible implications. Conservative MP Winston Churchill alleged their relevance to the question of Wilson as a potential security risk: 'The question mark that does arise in many people's minds . . . is the fact that he has paid no fewer than nineteen visits to the Soviet Union. And that does provide the other side with certain opportunities.'[22]

The second grounds for suspicion were the circumstances surrounding Wilson's accession to the leadership of the Labour Party following the sudden death of Hugh Gaitskell in 1962. The cause of death was an extremely rare virus for which there was no known cure, nor any information on what may have caused it. Disturbed by the unusualness of the illness Gaitskell's doctor called MI5, who sent Peter Wright off to Porton Down, the Government's chemical warfare establishment. What worried MI5 was that the Russians, who had been publishing one or two papers on the virus, had developed a means of inducing it in people; Gaitskell had recently been to the Russian consulate to arrange a visa to visit the country. What encouraged the thought of murder had been the arrival of Anatoli Golitsyn, a senior KGB official, on the doorstep of the CIA station chief in Helsinki in 1971. Golitsyn delivered the names of agents in France, the USA and Britain; he provided the final clues about Philby, opened up the leads on Blunt and dropped the first hint of Vassall. Golitsyn also told MI5 that he had contacts with the KGB's Department 13 which had been planning the assassination of a high-level political figure in Europe 'in order to get their man into the top place.' He did not know the country but pointed out that Department 13's head was General Rodin 'who had been in Britain for many years and had just returned on promotion to take up the job, so he would have had good knowledge of the political scene in England.'[23] Wilson was alleged to be such a man, a belief confirmed in MI5's eyes when James Angleton, then head of the CIA Counter-intelligence Division, flew to London in 1964 to tell Furnival Jones, then MI5's director of counter-espionage, that an 'unnamed' source alleged that Wilson was a Soviet agent. Thus Golitsyn confirmed his own allegations.

## The Plot Begins

MI5 suspicions about Wilson began to mount. On becoming Prime Minister in 1964 Wilson, who told MI5 that 'he had long believed (it) was staffed by people who could not tell the difference between a democratic socialist and a communist'[24], tried to appoint a police officer to head MI5 on Hollis's retirement. This was vigorously resisted internally and Hollis's deputy, Furnival Jones, took over. Wilson also demanded MI5 got his personal permission before it could investigate MPs or peers against whom, in any case, he had made it plain that he would not accept the word of a defector. 'These rulings', said Pincher, 'are tantamount to the granting of immunity to all elected politicians . . .'[25] What annoyed MI5 was that defectors *were* providing names of Labour politicians and trade union leaders who had allegedly been approached by Czech agents. Then, at the end of the 1960s, another defector, Oleg Lyalin, alleged that Richardas Vaygauskas was a KGB officer working in London under cover in the Soviet Trade Delegation. One of his contacts, said Lyalin, was a Joseph Kagan, friend and confidante of Harold Wilson. Here, for the MI5 faction, was proof of the 'enemy within'. Both Wilson and Kagan were interviewed – the former at his own request – and both denied the possibility of any espionage. Wright went to the new Director-General (Sir Michael Hanley, who had taken over from Jones) and showed him the Wilson file. 'There's lots of smoke, but not a lot of fire', said Hanley but the imminent election and persistent calls from Angleton about Wilson persuaded MI5 to keep the file open.

Wilson's victory as leader of a minority Labour Government in February 1974 saw, as Wright put it, MI5 sitting on information 'which, if leaked, would undoubtedly have caused a political scandal of incalculable consequences. The news that the Prime Minister himself was being investigated would at the least have led to his resignation.'[26] Some of his colleagues shared that opinion, badgering Wright for information to be leaked on Wilson and other leading party figures to sympathetic journalists and to politicians, and to have 'the matter raised in Parliament for maximum effect.' Wright refused to release the information but said later that, 'although the full Wilson story never emerged, it was obvious to me that the boys had been actively pushing their plan as much as they could.'[27] It would appear, however, that the extent of their great destabilisation exercise was planting whispers about a 10 Downing Street communist cell in the ears of known sympathisers and a forged Swiss bank account purportedly belonging to Ted Short in the hands of selected journalists. The other major controversies – particularly Poulson and the Land Deals stories – needed no help from MI5. There were further allegations – such as the thirty 'active communist' Labour MPs, Marcia Williams's refusal to be vetted and the question of the fatherhood of her children (this was whispered among some Tory MPs as the 'Babygate' scandal) – which never reached the electorate. The public effect was negligible: Wilson won and increased his Party's majority in the House.

Wilson learnt of the rumour from Oxford historian Martin Gilbert, who spent a lunch-party in the company of Chapman Pincher. Pincher had talked about most of the allegations against Wilson and claimed that the Tories were keen to use them. Wilson, outraged, called in Maurice Oldfield, the head of MI6, and told him of the allegations. Oldfield passed the conversation on to Wright, who after prompting by Oldfield, went to his MI5 boss, Hanley, and told him the story: 'now he was learning that half his staff were up to their necks in a plot to get rid of the Prime Minister.' Hanley was then called in by Wilson and admitted the existence of the rumours. Wilson was so jumpy as to who he could trust that, in 1976, he sent his publisher Lord Weidenfeld to have Hubert Humphrey check with George Bush, then head of the CIA, to see if it was the CIA that had him under surveillance. Bush actually flew to London to reassure Wilson who had, by then, resigned. There had also been an internal review inside MI5: Hanley wrote to Wright that 'the firm is doing quite well: it has passed its recent examinations.' Wilson was still not satisfied and wanted a Royal Commission, something for which he found no takers in the media because of his lack of evidence. His last throw was to invite Penrose and Courtiour to 'investigate the forces that are threatening democratic countries like Britain.' Wilson may have had enough of the bruising he had taken throughout his political life and wanted to go early enough to enjoy his retirement. On the other hand, he may have decided that he had had enough of the behind-the-scenes whispers about himself and his friends that were clearly not going to stop if he remained in office. Certainly Wilson's 'firm decision' to go appears to have been taken around the time he confronted the Head of MI5 in August 1975 over the allegations that he was being investigated by officers from MI5 *and* MI6 but, as David Leigh suggests, 'whether Wilson's feelings of disgust and alarm about MI5 altered his timing or increased his determination to go is still an open question'.[28]

# Chapter 16

## 'Sex Please, We're British'. The Parkinson Scandal

### High Risks: High Stakes

When he learnt that his mistress was pregnant and that the media were taking an interest, Cecil Parkinson, Minister of Trade, Tory Party Chairman and architect of the 1983 General Election victory, had two sets of choices, the one concerning his future in public life and the other concerning his future private life. The permutation that would cause the highest public profile would be to rely on his Prime Minister's advice to stay in office and to stay with his wife while riding out any criticism after making a full admittance of, and financial provision for, his behaviour. Thatcher did not want him to resign because she believed that his conduct was a private matter which was far outweighed by his abilities as a Goverment Minister. Of course she was thoughtful enough to lift the burden of Party Chairman from his shoulders (and drape it over the shoulders of the unimpeachable John Selwyn Gummer) which ensured that the Tory rank-and-file would not be too upset should the affair become public knowledge. It was, however, 'a high-risk course which was vulnerable to the latest development, and the unexpected.'[1]

In so doing Thatcher was ensured of the support of the Tory press, never slow in picking up the signals of the leader's loyalty to rally behind her. On the other hand both they and the rest of the media 'also had a natural journalist's desire to cover every twist and turn of a story their readers were devouring, thereby keeping the scandal alive and making Mr Parkinson's position increasingly untenable.'[2] During the first week of October 1984 *Private*

*Eye* ran a speculative gossip column story: 'why was Cecil Parkinson asked to step down as Tory Party chairman? I can assure readers that it had nothing to do with his marital difficulties which have recently caused raised eyebrows in Tory circles. Now comes the news that Parkinson's fun-loving secretary Ms Sara Keays is expecting a baby in three months' time.' The item then went on to name the wrong MP as the other party in the 'Ugandan' activity, statements that were later to cost the magazine damages and apologies to those concerned. That drew wider media attention, a formal joint statement from Parkinson's and Keays' solicitors on the parentage of the child and the Prime Minister's announcement that she wished him to stay in office. Between the original *Private Eye* story and the Party conference a week later the twin pursuit of the story – Thatcher's endorsement of her loyalty to Parkinson and the media's enthusiasm of a sex-and-politics thriller – ran heavily in Parkinson's favour. The Party's sympathy machine cranked out signals of 'expected warm tributes' at the conference, with many unattributable media comments on the temptations of the Palace of Westminster where pressure of work, long hours, the aphrodisiac of power and the warm blood of the Minister of Trade were mulled over for causing 'a sad and silly blunder.' Some writers were clearly hostile to Sara Keays, with portrayals ranging from a Sloane Ranger with sex-appeal, to a middle-aged single woman avoiding being left on the shelf, whose pregnancy, in the age of the Pill and the abortion, might be considered careless or even a ploy to turn an affair into something more permanent.

## Reputation's High-Ground

By the time Parkinson sat down after his anodyne Conference speech to the massed ranks of the media and the Party faithful, the response was sufficient to suggest that the Party could forgive even if it could not condone his behaviour. Parkinson certainly believed he had survived but then he clearly underestimated the consequences of the tactics adopted by his supporters in the party and the media. To defend his political reputation the affair had to be marginalised as a temporary aberration in which he succumbed to the temptations of a high-pressure job in a particular environment from which his 'fall from grace' was sufficiently punished by a full admission, financial restitution and an acceptance that higher office was no longer achievable. In that he was buttressed by the loyalty of those who felt he had taken the right course of action, his wife and his leader, and by a statement agreed with Keays' solicitors giving the bare outline of the affair (issued after the *Private Eye* story) on which both sides stated that they would not answer questions.

Unfortunately for Cecil Parkinson, this exercise in damage-limitation misunderstood the nature of the case he was proposing. In a sense Parkinson was in the middle of a contested rather than an uncontested divorce. Rather than either side accepting full responsibility for ending the affair, or both sides agreeing to its mutual ending, one side had gone for partial responsibility but was claiming, instead of a disproportionate share of savings or posses-sions, that of reputation and career. As is often the way with contested divorces, the other side was having none of it. Sara Keays had her reputation and her career to think about and she was determined that, in protecting them, she would make sure that the circumstances of her pregnancy should be made known in their true perspec-tive. Whether or not the pregnancy was the catalyst that forced a decision out of Parkinson to end their relation-ship, the end of that relationship would have been equally traumatic without the involvement of the baby. Despite the attention given to it, the question of the baby's paternity was never in doubt. What was in doubt was the quality of the relationship and the question of Keays' future. What Parkinson and his supporters attempted to do was to marginalise both. Given both Keays' emotional investment in the relationship and her determination to assert her own, undeniable aspirations and strength of character, this was both unwise and, ultimately, disastrous.

Sara Keays was born in 1947 into a comfortably-off, closely-knit family who lived in a country vicarage near Bath. Moving to London in 1967 with her sister, she took various secretarial jobs before beginning work in the House of Commons as, in journalist Simon Hoggart's words, 'one of the scores of nice, well-bred middle class girls who work for Tory MPs.' Little over a year later she became secretary to Cecil Parkinson, who had been elected in 1970 as Tory MP for Enfield West. Son of a Lancashire railwayman, Parkinson had progressed from grammar school to Cambridge and then to a job as a management trainee for the manufacturers, Metal Box. There he met Anne Jarvis, the privately-educated daughter of a self-made building contractor in 1955: 'so when the vivacious sporty home-counties girl met the ambitious, suave Cambridge graduate, the attraction was almost instantaneous. They were married the following year.'³ Parkinson's father-in-law encouraged him to take up accountancy and set him on a business career by offering him a Stockport building firm which Parkinson bought in association with the grandson of Woolworth's chairman. They set up their own company, Hart Securities Ltd, which put Parkinson on his way to a modest fortune and homes in a former rectory in Hertfordshire, in Pimlico and in the Bahamas. He became a Conservative through personal conviction, joining the Party in 1956 and, by 1966, chairing the Hemel Hempstead association with the young Norman Tebbit as his deputy.

The affair with Keays began shortly after their meeting – 'a long-standing, genuine love affair', says Keays. It was marked by regular conflicts over what each wanted from the relationship. Clearly Keays wanted her independence and her career and did not want to continue indefinitely as Parkinson's mistress. On the one hand she 'loved him wholeheartedly and wanted nothing more than to spend the rest of my life with him.'⁴ They did not hide the affair: 'Parkinson made hardly any attempt to hide the relationship and in some circles the two were known as a couple as early as 1976.'⁵ There were presents and holidays (which Parkinson did not conceal; Keays later published a happy photograph of the two in the Bahamas in 1980). On the other hand there were also doubts about Parkinson's intentions. Despite his promises of marriage and undying affection he appeared content with the existing relationship: 'he was doing well in politics, his work was very demanding and our affair made up for the shortcomings of his domestic arrangements.'[6] Keays saw a stark choice of marriage and children or an interesting career. In 1979 Parkinson was appointed to Ministerial office as Minister of Trade. Keays decided to end the affair at that point. She took herself off to Brussels as secretary to Roy Jenkins, then President of the European Commission, leaving behind the 'wretchedly unhappy' Parkinson. Not for long, however, because the Government Minister popped up in Brussels to resume the affair, only to announce at the end of 1980 that marriage was out of the question because of family problems (one of his daughters was a drug addict). Up he popped again in 1981 on Keays' return to London, this time able to announce that:

it was because he loved me that he had to see me. He was very tender and reassuring, begging me to believe that he truly loved me and wanted us to be together more than anything in the world. He said his personal life had been fraught with difficulties, which was why he had not been able to keep his promise before, but that in due course these would be resolved and he would give up politics after the next election when he would be able to marry me, if I still wanted him and would agree to wait.[7]

Keays agreed to wait, but three events then occured to dramatically threaten that promise. In living her undoubted enthusiasm for politics, (as she herself accepts), vicariously through talking to him about his work, she wanted to become 'involved in politics in my own right, especially if it transpired that we had left it too late to have children', by becoming accepted on the list of approved Tory candidates. Parkinson in fact tried to thwart that, much to her fury. But then Parkinson was worried that her 'name would be linked with his', particularly in view of the success of his own career. Party chairman and a Cabinet seat in 1981, a member of the Falklands Inner Cabinet in 1982, he was a Thatcher favourite and protegé with potential for future advancement. Unfortunately for Parkinson just as he was winding-up the successful campaign for the June 1983 General Election and casting hopeful glances in the direction of the post of Minister of State at the Foreign Office as the penultimate step towards 10 Downing Street, Sara Keays found she was pregnant.

Parkinson was worried and confided in Tebbit, now Minister for Employment, who advised him to 'say nothing to anyone and do nothing except play for time'. When they met again Tebbit promised to stand by Parkinson whom he thought was now 'clearly worried', torn between loyalty to his wife and a sense of responsibility for the baby. Unfortunately things were less comradely with Sara Keays, who claimed Parkinson proposed an abortion and alleged that he accused her of 'using the threat of a scandal to try to force him to marry me . . . he seemed not to give a thought to the consequences for my reputation and career.' Meanwhile Sara Keays' father had written to Mrs Thatcher about Parkinson's persistent pursuit of his daughter. Thatcher was somewhat dismissive of his concern but now Parkinson told Thatcher; she was not willing to lose him from the Cabinet but accepted that it would be unwise to appoint him Foreign Secretary. Instead she gave him Trade and Industry, the post Tebbit had been hoping for; Tebbit himself said he was 'pretty fed up'. Parkinson told Mr Keays that he was speaking to his 'future son-in-law', paid Sara £5000 and advised her to exercise discretion and secrecy until he told his wife. On the day of the General Election Keays then claimed he gave 'my solemn word of honour' he would marry her (there is some doubt whether he passed this piece of information on to his Prime Minister).

In August 1983 the *Daily Mirror* had picked up rumours of the pregnancy (its reporters were once involved in a dangerous car-chase with Keays). At the start of September Parkinson returned from holiday to announce he was staying with his wife. Tebbit believed that Keays was annoyed and that the story was soon likely to break in the media. Parkinson clearly thought so and wanted to resign. Tebbit says he implored him not to do so, just because his marriage had outlasted his mistress: if 'they get you, they'll want to go on and drag someone else down . . . if they drag one of us off, the bloodlust will be worse and they'll be after the rest'. Nevertheless Tebbit told the Prime Minister of events and suggested that Parkinson should step down as Party Chairman to 'avoid difficulties at the Party conference'.[8] Keays' father wrote again to the Prime Minister warning her of the imminent public scandal while solicitors from both sides wrangled over a suitably-worded announcement in anticipation. Released immediately on the publication of the *Private Eye* story, the formal announcement stated that Parkinson acknowledged the relationship, had proposed marriage but had changed his mind. He and his wife would be staying together but he would be making financial provision for his unborn child. The statement precipitated the onslaught of the media circus. Fortified by a Downing Street announcement that the affair was a private matter and that 'the question of resignation does not and will not arise' Parkinson headed for the Party conference in Blackpool a week later still clutching the Trade appointment and a foothold in public life. Not unnaturally, the media enthusiastically dissected his chances of survival which, following a dignified appearance on *Panorama* and a workmanlike speech at the conference, appeared a possibility. The unexpected was Keays' reaction to the increasingly-pointed media comments on her motives, the references during the *Panorama* interview to 'the other person' and the benign focus on the consequences of the scandal on Parkinson. Keays chose the evening of the day he addressed the Conference to publish through *The Times* her own unexpurgated version of events that talked of a long relationship and showed Parkinson as a vacillating creature of conflicting emotions who made promises he did not appear to keep. His resignation was inevitable and immediate. Tebbit was appointed to Trade and Industry. His colleagues were privately relieved; the background presence of a former mistress and a child would always dog his, and the Party's, public image (indeed, during early 1988 the child's illness brought a spate of press reports both on the illness and on whether or not Parkinson was concerned). Publicly there was fury at Keays' reaction and the media coverage, with colleagues accusing 'pygmies' of bringing down a man who appeared to be hounded from office for refusing to break up his marriage. That weekend two newspapers, the *News of the World* and the *Sunday Times*, launched the same attack on Keays (the former borrowed the latter's story for its front page while, remarkably, its inside story took the opposite line and criticised Parkinson for adultery, loss of nerve and deceit). The *Sunday Times* report, based on information from Parkinson's 'friends', denied Keays' version of a longstanding, loving relationship in which the child was conceived and claimed the last offer of marriage was made out of a sense of duty rather than rekindled love.

## Getting A Word In Edgeways

The aftermath of the scandal was punctuated with acrimony and agonising over why Parkinson's behaviour should require his resignation. Apart from some nonsense about a ten-year cycle of Tory scandals (even Parkinson could not claim fate as a mitigating circumstance), many politicians and commentators sermonised about the prevalence of double standards that required public figures to behave differently from the rest of the population. Yet the Tory Party had made a valiant effort to capture the electoral high ground of decency, morality and the value of the family. It is hardly surprising therefore that 'if you use your private life, as the public thinks it is, to sell yourself to the voters, you can hardly complain if they show an indecent interest in its collapse.'⁹ Parkinson in fact had ridden those double standards because Thatcher is prepared to defend the presence of those whose abilities outweigh their failings. Even she, however, cannot protect those whose failings, however tenuously, will be used to contrast with party policy and preoccupations. Indeed, the periodic media trailers for a Parkinson revival has floundered on that contrast; the 1985 party conference was enlivened by surreptitious reading of Keays' autobiography in the *Daily Mirror*. The 1986 conference was presaged by a Keays interview in *Good Housekeeping* which talked of 'the hypocrisy, the lying and the arrogance of the other people who interfered – Conservative politicians who were prepared to destroy me to protect themselves.' And that raises a more important issue about the behaviour of public life and the question of double standards. In all the talk about Parkinson's 'fall from grace' little was made, wrote Katherine Whitehorn, of how Keays should have behaved apart from remaining silent and not 'tastelessly embarrass the men they have embraced.'¹⁰ Even less was made – and Parkinson's rehabilitation would, whatever the Tory voices say, raise the question – of the efforts to stave off the scandal. Professor Graeme Moodie says: '. . . the most remarkable and disgraceful events and conduct . . . are these: the use of the "Lobby" system and the Conservative party grapevine to mount a campaign of vilification (based at best on misunderstanding and at worst on conscious fabrication), of her, and to mobilise sympathy for the suffering *he* (alone) had undergone . . . and the intrusiveness and irresponsibility of the popular press (with some allies in the quality press) as it sustained its misrepresentations and animosity over the months.'¹¹

Henry Porter has written, eighteen months after the scandal, about the circumstances surrounding the *Sunday Times'* attack on her following his resignation. Editor Andrew Neil asked for a telephone interview which he got, but only on 'lobby' (non-attributable) terms. 'The Case For Parkinson – Ex-Minister's Friends Speak Out' was, says Porter, 'almost without exception', supplied by Parkinson himself. One journalist told him: 'The Lobby system is invidious enough anyway but when someone like Parkinson uses it to settle some score with a girlfriend whom he got pregnant that is a real abuse. The whole final edition story was based on Parkinson's phonecall and that was not good enough. I would say that it was an extremely injudicious story. We could have done one on how Parkinson was trying to manipulate the press. The *Sunday Times* was not the only paper phoned on that Saturday.'[12]

While Hugo Young in the *Guardian* might claim that 'politics is so full of real charlatans that is seems wrong to punish with eternal damnation a man who, most of the time, is not one'[13], such behaviour can only raise questions about motives and methods. Nevertheless the Prime Minister kept faith and kept in close contact with one of her favourite colleagues and friends. Parkinson was again at her elbow after the success of the 1987 General Election. Despite further criticism from Keays during TV's *Wogan* show – during which she alleged that 'the scandal where I was concerned arose out of the deception of my family and the fact that the Prime Minister, if she didn't actually connive at it, condoned it' – Thatcher had decided that she wanted him back in the Cabinet. In 1987 he was appointed Minister for Energy. He had paid his party dues, undertaking a large number of speaking engagements and travelling across the country during the campaign – 'slicing turkeys in plastic pubs, posing by a large cheese in a market stall and persuading pigeons to eat out of his hand, in the hope of getting a Conservative candidate's picture in the local paper.'[14] He had always been welcome at 10 Downing Street and at Chequers, a consequence as one insider put it, of her weakness for 'amiable, smooth-talking and handsome men who can both flatter her and stand up to her' and of her preference for his advice, without which 'she's like a boat bucketing around without an anchor. He's always been good at calming her down, making her see the political side of things behind her ideological fervour.'[15]

While, as Professor Moodie suggests, the real political story lay in the damage-limitation tactics of Conservative politicians and the Conservative establishment, not to mention the press, 'when presented with the facts of a leading politician's infidelity with his former secretary and his fathering of their, then unborn, daughter' against which the 'supposed scandal of the relationship between Mr Cecil Parkinson and Miss Sara Keays is of little public significance'[16] it is the latter scandal that is unforgettable to the public.

The impact of the Parkinson image, the scandal and the startling contrast between the two (highlighted by the circumstances of the revelations and the dramatic unfolding of subsequent events) has fixed this particular scandal firmly in the public consciousness. As with the Profumo affair, the participants themselves are news and their names inextricably linked as Parkinson continues a public career: 'he seems', said the *Independent* 'to exist only as a reflection of other people's ambitions and emotions'.[17] He radiates seriousness in public but in private is known to be less than sanguine at the periodic statements from Sara Keays that jolt the public memory.

Unfortunately, their daughter Flora is epileptic and needs both hospital attention and financial support. When she was in hospital in January 1988 the media were there in the expectation Parkinson might visit. When her solicitors asked in October 1987 for financial support with nursing care, the press quickly picked up the story. Yet while Parkinson would like to see both settled, secure and invisible, events conspire to revive the memories. Norman Tebbit's autobiography in October 1988 was redrafted and, subsequently, damages paid on the basis of extracts printed in the *Mail on Sunday* which Keays called 'untrue, defamatory and a grave libel' (a reference to her angry reaction to his paragraph on the settlement in which he alleged that Keays broke an agreement not to comment on it with a 'highly coloured' story in *The Times*: this disappeared from the book). One month later Parkinson's daughter Mary was filling the centre pages of the *People* with tales of sex, drugs, drug-smuggling and a brush with the police: 'Daddy spurned Sara Keays because his love for me was greater', read the banner headline.

Meanwhile Parkinson worked away at the Department of Energy, on the privatisation of the electricity industry, with more than one whisper that, under the benign guidance of his patroness, his dream of reaching No. 11 (but not No. 10) Downing Street was on the agenda. In the July 1989 reshuffle, he was moved on to the Ministry of Transport but the man known for his likeable conviviality among colleagues and party members was not a happy man at the October conference. Shortly before, he had been asked questions about his shareholdings by an independent TV company, Fulcrum Productions, run by Chris Hird and Richard Belfield. Hird had been editor of the Insight team on the *Sunday Times*; Belfield with *World In Action*. Having completed one programme for Channel 4 about two businessmen allegedly involved in insider trading (one to buy into a firm, the other to make a takeover bid to push up shares) in which other stockbrokers were involved, the pair were preparing a second story. It would appear that, under the conventions governing Ministerial shareholdings that require the divestment of controlling shares or those that might atttract criticism, Parkinson had put his shares in a 'blind' trust – that is, in the hands of a third party with authority to buy or sell to maintain, not those specific shares, but the value of the holding without reference to the owner. It would appear that the nominee company used for this purpose may have been part of the various share manoeuvres.

The skeleton of the story broke in the *Scotsman* on 2 November – 'Scandal Threat to Tories' – which warned of a financial scandal that involved a share-purchasing group which numbered 'at least one senior member of the Goverment among its clients'. Rumours of the scandal and Parkinson's name were running the previous evening in Westminster; the Stock Exchange visibly rattled on Thursday (13.8 points down) and Downing Street was receiving calls asking if Parkinson was to resign. He was not: he was instructing Peter Carter-Ruck to issue a statement that he was not involved in share-dealings, let alone insider dealings, and was not intending to resign. The statement ended that 'in the event of a repetition of any of these baseless rumours, he will not hesitate to sue'. Clearly the rumours upset him and the Party; there were claims of smears about Parkinson and attempts to exploit the embarrassment of the recent resignation of Chancellor of the Exchequer Nigel Lawson. The Prime Minister snapped at a Labour MP who tried to discuss it in the House 'that she had nothing to add and was frankly amazed at him raising it'. The affair with Sara Keays was helpfully mentioned by several newspapers as background to the story. It was, as the *Independent* put it, 'Mr Nice' back at the centre of speculation and rumour.

# Chapter 17

## *Keith Hampson and A Night at the Gay Theatre*

### *Doctors Of Philosophy And A Sense Of Devilment*

Entry to the small Gay Theatre in Berwick Street, Soho, cost £5 in 1984 (£3 for pensioners and students). Down the narrow stairs, in four rows of four seats, was a sixteen-seater, flock wallpapered auditorium facing a small stage lit by a single bulb. It opened from midday to midnight on six days a week, and from 2 pm to midnight on Sundays. It had no drinks licence and served no other refreshments.

Outside, a poster of a reclining male in blue pants with the words 'Adults Only' advertised the club to passers-by. Before walking down the stairs another poster warned customers that the management would ask anyone acting or suspected of acting in an indecent manner to leave. Next to it a sign on the lavatory door proclaimed that access was limited to one person at a time. For their drink-free five pounds customers were treated to a continuous two-hour show of male dancers – the tall slim young variety – performing a full striptease to pop music. The club employed five dancers at £20 each a day to entertain an average of sixty customers. Its Glaswegian manager complained of harassment by the police, who came in in plainclothes and 'attracted attention' to themselves, making an arrest when they 'get the response they are seeking.'

At 10.30 pm on Thursday, 3 May 1984, the police arrested a customer for an alleged indecent assault on a plainclothes police constable from Scotland Yard's Club Squad who was on routine surveillance duty with a woman officer. The customer was Dr Keith Hampson, a Conservative MP. A former teacher and lecturer in American History at Edinburgh University, he had been elected as MP for Ripon in 1974 and then for Leeds North-West in 1983. In June 1983 he had been appointed Parliamentary Private Secretary to Defence Minister Michael Heseltine. On the following Saturday, 12 May, Hampson resigned his Ministerial office to 'avoid embarrassment' to Heseltine and the Government. Immediately the press began doorstepping his £180,000 London home in Markham Square, Chelsea, and his whitewashed stone cottage, Pear Tree Cottage, in Darley in the North Yorkshire Dales. What, they wanted to know, was Dr Hampson doing in the Gay Theatre?

Official reactions were essentially one of surprise that an outgoing young man who lived for politics – he began his political career as personal assistant, at the age of twenty-two, to Edward Heath in the 1966 General Election – should be found in a seedy Soho club. His second wife (the first, a model, was killed in a car crash in 1975), a *Financial Times* journalist, announced he was not gay and that they had a 'perfectly normal sex life.' The landlord of the local pub in the Dales thought that 'he was a doctor of philosophy and on a different plane to the rest of us.' A colleague, Marcus Fox, MP for Shipley, was 'staggered that he was in a place like that' while his constituency party chairman, after talking to Hampson, promised 'our confidence and support at this rather distressing time.'

Hampson announced at the time of his arrest that his behaviour resulted from personal problems and that he was 'totally fedup and drank too much.' On the other hand the club's manager alleged that Hampson was a regular customer (as, he added gratuitously, were three or four other MPs) who had come once a week since the previous December when the club started doing live shows, staying a couple of hours and leaving. Hampson was to claim that he had only been there once – on the occasion he was arrested.

After his arrest – he was subsequently released on police bail pending the outcome of a report to the police solicitors – a flurry of senior officers arrived at the West End Central police station. They did not inform any Government official, nor did Hampson. On Friday 11 May, however, Chris House, crime reporter for the *Sunday Telegraph* which eventually broke the story on Sunday 13 May, was asking questions about the arrest. Hampson told Heseltine late on Friday and, after a hurried series of telephone calls between the Minister and senior Party officials, Hampson announced his resignation. The delays triggered off a barrage of Labour questions about, as Ted Leadbitter put it, the insufficient vigilance in monitoring people with duties that could involve them 'in intelligence or sensitive security matters.' Hampson was charged with indecent assault on 18 May, with the Tories split over whether or not he should resign (and cause a by-election) but he sat tight and opted for trial by jury in October. The prosecution's case rested on the police officer's statement which alleged that Hampson put his left hand on the officer's right buttock while his right hand grasped the officer's groin.

Hampson's defence was that he spent the evening drinking, (he blamed the potent draught Bass), and later went to Soho to a pub before deciding, since his wife was at a party, to visit a club while waiting for her. He picked the Gay Theatre as he parked in Soho because, as he said, he had never been in a place like that before and there was a sense of devilment in visiting it although he did accept he had visited female strip clubs occasionally. Saying he had an ebullient, carefree attitude at the time he became fascinated by another customer – this was, apparently, the plainclothes woman police officer – whom he thought could be either a woman or a man in drag. He decided, he said, to take a closer look because he was genuinely interested in the person. But, inadvertently, his left hand brushed the male police officer's thigh in bending forward to look at her (or him).

After five hours deliberation the jury could not agree on a verdict. During his summing-up the judge had pointed out that witnesses had said Hampson was of good character and that to suggest he was homosexual or had such tendencies was absurd and unthinkable. The judge himself told the jury to remember that 'the history of mankind is littered with debris of men who have acted more stupidly than anyone else would have thought possible at the time.' Subsequently the Attorney-General Sir Michael Havers decided not to press for a retrial, partly on the grounds of the widespread publicity given to the case and partly because of the 'exceptional circumstances of this particular case.' The judge then directed that a verdict of not guilty be recorded.

# Chapter 18

## Jeffrey Archer's £500,000 – Not A Penny More, Not A Penny Less

*A Case of Mistaken Identity*

Monica 'Debbie' Coghlan was a middle-aged single woman with a young son to support. Self-employed, she responded to the Conservative Party belief that those who want to work should go out and get work, by catching the Inter-City train from Manchester to London each week. There, she put on her work-clothes – fishnet tights, a PVC black wet-look miniskirt, a white sweater – and went off to Shepherd Market, near Park Lane, to ply her trade as a prostitute. Herself the child of a single parent, she had begun her work while a teenager in Manchester. She had moved to London in 1980 and worked from a flat near Shepherd Market. She met and lived with a small-time property developer who bought her a bungalow in her hometown of Rochdale. When he died she returned home, had a child by another boyfriend and commuted weekly to London to continue her work. By her own account she found the work congenial, occasionally dressing up as a maid or a matron for some clients. She averaged three or four clients a night at £50 to £70 a time, for the three nights she stayed in London. Out of this income she paid £25 a night for a hotel room – and £5 to come and go as she pleased, together with her travel and other expenses, and a regular amount for fines for soliciting.

What happened on 8 September 1986 is not in dispute. Coghlan was in Shepherd Market around midnight. She already had had sex with two clients (£70 at a hotel in Belgravia, and £50 at a hotel in Victoria). A third man approached her, agreed the £50 price and said he was going to get his car. While he was away a fourth man, Aziz Kurtha, got out of a Mercedes and, because the earlier would-be client hadn't returned, Coghlan went off with Kurtha for £50, fifteen-minute sex in the hotel. Coghlan then asked the man to take her back to the beat. On leaving the hotel the man pointed out that someone in a car was flashing his headlights. Coghlan went over; it was the man who had gone to get his car. As they returned to the hotel Kurtha called her to him and allegedly said: 'you have hit the jackpot, young Debbie, that is Jeffrey Archer'. Coghlan then returned with her new client to room 6a in the second hotel where he paid £50 for the sex and a further £20 to 'make it last longer.' They undressed, the man expressing surprise at Coghlan's nipples (they were large), and sex took place with Coghlan on top; it took 10 minutes, and because it was over so quickly, Coghlan offered him another try after cleaning him up. She lit a cigarette, lay on the bed beside him and asked what he did. He said he was a car salesman, then said he had to go and move his car. He never returned. When she telephoned later that week to book her room the hotel receptionist told her that a man had been trying to contact her. It was Aziz Kurtha.

Kurtha was an Indian-born, LSE educated lawyer who had married wealth and developed a profitable legal practice in Dubai for his fellow-countrymen. He expanded the practice in London, earning enough wealth for a large house in Richmond, private education for his children, and an art collection. He liked the public limelight, acting as an emissary of the Pakistan Government in the USA after the Bangladeshi war and presenting TV programmes in Dubai and Pakistan. He offered himself, and was appointed, as a presenter in 1983 for Channel 4's *Eastern Eye* Asian programme, supplementing his fee himself in order to fly regularly from Dubai to London. He enjoyed the attention and hoped the media exposure would facilitate his ambition to become a Labour MP. Those dreams collapsed when *Eastern Eye* was axed in 1985 and he failed to win a seat on the local council. Bored, he indulged himself with gambling and the occasional prostitute, one of whom was Monica Coghlan.

That day, after he was convinced he saw Jeffrey Archer go with her into the hotel, Kurtha went to *Private Eye*, for whom he had written gossipy pieces on Dubai. Then he met with Coghlan and tried to persuade her to tell her story to 'a couple of friends' of his for £600. Coghlan demurred but Kurtha was persistent. Kurtha was convinced he had a major scoop and was determined to have it published. Part of that determination clearly lay in his simplistic assumptions about good guys and bad guys, and his misunderstanding of the nature of exposé journalism in Britain. Certainly he was to allege later: 'I saw his private activity to be totally hypocritical, in direct contradiction to his party's policy and was humbug . . . it had to be exposed.' On the other hand he may have become carried away over his own rôle in 'a matter of "considerable journalistic and public importance" . . . and in the process lost his sense of proportion.'[1]

A *Private Eye* journalist passed him on to the *News of the World*, who saw him as an intermediary and, after extracting Coghlan's whereabouts from him, squeezed him out. Kurtha took his story to other Fleet Street newspapers, making no secret of landing a 'valuable deal', and from there the rumours percolated to the annual Tory Party conference in October. One man particularly concerned with the rumours was the Party's Deputy Chairman, Jeffrey Archer.

## The Rise and Fall of Jeffrey Archer

Archer had learnt some of the basic ground rules for political survival the hard way, by personal experience. The first was not to do anything that invites criticism, particularly if it involves behaviour that may be perfectly acceptable in the private sector but may be misinterpreted in the political arena. From his days at Oxford University, doing a Diploma in Physical Education, he had developed a flair for fund-raising and publicity: he brought the Beatles to dine at High Table. On graduation he took his talents to the United Nations Association, then run by Humphrey Berkeley, but left somewhat acrimoniously after fifteen months (there was a small matter of a libel action brought by Archer against Berkeley over the latter's comments on his expenses' claims). By then, however, he had become a member of the GLC, a personal assistant to Tory MP Chris Chataway, a friend of such Establishment figures as Lord Harlech and Lord Mountbatten, a co-owner of a Mayfair art gallery and chairman of Arrow Enterprises. Arrow was a professional fund-raising firm that took a percentage of money raised. It won the lucrative PR contract for the pro-Common Market European Movement and one of its major fundraising events was to invite the three Party leaders – Edward Heath, Harold Wilson and Jeremy Thorpe – to speak at the Guildhall in London. Wilson protested:

> A few days before it took place I decided to withdraw, as I had heard that the fundraising firm, Arrow Enterprises, which was in charge of the fund-raising activity, had been promised ten per cent of the proceeds. Recalling all the thousands of voluntary workers who organised functions, for charities and other worthwhile activities, I revolted against this form of professionalism. I particularly disliked the principle that if either of the other two party leaders or I succeeded, through our eloquence, in persuading some rich fellow-diner to contribute £10,000 to the cause, the fundraising organisation concerned would benefit to the extent of £1000. My refusal, backed by Jeremy Thorpe, led to a change in the arrangements, under which the fundraiser was promised a flat fee, which I accepted as reasonable.[2]

For the young Archer, whose accomplishments now included a seat in Parliament, after he had retained the Louth constituency for the Conservatives in a 1969 by-election, it was a public rebuke that stuck. When Michael Sobell, father-in-law of GEC chairman Arnold Weinstock, was knighted for his services to charity, the coincidental matter of his payments to the European Movement was raised in Parliament – 'for which charity', said one MP snidely, 'the Conservative MP for Louth . . . was the principal sponsor, taking his usual cut.'[3]

Worse was to follow as Archer disregarded another ground rule; don't take risks and do something stupid. In 1972, acting on what turned out to be a dud tip, Archer borrowed heavily to invest £195,000 in the Canadian industrial cleaning firm, Aquablast, which had acquired the rights to an exhaust emission control device. This, the Weimann Idle Arm Adjuster Valve, was hailed as the solution for controlling exhaust fumes from American cars. Unfortunately Aquablast defaulted on payments for the rights – there was speculation of a Mafia-inspired swindle – and went bankrupt with its shares sliding from $5 to 10 cents in a year. Archer said farewell to his Daimler with the personalised numberplate (ANY 1), the Chelsea home which was the scene of many glittering parties and, more seriously, his constituency. Surviving on his wife's salary as a Cambridge academic, Archer turned his experiences into a novel. *Not a Penny More, Not a Penny Less* was highly successful, as were Archer's subsequent novels. With his debts paid off he bought a penthouse overlooking the Thames (and the House of Commons) where, amid his expensive collection of works of art, he cultivated the rich and famous. He and his family also lived at the Old Vicarage at Grantchester near Cambridge. He never made any secret of his political ambitions, however, considering life as a famous author boring and unfulfilled.

## The Party Calls

In 1985 the call came. To the surprise and mumbled concern of senior colleagues Prime Minister Margaret Thatcher invited Archer to become Deputy Chairman of the Conservative Party. As a self-confident, self-made man with good looks, charm and drive he was intended to revive the party faithful in the middle of a jaded and drifting government performance. While close to Thatcher he was not closely involved in policy-making at Party headquarters and more than once warned for indiscreet remarks. Nevertheless, financially secure, free from constituency demands and unencumbered with Ministerial duties, he worked tirelessly and unpaid as the Party's fund-raiser and morale-booster for fourteen months. His good-humoured enthusiasm and unaffected interest gave him the limelight he enjoyed. Indeed, with Party Chairman Norman Tebbit thinking of retiring to look after his wife, who had been badly injured in the IRA bomb attack during the 1984 Party conference in Brighton, he had hopes either of succeeding him or taking up even a 'minor' political office which would require a seat in the Lords. He may not have been aware that many of his colleagues would be not particularly keen on either eventuality but he must have been very aware that he had to avoid doing anything to jeopardise his second, and probably his last, attempt at a political career. Which is why he cannot have been a happy man when the telephone rang on 25 September 1986. It was Monica Coghlan.

## Plotting The Plot

When the *News of the World* found Coghlan they sent John Lisners, who, Coghlan claimed, pretended to be Archer's friend to coax the story from her; Kurtha had repeatedly told her that the client was Archer. Believing both Kurtha and Archer powerful enough to make life miserable for her, she repeated what happened on 8 September. When another newspaper called, after a visit from Kurtha, the *News of the World* took her off on a tour of English and overseas hotels as they worked on the story. Unprovable as it stood, the newspaper decided to use Coghlan to try and make Archer corroborate her claims.

Coghlan telephoned several times: coached by the *News of the World* journalists not to say she was working with them and not to sound as though she was blackmailing him, she was told to spin a story of harassment by Kurtha and the media over rumours of his relationship with her ('this is the way it has to be done,' said one when Coghlan complained about lying). Hoping to coax some signs of recognition or reaction from Archer the do-it-yourself telephone eavesdroppers were rewarded with a pay-off they could hardly have anticipated. Archer offered to pay £2000 for Coghlan to go abroad on holiday. To make it easier for them Archer explained in detail how the payment was to be made; Platform 3, Victoria Station at 11 am the next day, a Saturday. Since the *News of the World* had heard that the *Sunday People* were considering a 'Mr X and the Vice Girl' lead story, Archer's efficiency was a godsend. Coghlan had a tape-recorder strapped to her thigh with the microphone in her cleavage and was sent to Victoria Station in full view of the telephoto lenses of prearranged and positioned *News of the World* photographers. At 11 am the surveillance team were on tenter-hooks; one version had it they suspected a police trap, another that the *Mail on Sunday* was about to expose *them*. Then Michael Stacpoole arrived with a package containing forty £50 notes and handed it to Coghlan with the immortal words: 'I'm here to do a favour for a very important political friend.' Stacpoole was Archer's PR man. The newspaper had its story.

## Archer Strikes Back

Archer's later explanation of his generosity was that he wanted to help the unfortunate woman despite the fact he had no idea whom she was. This is unlikely. Whatever else he was Archer was no twentieth-century Scarlet Pimpernel rescuing a fallen woman in distress, as the *Mail on Sunday* extravagantly suggested, by 'a willing quixotic, romantic gesture.'[4] More prosaically but much more real-istically Archer was all too well aware that any allegations, however baseless, could shatter his political reputation and that it would take years to win retribution in the courts. Accordingly he tried to outwit Kurtha, realising that, since Kurtha was a solicitor, he had to act decisively and quickly. He realised both the pressures on Coghlan and her predicament. Thus, 'in the belief that the woman genuinely wanted to be out of the way of the Press and realising that for my part any publicity of this kind would be extremely harmful to me and for which a libel action would be no adequate remedy, I offered to pay her money so she could go abroad for a short period and arranged for this money to be paid over to her.' He wanted her to stay away from the press so he could deal with Kurtha: 'it might help if you were able to pop abroad, after today he'll be a very frightened man . . . the longer you can go abroad the better.' The fright for Kurtha was a letter from Lord Mishcon, Archer's solicitor, which read:

> Our client has instructed us that it has come to his knowledge from unimpeachable sources that offers have been made by someone giving your name . . . against payment to be made to you to pass on for publication a most serious and damaging libel of and concerning our client. If you are in fact responsible for these offers, and we would ask you to inform us in writing by return if you are not, we are further instructed to inform you that if there is any repetition of this conduct, or any further defamation of our client of any kind for which you are directly or indirectly responsible, immediate steps will be taken on our client's behalf.

That letter was agreed on 23 October and Coghlan received her payment the next day but Archer was still not certain he had effectively dealt with the threat because he knew the rumours were all over Fleet Street.

## Publication

Archer had learnt of the rumours from the *Mail on Sunday*'s editor at the Tory Party Conference which, said one journalist, was awash with ribald schoolboy jokes about the matter. More importantly he already knew from a friend in the newspaper world that the *News of the World* were pursing the story. David Montgomery, the *News of the World* editor, alleged Archer called twice before the Conference to find out if 'I was intending to run a dirty story about him.' The third call, on 4 October, was to arrange a conference meeting with Montgomery and his political editor. Everyone else's version was that Montgomery used the meeting to float the possibility of another Parkinson-type scandal to see if Archer reacted. Montgomery's version was that Archer wanted to warn him off, saying he had the Prime Minister's ear and could either arrange for her to 'speak to him from time to time' or have her tell Murdoch, the newspaper's owner, that he was 'a thoroughly bad lot.'

After the conference the interest on both sides faded until Coghlan telephoned Archer again. He put his plan into action. Archer was, however, to speak to Montgomery again. The day Stacpoole met Coghlan, Archer was telephoned by Michael Dobbs, head of the Conservative Central Office, and was told that the *News of the World* intended to run the story the next day. Archer called David Montgomery, the newspaper's editor, several times, and spoke to him and journalist John Lisners. Archer denied the payment and began by warning presciently 'I shall sue. I will win but you will ruin my career.' He then withdrew the threat to sue, admitted he had been foolish but pleaded with Montgomery to be allowed 'an outside chance of doing some work in my life that I would be proud of.' Montgomery asked for time to think it over but then said that he would 'have to go the way my conscience dictates . . . it is a very unfortunate episode indeed, for me as well as for you.'

## The Tabloids Go To Court

The next day, after preparing a 'rogue' front page to fool the rest of Fleet Street (newspapers exchange copies of each other's first editions), the *News of the World* splashed the story – 'TORY BOSS ARCHER PAYS OFF VICE GIRL' – while Archer telephoned Norman Tebbit and announced his resignation. At once the Fleet Street circus was on his trail, jumping traffic lights and forming a convoy for the journey back to Grantchester before settling down on his doorstep – 'the paraphernalia of scandal', one newspaper called it. Archer was invariably courteous to the waiting journalists, posing for photographs, bringing them coffee and apologising for the awful weather. Meanwhile other journalists were scouring the country for leads. The *Star* unearthed Monica Coghlan's nephew Tony Smith who offered them for £400 a tale of kinky sex with Coghlan dressed as Little Red Riding Hood. This they published five days after his resignation under the headline: 'Poor Jeffrey: vice-girl Monica speaks: Archer the man I knew.' This was unfortunate for the *Star* since it took the *News of the World* story at its face value and explicitly alleged sex took place; in the latter's story sex was implicit (that is, the payment to Coghlan could suggest that there might have been a sexual relationship). Archer promptly sued and it was the *Star* who found themselves in court defending another newspaper's story and journalistic techniques after some negotiations for an out-of-court settlement. Both sides thought they stood a 50/50 chance of success but the possibility of a settlement foundered on Archer's demand for a suitable front page apology – 'why should we give in to that little shit?' said the *Star*'s owner – and a lack of enthusiasm on the part of the newspaper to offer a deal. In court, the *Star*'s star defence witness, Monica Coghlan, by pointing out that she had had little contact with her nephew and that his information was fantasy, demolished most of their case – apart from the sex with Archer. The jury then had a straightforward choice; either Archer or Coghlan was lying. Archer's defence was that he had had dinner with his book editor, then left the Caprice restaurant around midnight with his theatrical agent, who had no record such as a cheque-stub or diary entry to confirm the meeting but was certain that the date was right. Archer then drove him home to Camberwell, arriving there around 1.45 am. Neither Coghlan nor Kurtha made good witnesses but Archer's counsel chose to take the case away from the issue of identification and details to the ethics of the tabloid press. He did not get the *Star*'s editor into the witness box – part of the 'most astonishing defence ever offered' he called it – but he accused the *News of the World* of deception, deceit and lying and the *Star* of cynicism, titillation and peddling degrading accusations. Mr Justice Caulfield in his summing up chose not to dwell on the iniquities of the tabloids but rather devoted himself to Mary Archer's fragrance, elegance and radiance and to Archer's worthy healthy and sporting history. Since they had a 'full life', said the judge, was Archer 'in need of cold, unloving, rubber-insulated sex in a seedy hotel?' (If he was, suggested the judge, his sexual urge must have been very sustaining and may not have been very discerning). It would seem Mary Archer's demeanour and changing appearance each day during the trial[5] was noted by the media. Certainly her presence and evidence, including the state of her husband's back and the extent of his suntan (Coghlan was wrong about them), were important factors in the trial that underlined the enhanced rôle of the family ideal which now, as the judge seemed to imply, should provide sexual as well as moral satisfaction.[6]

## How To Win And Lose At The Same Time

Archer won the case and £500,000 in damages, together with costs of £230,000. The *Star* pondered on an appeal, particularly on the basis of the judge's summing-up (he made several factual errors he had to correct), but decided against it. The *News of the World*, originally claiming its intention to defend its actions, also chose discretion and settled out of court: this time Archer received £50,000. The case was over and the queues of crowds in and around the courtroom dispersed. While the serious newspapers ground their teeth over the judge's partiality and the dismissal of journalist Adam Raphael's claim that Archer had said to him he had previously met Coghlan 'very casually', they were universally annoyed at the criticism of the journalistic methods employed, rather than the ends to which they were put.

For Archer, however, the success of the court case spelt the end of his second career in politics. Senior Tories had never been too happy at his re-emergence in the upper echelons of the Party and were concerned that his off-the-cuff remarks could be an electoral liability. Even when the case was over and Archer vindicated there was no official word of congratulation and certainly no offer of a new post. The whole story is, however, an interesting lesson in the power of conventional morality. It was obvious that Archer's real error of judgement was not the alleged sin of fornication but his efforts to conceal or deflect the making of the allegations. Little attention was given to what he was trying to do – 'nail the lie' – but much was devoted to his foolishness in adopting the tactics he did or at least adopting tactics that put him in the headlines. The tabloids were condemned for pursuing 'a private peccadillo' for the purposes of sensationalism and Archer considered unwise for believing that the allegations, however ill-founded, had a public value. The *Observer* argued that his 'attempt is in itself a genuflection to conventional morality – and that morality lies in ruins all about us.' It compared the activities of the tabloids to a traditional dance 'whose movements and gestures have been lovingly handed down from generation to generation . . . but whose symbolic meaning has been lost.'[7] But that was the whole point; Archer, Kurtha and the *News of the World* knew that it was the symbolism of conventional morality which had *not* been lost. Kurtha thought the alleged hypocrisy should be exposed, the *News of the World* knew that the symbolism was still a benchmark people believed in (even if they were no longer shocked by its transgressors) and Archer knew the damage the allegations would cause. The Tories have made a great play of the 'simple moral values of Christian family life' because they knew the electoral value in promoting that symbolism. Archer knew only too well the consequences of being accused of being out-of-step and, in attempting to keep himself within the Party's symbolic mantle, failed to make the right moves to defend himself.

# Chapter 19

## *The Trivial Pursuits of Harvey Proctor*

*Political Character Assassination*

The most interesting feature of Harvey Proctor's downfall as an MP lay in the total absence of any comment on his behaviour from his Party leadership. Neither his strident right-wing politics nor his enthusiasm for spanking young boys brought a rebuke or condemnation. Of course Prime Minister Margaret Thatcher had long made it plain that MPs' private lives were their own affair and there was never much likelihood of Proctor achieving any sort of Ministerial office. On the other hand it was surprising that a Party that marched into electoral battle proclaiming the sanctity of the family and reviling the excesses of the permissive society should not think it prudent to restrain, if not disassociate itself from, an MP whose public and private behaviour hardly reflected the values the Party appeared to hold dear. The knowledge both of his personal and political preferences was already on the fringes of the public arena in 1981 when *Private Eye* attacked the 'deeply unpleasant' MP for his right-wing views and for being a 'raging homosexualist'. It was one of the first to seek out Terry Woods, a longstanding boyfriend of Proctor's, who had rung around Fleet Street after he had been thrown out of Proctor's flat. Woods was also to appear in court in 1981 where he was fined £20 for breaking windows at his parents' house in Frisby, Leicester. Woods' explanation then was that he had had too much to drink as a result of the ending of his seven-year relationship with Proctor. 'My client', Woods' solicitor told the court, 'says that they are both homosexuals and that he was shattered by the end of the relationship.' Proctor emphatically denied the relationship: 'Mr Woods is engaged in a sustained campaign of political character assassination and I utterly repudiate his comments in so far as they concern me.'

Proctor clearly thought he was politically safe. He kept his private interests in London and worked hard as a personable, competent constituency MP for Billericay where he had a 14,615 majority and where his right-wing views found a ready audience among the blue-collar, East End emigrants. He felt so secure that he was able to deny emphatically the successive revelations that suggested he was a keen practitioner of the corporal punishment he apparently advocated for schools.

The first major allegations were published in June 1986 in the *People*, alleging kinky sex games, spankings and cane beatings with a young male prostitute in his London flat. 'A monstrous attempt to blacken my name', said Proctor. He repeated his denials, looking 'shaken', in September when the *People* published further information. It alleged a gay massage parlour boss met Proctor in 1983 and began supplying him young boys for £35 each. These would act out the rôle of naughty boys, usually in tight white shorts, who were to be punished by 'headmaster' Proctor with bare-bottom beatings administered by hand, slipper and cane. The beatings were severe – Proctor allegedly took Polaroid photographs of the weals – but, once in bed, Proctor 'reverted to someone quite pleasant and civilised.' Proctor dismissed the allegations which were supplied, together with photographs, by a 20-year old homosexual 'sickened by the brutality used by Proctor in bizarre sex games.' Proctor called them a monstrous slur, a tissue of lies.

## 'I Can Spot A Homosexual At 50 Feet'

Down in Billericay, however, the local Conservative Association had a new chairman, Frank Tomlin, who was a computer systems manager and Vice-President of the local Community Relations Council. An articulate member of the middle classes, he was less enthusiastic about Proctor than his predecessor, of whom it was said that he 'thought old Harvey was some sort of God.' Billericay is a constituency of two worlds, intolerant working-class conservatism of the large housing estates and middle-class moderation, which was further complicated by the strong presence of the right-wing Monday Club, in which Proctor served on the executive council. Frank Tomlin wanted an explanation from Proctor about his private activities; Proctor hardly endeared himself to Tomlin by turning up in October at the annual Tory Party conference in Bournemouth and attacking official party policy on immigration. Within two weeks it was Tomlin, together with his wife, who had acted as Proctor's agent, the Association's Vice-Chairman and the Treasurer, who resigned after a stormy meeting of the constituency executive committee voted thirty to ten to support Proctor. The Treasurer alleged that there had been a well-orchestrated campaign to discredit the meeting and the chairman by swamping it with Proctor supporters. Proctor, who had told the meeting that he would not sue the *People* because of the costs involved, was then accused by the newspaper of deliberately lying in denying their allegations, as it turned the information over to the Serious Crime Squad for investigation. In the meantime Proctor continued to voice his political views, asserting that multi-racialism 'had acted as a catalyst to the growth of crime by destroying the sense of community, solidarity and identity', and attracting press attention as police visited his flat to sort out a noisy domestic dispute with an art dealer in his underpants. The dealer, none other than Terry Woods, told the *Daily Mirror* in March of Proctor's Agadir holiday the previous January, and the discovery of a naked Moroccan under Proctor's bed in the Ali Baba Hotel. 'Completely untrue', said Proctor, 'I have never used the services of a prostitute, either male or female.' In a matter of weeks Proctor was helping the police with their inquiries and the Billericay Conservative Association had another meeting on Proctor's fate. To the right-wingers who now dominated the Association, Proctor was either not a homosexual ('I was in the Navy during the war', said one, 'and I can spot a homosexual at 50 feet, Harvey Proctor is not one of them.') or, if he was, he should keep it quiet rather than risk losing the seat. Proctor still retained the support of the Association but resigned shortly after being charged with gross indecency offences.

## Trivial Pursuits

At his trial in May 1987 Proctor pleaded guilty to four charges of gross indecency and was fined £1450. The charges all involved sessions with rent-boys obtained by an escort agency in which he spanked them in 'schoolboy punishment' rituals for getting the answers wrong in the Trivial Pursuit quiz-game. They wore shorts; he used canes, a training shoe and his bare hands (six strokes of each). The youths with whom the acts took place were aged sixteen and nineteen at that time; they were paid £15 or £20 a session. Proctor appeared to have a collection of canes and took polaroid photos of the youths. He also masturbated himself and fondled the youths. His defence solicitor, David Napley, pointed out that the youths were willing partners and blamed everything on the press by claiming that the case was instituted by a journalist who offered money for people to give evidence, and not in the pursuit of justice, but in pursuit of copy in order to sell newspapers.

# Chapter 20

## *BT Shares and The Many Names of Keith Best*

### *A Rare Welsh Tory*

At the age of twenty-nine Keith Best achieved the greatest success of the 1979 General Election when he turned a 5900 Labour majority into a 2800-vote success for the Conservatives in the Anglesey constituency. A former army captain with a barrister's business in Brighton, his uneventful political career was disrupted in 1980 when he crashed his silver VW Sirocco into the back of a broken-down van on the Holyhead road. Best had been returning to his home after an evening in an Anglesey hotel. With him was Brenda Rodgers, a divorcee who worked as a clerk in his Brighton chambers and had come to Holyhead for the weekend to help Best fix up his house. After spending the evening having a meal in the hotel the couple had left about 11.30 pm. Shortly before midnight Best collided with the van, hitting it 'with such force that the fully-laden Bedford was pushed forward six feet, up onto a pavement and into a wall. The car was a total write-off.'[1] Best suffered broken bones; Brenda Rogers was killed. Best was acquitted of driving without due care and attention; the van driver was fined £100 and £587 costs for having defective tyres and failing to display the correct rear lights. Best recovered from his injuries to pursue his career, becoming PPS to the Secretary of State for Wales and supporting his Government's enthusiasm for denationalising large parts of the public sector to return them to the private sector.

The facade of public participation in this massive realisation of a major Tory objective was created by encouraging the public to buy shares in previously state-owned firms. To ensure that the shares were spread amongst the widest number of people, restrictions were introduced on the number of shares that could be purchased by any one person. This, it was believed, would discourage speculation, avoid the dominant influence of a handful of large financial institutions and promote a share-owning democracy.

At first the restrictions relied on warnings and 'accepted business practice' to deter would-be speculators hoping for a quick profit. One of the first sell-offs was Jaguar Cars. Its prospectus warned that 'the right is reserved to reject any application in whole or part, in particular multiple or suspected multiple applications.' As the success of sales became evident, and justifying the creation of a share-owning nation became pre-eminent, so the restrictions were tightened. In the 1984 British Telecom flotation prospectus applicants were required to 'warrant that no other application had been made on your behalf.' This could be used against those who used others or aliases to apply for shares because they could be charged with deception under the 1968 Theft Act. Less clear was the position of those who used permutations of their own name (initials of forenames, one forename, then another forename) or different addresses they could claim as their own. This ambiguity was clarified in later sales where it was clearly stated that 'criminal proceedings may be instituted if you make more than one application.'

## Trawling For The Wrong Fish

As a barrister, Keith Best should have been aware of the import of the restrictions and, as an aspiring Tory politician, even more aware of the Government's purpose in spreading share-ownership – which makes his subsequent behaviour all the more surprising. In 1987 the Labour

Research Department, the trade union-funded research organisation that painstakingly tracks down the relationships between business and the Tory Party, trawled 51,000 pages of British Telecom applications and found the names of 101 MPs and 34 MPs' wives. They were looking for any Labour MP unwise enough to indulge in personal gain from privatisation. Included among the names they came across that of Keith Best, or rather three variations of his name using four different addresses in pursuit of six applications for a total of 4800 shares (the limit was 800 per person). Against the background of official Tory support for the widest possible share distribution and regular revelations of insider dealings in the City, Best was a prime target for Parliamentary criticism. Labour MPs were quick to demand his resignation and immediate prosecution. Best had party support at first – John Biffen called the demands 'sanctimonious and distasteful' and the local Conservative Chairman announced that Best had the support of his local party executive 'for the time being.' What fuelled the criticism was the suspicion that Best might not be prosecuted because he had used permutations of his own name; only the use of bogus names was clearly an attempt at deception. Worse for Best was the *Observer*'s revelation in April 1987 that Best had made four applications for 1000 Jaguar shares. Best had not brought this to his local party's attention when he had been making a 'full and frank explanation of his action' and assuring them that 'examination of other privatisation issues will not yield any further embarrassments about his share dealings.' With prosecutions of ten people who had used bogus names for BT applications, Labour MPs pressed for a government statement on whether or not Best was to be prosecuted. On the grapevine they had learnt that, while Treasury officials and Fraud Squad officers wanted to charge those who used permutations of their own names, the DPP was reluctant to proceed because of the ambiguous wording of the BT prospectus.

A few days later, on the day Harvey Proctor was charged, Best announced his intention to resign his seat at the next General Election. This was seen as an attempt to limit the damage to the Conservative Party by their avoiding having to make a public statement on the matter and by avoiding an embarrassing by-election. (In the event Plaid Cymru won the seat in 1987). In the House, Labour's attempts to publicly arraign him ran into a Speaker's ruling that his behaviour did not relate to proceedings in Parliament. Brian Sedgemore called the resignation decision 'political expediency at the expense of the integrity of Parliament' as Labour leader Neil Kinnock taunted the Party Chairman: 'I am just waiting', he said, 'to see if we get a sermon on moral values from Mr Norman Tebbit over the next few days. He has fallen strangely silent.' Meanwhile the media had also begun trawling the privatisation sales and found that Best had been an assiduous if legitimate gatherer of shares in the TSB, British Aerospace, British Gas, Cable and Wireless, Britoil and Enterprise Oil. Best spoke briefly after resigning. He had put in multiple applications for BT shares because, where there was an over-subscription, bids were likely to be scaled down. The more applications he put in, he believed, the more likelihood of getting his entitlement. He then announced that the profits from his 4800 BT shares (bought at £1.30, now trading at £2.40) would go to charity.

In October 1987 Best was prosecuted in the courts for his BT applications. At his trial, where the charge was changed from deception to dishonestly attempting to obtain more shares than his entitlement, prosecution counsel underlined the care and extraordinary lengths Best went to, to arrange the applications. Defence counsel argued that Best was unlikely to be acting dishonestly and risk his promising career (at this point Best broke down in tears). Nevertheless the court accepted that the planning of the applications – to hoodwink the scrutineers – was a deliberate ploy to net as many shares as possible. He was stunned to receive a four-month jail sentence, a £3000 fine and ordered to pay £1500 in costs. The judge told him: 'You engaged in carefully calculated acts of dishonesty, designed to provide a substantial profit. Nor have you expressed one word of regret. I realise your career is now in ruins. I bear in mind your previous exemplary character. But conduct of this kind is all too frequent, and I would add that all those who might be considering behaving as you did, must be made to realise this does not pay.'

## A Warning To Dissuade Others

Best's lawyer immediately applied for bail pending an appeal but Best had to spend the weekend in Brixton Jail – in the hospital wing before he knew the outcome. On Monday, 5 October the prison sentence was quashed by the Appeal Court and the fine raised to £4500 – a decision reflecting the fact that fines had been imposed on ten others who had been convicted of making multiple BT applications: 'It is only by the skin of his teeth this appellant escapes gaol', said the judge, sitting to hear the appeal only days after the original conviction.

One other Conservative MP also found his political career at an end. Eric Cockeram, MP for Ludlow and a Member of Lloyds, trustee of the TSB (North-West) and director of the Liverpool Building Society, admitted to more than one application for BT and British Gas shares after the Labour Research Department had unearthed his name along with Best's. Cockeram said that he had bought the shares for his grandchildren – 'I much regret that these two Christmas gestures to new arrivals in the family have caused so much trouble.' Admitting he might have committed a 'technical breach' he chose to resign his seat at the 1987 General Election.

Interestingly, Best was the only individual prosecuted for this method of application, although applications from 6600 others were rejected as being potential multiple applications. The Goverment promised to 'crack down hard' on future multiple applications. It was obvious that what was a common practice had, in the light of less savoury City activities, become, in the general climate of opinion, unacceptable behaviour: 'those' said the judge, 'of exemplary character do unhappily fall from their own standards.' Unwise and unhappy as Best was, he was clearly an official warning to others as well as guilty of the crime for which he was convicted. As the judge said in March 1988, on dismissing his appeal against conviction; for the jury to have reached any other conclusion in the original trial 'would have been perverse'.

# PART FIVE

## *PUBLIC STANDARDS, PRIVATE MORALS*

# Chapter 21

## *The Private Lives of Politicians*

### *The Dividing Line*

The label 'MP' is always good for a story. Why else would
the *News of the World* run a front page headline 'MP's
Husband and the Vice Girl'? Clearly the allegations from
a 'busty 27-year-old brunette' that John Golding, General
Secretary of the National Communications Union, had a
small penis, liked oral sex, noisy sex sessions and called
her Cocoa (hot, sweet and good to take to bed) is good
entertainment. What makes it a front page story is the
political link, however tenuous, and, for the former
Labour MP, the story that was to result in early retirement. The media love stories about politicians and those
connected with them, because that distinguishes them
from the generality of society in the same way that group
membership, be it royalty or the cast of a popular soap
opera, identifies the individual in the public's mind. As
Woodrow Wyatt, a columnist in the *News of the World* put
it – 'we may say this is distasteful. But most of us enjoy
these revelations' – while denying the allegations had any
bearing on the ability of those involved to perform their
jobs. But, as the *Observer* suggested in one case where
disciplinary action was taken as a result of newspaper
allegations, 'the greatest case for concern is that they have
legitimised another scurrilous and offensive campaign by
the tabloid Press.' The question is, where should the
dividing-line be drawn between media entertainment,
public standards and private morals? Said the *Independent*:
'genuine public figures have a responsibility to comport
themselves in public in a manner which does not bring
discredit on the organisations which employ them and

the press has every right to expose them when they fail to live up to their obligations. Beyond that, however, they should be left to conduct their lives as they see fit.'[1] Nevertheless, the mix of the media's traditional enthusiasm for the salacious and the sensational, together with a tradition, whether right or wrong, that any aspect of a politician's life may be a matter of public debate and have a bearing of their political position, has focused attention on their private and in particular their personal conduct.

## The New Dark Age

Sex, controversy and black-and-white sanctimonious moralising are the stock-in-trade of the tabloid newspapers. There are those, however, who think that the justification for stories about public figures – the relevance, the public interest, the exposé of hypocrisy or double standards – has gone. 'If a Martian came down and looked at our papers', says Eve Pollard, editor of the *Sunday Mirror*, 'he would think that all people are worrying about is sex: where are the stories about major financial developments, social affairs, even food poisoning?' After wading through the endless titillation about showbusiness and pop stars, the tabloids have turned this successful formula – and no-one is denying that sales have not increased – onto the Royal family and public figures, stretching out far and wide to encompass in any of these groups anyone who can provide the story that is, as Nick Lloyd, former editor of the *News of the World* says, 'more dramatic than the last'. When painter Francis Bacon went to Moscow in 1988 and gave a press conference, Lord Gowrie recalls that 'the Russian journalists asked questions about Bacon's work; the British about Bacon's private life'. When British athletes were in Seoul for the 1988 Olympics, sports writer Hugh McIlvanney complained about 'the squalid eagerness with which the more scurrilous tabloids ferret around the lives of the well-known'. Increasingly, many are concerned about this development. Terry Lovell says he left the *People* because of his 'sense of disgust and anger at its brutal treatment of people's lives'.

Lord Cudliff, former chair of Daily Mirror newspapers, condemns the shift from investigatory journalism in the public interest to intrusive journalism for the prurient. Talking of a 'dark age' where sleazy stories about 'bonking bimbos' achieve a dominant influence in the circulation charts, he warns of significant national and international events being nudged aside 'by a panting seven-day and seven-night news service for voyeurs'. The result, says David Steel, the former leader of the Liberal Party, is that 'our sewer-oriented journals . . . compete to entertain their readers with titillating stories . . . told with a reckless disregard for the need to check the truth or accuracy of their stories'. But sex – and scandal – sells most products (most of the audience watching the recent film about Profumo were not there to brush up on their history), and, in the media, it is not only the tabloids who use sex to attract readers. When in October 1988 the *Mail on Sunday*, a partly-serious newspaper, began its serialisation of Norman Tebbit's autobiography it chose to publicise it twice on the front page with 'EXCLUSIVE: NORMAN TEBBIT TELLS THE REAL STORY OF THE MINISTER AND THE MISTRESS' and 'WHY I HUSHED KEAYS SCANDAL'. One week earlier the portentous *Sunday Times* had begun its serialisation of the equally serious official biography by Alistair Horne of Harold Macmillan – and the subject of the first extract? 'MACMILLAN: THE ANGUISH OF HIS WIFE'S INFIDELITY'. Even the more restrained *Observer* offered its readers at this time 'NEHRU AND THE LADY', the hoary old story of whether Edwina Mountbatten slept with him (it is more than likely she did), as its only extract from a new biography of the Indian leader. If this was not enough upmarket excitement there was a recent diary item in the *Sunday Times* book section that revealed, in the race to produce the latest Harold Wilson biography, one author had obtained some exclusive material – Wilson's love letter to his first girlfriend 'who will not be named until publication.' Wilson was seventeen at the time.

## Fair Game?

With sex now a front-page media preoccupation, it is, therefore, hardly surprising that politicians' sexual relationships are considered fair game. How far a politician may be pursued or how he or she may react will depend on that politician's status, the behaviour in question, the degree of embarrassment that could be caused and the degree of support that his or her party may be prepared to offer, but sex scandals therefore will always find a ready market in the mass sales end of the media, which has been traditionally predisposed to such highly-marketable and profitable stories. Such stories are passed on by those who relish the notoriety, the publicity and the benefits of cheque-book journalism and who have a lot less to lose than those they talk about. Furthermore the cumulative effect is that such stories now satisfy a demand they created and tend to dominate other types of stories about MPs' private activities.

Private finances receive less attention, partly because nearly all means of enhancing one's Parliamentary salary are acceptable even though, as in the case of consultancies and lobbying, the ends to which they are put often raise issues of Parliamentary independence and integrity. They will also receive less attention because financial, as opposed to sexual, probity has traditionally been focused on Ministers rather than Parliament as a whole. Financial misconduct is also less interesting to the media and the public unless, like the case of Keith Best, it involves a court case or, in that of John Stonehouse, it also involves sex. This is because of the lack of clarity in the rules, the problems of ambiguity, the lack of definitive information or the lack of Parliamentary decisiveness.

It could be argued that the media should concentrate on the more serious issues of misuse of power, lying and deceit by governments, but, as Peter Jenkins wrote of the Westland Affair: 'In general all such questions of constitutional or parliamentary procedure or propriety interest the governors more than they do the governed. Leaks in particular are a subject of endless fascination to politicians and the press but of little interest to the public. The

Westland Affair was an in-house scandal and in that way a very British scandal, except that for once it lacked sex.'[2] Furthermore, politicians in such cases are protected by the Official Secrets Act, the Lobby System, the obligation of silence for civil servants, the requirements of confidentiality on the part of Cabinet Ministers, the D-notice system, the tendency for cross-party collusion on issues of political sensitivity and the secretive environment of Westminster and Whitehall that excludes outsiders and, club-like, binds those on the inside to the unwritten but generally-understood conventions of discretion, accommodation and compromise. Taken together they make investigatory journalism into the political activities of politicians difficult. As the *Observer*'s editor, Donald Trelford, put it: 'The law doesn't touch papers who libel poor people, make up interviews, invade privacy, and engage in general muck-raking. But it makes life impossible for papers who want to investigate the rich and powerful, to probe the waste in government departments and to find out about the financial connections of politicians and their families',[3] a consequence noticeable when comparing the attention given to MPs' private lives or private finances.

## The Price Of A Free Lunch

On a hypothetical Tuesday, says Austin Mitchell MP, 'lunch can be at the expense of some pressure group, firm, embassy or any organisation unimaginative enough, or ill-informed about political realities, to want to impress MPs . . . "Gastronomic pimping", Aneurin Bevan called it.'[4] Some groups go further; they invite the MP to join their payroll. Parliament has never come to terms with whether being an MP is or is not a full-time, if precarious, occupation. At present the pay is modest but the facilities and resources are woefully inadequate. To ameliorate all three would not please Governments, who would not take kindly to finding themselves under permanent Parliamentary scrutiny. Furthermore, to do so would cut across the tradition of allowing MPs the independence and freedom to order their lives as they so wish. Of course many MPs enter Parliament after establishing careers elsewhere and would be loath to forgo the benefits and the income. It is also argued, somewhat spuriously, that continuing outside occupations puts MPs in touch with the 'real world.'

MPs have a public position – and a modest amount of political influence – that has its attractions for parts of the business world. Those in office who seek additional financial income occasionally find themselves embarrassingly caught up in some venture for which their image of trustworthiness has been of more value than their business expertise. On the other hand, the rules for the business interests of Ministers are designed to avoid that type of embarrassment. It is rare to find a political career, especially a Ministerial career, ended as a result of an ill-judged financial venture or financial interests which may overlap with their political duties. The only Minister in recent years to run into serious criticism was the tenth Lord Polworth, a Conservative Peer appointed a Minister of State at the Scottish Office in 1972 and given the responsibility of chairing an inter-departmental task force on North Sea oil developments. He and his family had a modest part of their trust holdings invested in oil-related companies. That interest was raised in the House, where Prime Minister Ted Heath pointed out that the trusts were independently managed and that the peer's small holdings in the trusts did not indicate a direct financial interest in oil companies: 'I do not regard Lord Polworth's shareholdings in these trusts as rightly to come in conflict with his duties and I do not see how it could be seriously argued that they might.' Nevertheless Polworth chose to sell his shareholdings to allow him to continue his work 'unhampered by a continuing campaign of unfounded innuendoes.'

Thus criticism of politicians' financial activities tends to be restricted to serious newspapers, whose readers are more likely to read such stories, and to those politicians involved with companies whose commercial practices are considered unorthodox or unusual. Thus Lonrho's payments of fees through tax havens to a Tory MP and former Minister, Peter Walker's involvement in the investment firm of Slater Walker, and the funding of a property empire by Keyser Ullman when chaired by Edward Du Cann attracted occasional critical media comment, much to the annoyance of those involved, inadvertently or otherwise. As Du Cann told reporters when asked about the 'social responsibility of property developers'; 'the mere fact I'm a politician doesn't mean I'm the particular chap you want to answer the question in order to expose myself to all sorts of situations – you won't get any embarrassing views from me'.[5] Similarly Peter Walker was adamant that 'I have always kept my political and business life totally separate. The description . . . that the business life benefited my political career and the two were interlinked is totally false . . . I have always refused to transact business for my insurance broking firm with any Member of Parliament or with any person or firm living in my constituency . . . I had numerous offers of business which I rejected on the grounds that I never wanted to be in a position of having a business relationship with someone I was representing in Parliament'.[6]

Nevertheless, there is evidence of growing concern at the increase in those MPs whose business interests may overlap with their Parliamentary position. 'It is evident', says Sandra Williams, 'that conflict of interest is not in itself an *act* of wrongdoing. It is a *situation* which might raise questions of improper motives, whereby an official has a direct or indirect private financial interest which might influence, or appear to influence, the performance of his public duties and responsibilities.'[7] The preference for the 'aura of collegiality that envelopes the House', protects it from further reform and ensures toleration of colleagues' activities is, by some, felt to be ineffective. Problems can arise because there are no clear rules on advocacy versus interest-representation and because the poverty of the information currently available does not allow anyone to judge whether an MP is working for an interest just for the money – a paid lobbyist – or because that is where his or her own interests, experience or expertise lie. It is equally difficult to judge whether the pursuit of the interest is complementary to, or conflicts with, the wider public interest. On the other hand there are many who believe outside interests encourage shared expertise and dialogue. In 1980 Tory MP Anthony Steen was talking to the Association of Consultant Architects about the value of having an MP on their side. In an internal aide-memoire, the Association were apparently told that 'MPs have little opportunity on their own to concentrate on any one group's interests or problems unless they have a special reason for doing so . . . If, however, a special interest group is prepared to sponsor an MP, or group of MPs, to pay them fees for their care and attention, this has proved to be an effective method.' The benefits are, apparently, that an MP, or MPs, could, 'at the ear of government . . . explain problems with particular care to Ministers, take the extra trouble required to put down questions, to prepare speeches on special interests that would otherwise go by default'.[8] In 1986 a Tory MP with Ministerial experience, Sir Alex Fletcher, was negotiating with a UK car dealership interested in the potential sell-off of the British Leyland truck and Land Rover divisions. Fletcher offered to help in 'negotiations with HMG, BL and other parties regarding the proposed acquisition': he proposed a £5000 briefing fee, a £5000 monthly retainer and either a total minimum payment of £15,000 or a £25,000 bonus if the negotiations were successful.[9] As the chairman of the Motorcycle Association told Tory MP Keith Speed, whose Westminster Communications company had saved its members some seventy thousand pounds in backdated VAT on motorcycle tests, 'this is a good example of how having a friendly man in the House of Commons can be enormous assistance to us'.[10]

Another Tory MP, Marcus Fox, a co-owner of Westminster Communications, was hired by the leading figure in the association of private open-cast operators to push the NCB to relax restrictions on open cast coal mining. Fox, with the help of a few colleagues, started 'inquiring and pushing' so that there was 'no doubt that the Coal Board now understand that there is a strong feeling in Parliament that this is an area that's got to be encouraged'.[11] Certainly, outside financial interests are keen to persuade politicians of the political as well as the commercial aspects of their case, and thus raises the second area of concern; the intertwining of business interests with ideological attitudes.

Former Labour MP Maureen Colquhoun wrote of her experiences of an Oil Taxation Bill Committee, that the men from the oil companies 'wrote notes to the Tory members of the Committee. They were effectively advisors to the Tory opposition on the Bill. They slotted additional information to the Tory members of the Committee, who already had prepared briefs, during the process of examining the Bill'.[12] With the advent of a radical Conservative government committed to ending state monopolies and opening up the opportunity for commercial expansion, both MPs and special interests have been noticeable in their attention to the decision-making processes, something the Labour Opposition have intermittently queried (to no real effect). In the July 1988 debate on the Finance Bill Labour MP Nick Brown complained that 'it was companies, and not constituencies, that were being represented at this stage of the Finance Bill' with property – not people – motivating the changes being proposed by MPs on behalf, he alleged, of 'an extraordinarily long list of vested interests, interests that could not possibly be those of the majority of any of these Members' constituents'. In 1987 Labour MP Ron Lewis argued that Tory MPs with interests in the alcohol industry should not be on the Standing Committee of the Licensing (Amendment) Bill which would 'increase the profits of the drinks trade'. In April 1988 Labour MP Bob Cryer, a longtime critic of MP-lobbyists, wanted to know whether Tim Smith, a Tory MP and a consultant to accountants Price Waterhouse, was putting down questions on Whitehall spending on management and computing consultancy contracts that could be related to Price Waterhouse's development of a business plan. He also raised the issue of merchant bank Morgan Grenfell's Parliamentary consultant, Tory MP Andrew MacKay, when he claimed that the bank had urged more use of the 'considerable talents' of the MP who was apparently responsible for reviving the bank's 'political acceptability' following its involvement in the Guinness affair.

The strongest complaints have been aimed at the lobbying for the Channel Tunnel legislation and contract where nearly forty MPs and Peers have had links with the various consortia. A BBC *Newsnight* film revealed one MP, Tory David Atkinson, who had failed to register an interest while another, Tory MP Den Dover, apparently cast an important vote on the choice of construction schemes as a member of the Transport Select Committee while a declared consultant to one of the competitors.

The reason why this is not a major source of controversy is that, with the House responsible for such matters (but unclear about enforcement), there is no external scrutiny or external rules against which to judge Members' behaviour. Police and DTI investigations have provided information and assessable criteria which can see an MP in court (as in the cases of Stonehouse and Best) or severely criticised (as in the case of Thorpe). Otherwise, because the conflict of interest is a situation (that means it may or may not conflict with an MP's Parliamentary duties) the media may risk libel proceedings for misinterpreting that potential conflict, as in the case of Peter Emery (see pp. 129–30). In February 1990 the Select Committee on Members' Interests placed the issue firmly before the House when it called on it to take early action in the 'light of the serious nature' of those complaints it upheld against Tory MP John Browne, including a 'client' relationship based on a Selco retainer 'which influenced his parliamentary actions and conduct as a member and which should have been declared on the Register.'[13]

## Sex And Politicians

For the majority of the media, therefore, taking on MP's financial interests is not, and has not been, their preferred objective. Audience and readership ratings are the basis of commercial success and they are best achieved by a safe, secure product that identifies closely with the interests and activities of their market and provides a mix of entertainment and information that is easy to digest and to communicate. This formula has long determined the influences within the media upon the sort of story they publish. Overlaid is the traditional political bias pursued by parts of the media, partly the result of proprietors and editors with a preference for supporting a particular pattern of existing values or attitudes; 'The traditional image of corporate management is often bland, profit-conscious and even cautious. Their political inclinations tend to be conservative rather than right-wing in the ideological sense. They would prefer not to "rock the boat" politically . . .'[14]

Of more interest than an MP's financial interests are MP's personal interests, and politicians who appear to step outside the orthodoxy or deviate from the essential qualities as perceived by much of the media, are treated with suspicion. In the hands of the popular press that suspicion can be rapidly translated into 'facts', preferably as sensational or scandalous as possible to excite the interests of their readers. Although such tendencies are dismissed as turning politics into soap opera, the media has long been aware that, to capture attention, individualisation in terms of readily-identifiable behaviour strikes the strongest chord with their audience. Thus, rather than try and penetrate the walls of the Establishment themselves, they will rely on information available, or purchaseable, in the public arena that will embarrass or expose politicians in terms of everyday prejudices – hypocrisy, extremism or deviance (or, preferably, any combination of them).

As the media's treatment of Peter Tatchell in the Bermondsey by-election paved the way for the 1983 'Red Scare' attacks on Labour in the subsequent General Election, so the February 1987 Greenwich by-election established the format for the Election held in 1987. Deirdre Wood had been a member of the London Labour Party faction espousing 'left' causes, such as supporting the visit of Sinn Fein councillors and the twinning of London Schools with UN Palestinian camps. The *News of the World* dug up a story on her late father's life of drunkenness and violence, the *Sun* alleged that she lived in a council flat while owning a Victorian terraced house and the *Daily Mail* revealed that her husband ran a wine bar. Wood lost the election with the Party unanimous in blaming the defeat on the 'smear' campaign. Probably her 'left' image had already put off the electorate, with the smears reinforcing her poor image, but the attacks on her were mirrored in the 1987 Election with Kinnock's press secretary, Patricia Hewitt, warning (in a letter leaked to the *Sun*) that 'the "loony Labour Left" is taking its toll . . . the gays and lesbian issue is costing us dear.'

The *Sun*, the *Star*, and the *News of the World* all published material concerning unfounded allegations of an over-close friendship between Liberal leader David Steel and the wife of a personal friend (the settlements were out of court with Steel getting £10,000 from the *Star*). The *News of the World* ran a 'My Love for Gay Labour Boss' story about Labour's Director of Communication. The later story was notable for the scattering of key words( 'bizarre', 'strange', 'AIDS', and 'weird', for example) to push home the allegations. A week later the *News of the World* came up with 'HATTERSLEY DOUBLE LIFE SENSATION' that purported to show Hattersley living in two £300,000 houses, one with his wife and one with his 'bachelor' girl. The *Sun* picked up the story and, after Hattersley issued writs, the *News of the World* returned to it the following week to make even more explicit allegations. The *Sun* then unearthed a two-year-old story about the hip operation for the wife of Dennis Healey at a private hospital. Former Tory Prime Minister, Ted Heath, called it 'the dirtiest election ever' as Labour's National Agent, David Hughes, remarked that 'I have never known such attacks on characters and personalities.'

In a campaign that largely focused on the leadership styles of the party leaders it is hardly surprising that personalities should be an issue. That their private lives should be closely scrutinised is also not surprising given the media's daily preference for sensation, sex and sordid details of anyone in the public eye. As Edward du Cann said of the Parkinson affair: 'I think there has been too much talk of this affair – the old English vice of humbug and hypocrisy has reigned supreme'.

Unfortunately, if the media is to continue in its reluctance to investigate the MPs' official activities and act as a public watchdog, then controls on what the media *do* print about politicians will be increasingly promoted. Invasion of Privacy and Right of Reply legislation has been suggested but in terms of adjudication and implementation raise more problems than they solve. Recourse to the courts for libel is increasingly the politician's main course for dealing with media intrusion. Libel[15], however, is a minefield that may be best negotiated not by a fair consideration of the facts but by the differing qualities of counsel and a host of extraneous factors that make winning or losing a lottery. That 'lottery' aspect is exacerbated by the jury having the power to determine the size of the award (in criminal cases they only determine guilt or innocence while the judge determines the sentence) and, despite the warning in the Aldington case in November 1989 by the judge about 'Mickey Mouse' awards, the jury has continued a trend of awarding punitive damages on the basis of past cases and the enthusiasm for plaintiffs' counsels to encourage juries to punish allegations against public figures excesses of the media. Certainly the thumping libel awards handed out in 1989 have scared most newspapers into a voluntary code of good behaviour while the rumblings of the Right to Reply and Privacy Bills can still be heard.

Nevertheless, whether they like it or not – and many do not – politicians' private and public behaviour, and whether either type of behaviour is expected of such people with a public position, are unlikely to go away as a subject of media scrutiny or public interest.

'Those', says Geoffrey Marshall, 'who are in the public eye are now more than ever subject to the threat of adverse publicity by informants actuated by stupidity, a sense of grievance, or political partisanship. Ministers and senior public servants cannot be insulated from the adverse impacts of public feelings, and the risk of publicity and ridicule . . . If in consequence a higher or at least more conventional standard of morality is required of politicians than is expected of private citizens that may not elicit much sympathy for them. It may be seen as one of the responsibilities and burdens entailed in thrusting oneself into public life, and part of the heat that those who will not stay out of the political kitchens are often exhorted to endure'.[16] Marshall argues that as one consequence of this is that there would appear to be a tradition where Ministers at least are not to be allowed to 'treat deviation from conventional sexual morality as a private matter that need not impinge upon their continuance and effectiveness in office'.[17]

The problem today is that the idea of a 'conventional standard of morality' is hard to define and as standards change, as in the years preceding Profumo, so people's attitudes to change themselves alter. There are those who believe that a politician's private life may have only a tenuous relationship (and their families even less so) to their public position, and that only in terms of their Parliamentary duties. On the other hand there are those who, as with the Profumo era, feel things have gone too far and that there should be a reassertion of 'traditional' values. Within this broad spectrum, the media – with an eye on sales and on what stories *are* available – appear to consider that politicians' lives are acceptable quarry and that there are still conventional standards of morality in a climate where, in February 1988, the Chancery Division of the High Court ruled that there is now 'no generally accepted code of sexual morality' and 'no common view that sexual conduct of any kind between consenting adults was grossly immoral'.[18]

Nevertheless, the fact that there is no agreement on acceptable sexual behaviour does not mean there is agreement on the acceptability, suitability or tolerance of different types of behaviour. Rather, the lack of any common view has allowed those with a view – the 'moral' Right and the 'Victorian Values' tendency that dominates the Conservative Party – to exploit the divisions and attack 'unorthodox' behaviour. In doing so they encourage intolerance and associate sexual diversity or openness with permissiveness and moral decline.

In trying to reimpose a moral consensus on a society

that has allegedly gone into moral decline in the last twenty-five years and in trying to reassert the Family and its values as society's moral core, the traditionalists revive other Victorian 'values' – prurient curiosity, political double standards and dual morality of public and private behaviour. Even a traditionalist like Chapman Pincher can write that 'the sex drive tends to be compulsive, especially when tempting circumstances exist or can be contrived, and it cuts clean across normal intelligence so that people are often prepared to take sacrificial risks to indulge it. The instances where politicians and other public figures have taken ludicrous risks to satisfy a sexual craving . . . are legion. Such people do not seem to be deterred by the certainty that, if they are exposed, the media publicity will destroy their career'.[19] Parliament has been and is tolerant of the private lives of its Members, conducted discreetly within the confines of the small political world. Mrs Thatcher herself is known to be highly tolerant of colleagues' weaknesses, problems or private liaisons. The phrase 'it's a private matter' occurs regularly whenever a Conservative politician is not reflecting 'normal moral behaviour'.

Those who transmit or exploit the new moral fervour, the media, do not seek to distinguish the private matter from the attack on the permissive society, nor are they particularly prone to compassion or tolerance. They are, moreover, highly competitive commercial concerns and, if sex has always been a tradition as strong as that of gossip and curiosity about the lives of public figures then pursuit of the unorthodox and, just as often, the orthodox is almost axiomatic. Of course it is rightly argued that a public figure's private life is reportable if it is relevant to his fitness to hold office. Increasingly it is that relevance that is being lost. What is therefore left in its place is a simple prurient curiosity about *what* the public figure was doing, rather than an assessment of whether that behaviour may have a bearing on his or her official duties and responsibilities or of whether he or she was exploiting an official position to gratify personal wishes.

That curiosity is, paradoxically, enhanced because public figures know – and have known for a long time –

317

that public scrutiny of their private sexual behaviour will not be judged in terms of their fitness for public office nor in terms of their general political and public worth. Since, for many, unusual or different sexual behaviour may be a sporadic or episodic business, they will try to avoid scrutiny by concealment or denial. But – as in the case of Harvey Proctor – that excites curiosity and provides a motive for investigation. It focuses attention on a specific aspect of behaviour and that in turn colours the perception of the individual. Harvey Proctor concealed his homosexuality and insisted on playing the orthodox, right-wing MP. The denial of his sexual preferences put tremendous pressure on the demands of his sexuality and one can only speculate upon 'the strength of the urges which drove him to take such stupid, squalid and petty gambles when he knew that his alleged sexual proclivities were already attracting attention from parts of the press'.[20]

Proctor also attracted the attention of the police, and the subsequent conviction made his resignation inevitable. Since his Party and constituency appeared either to tolerate or affect an ignorance of his activities one must wonder for what market the press were actively pursuing Proctor's homosexual escapades. There are some Conservative MPs who belligerently affirm their intolerance of such 'evil'. Nevertheless the Prime Minister has often made plain her tolerance of colleagues whose sexual activities are unorthodox: her loyalty to Cecil Parkinson has only served to underline her insistence in believing political worth more valuable than private shortcomings.

It would appear that, despite the changes in the law and in general attitudes, perceptions of the private behaviour of politicians are, given the trust and status attached to their public position, still governed by a belief in a standard of morality that is 'far more severe and restricted than that of ordinary people.' In the hands of those parts of the media that have taken a traditional interest in the private lives of public figures, failure to adhere to that standard is in itself newsworthy. The more senior the politician or the more moralistic the party's official stance on general behaviour, the greater value the news story.

While both the Denning Report and the Security Commission Report on the Lambton and Jellicoe cases emphasise the security and blackmail aspects of concealed sexual preferences, it is the tried and tested enthusiasm of the British public for stories of sexual misbehaviour that is the prime motivator, whether relevant to the public position or not.

Therefore, any politician who decides to pursue his sexual preferences in the light of the present confused and fluid attitude toward personal morality will continue to run the risk of public exposure. 'We are all responsible for our own actions', say Margaret Thatcher, 'we simply cannot delegate the exercise of mercy and generosity to others'. A useful piece of advice for anyone entering or in politics today.

# REFERENCES

## CHAPTER TWO: REPUTATIONS, RULES AND FLAWS

1. David Steel, *Against Goliath*, Weidenfeld and Nicolson, 1989, p. 110.
2. *The Times*, 12.10.1981.
3. *Observer*, 11.1.1987.
4. Austen Mitchell, *Westminster Man*, Thames Methuen, 1982, p. 242.
5. *Guardian*, 21.2.1975.


## CHAPTER THREE: MPs AND THE TRADITION OF ESSENTIAL QUALITIES

1. E. J. Evans, *The First Industrial Revolution: The Forging of the Modern State, 1783–1870*, Longman, 1983, p. 280.
2. L. C. B. Seaman, *Victorian England, Aspects of English and Imperial History, 1837–1901*, Methuen, 1973, p. 13.
3. Ronald Pearsall, *The Worm In The Bud*, Penguin Books, 1969, p. 19.
4. *Victorian England*, op.cit., p. 14.
5. T. O. Lloyd, *Empire to Welfare State: English History 1906–1985* (3rd Edition), OUP, 1986, p. 24.
6. H. G. G. Matthew, *Gladstone*, OUP, 1986, p. 91.
7. ibid., p. 92.
8. Henry Blythe, *Skittles*, Victorian and Modern History Clubs, 1972, p. 186.
9. Richard Deacon, *The Private Life of Mr Gladstone*, Frederick Muller, 1965, p. 171.
10. Meredith Etherington-Smith and Jeremy Pilcher, *The 'It' Girls*, Hamish Hamilton, 1986, pp. 141, 181. See also Kenneth Rose, *Superior Person: A Portrait of Curzon and His Circle in Late Victorian England*, Weidenfeld and Nicolson, 1969.

11. James Lees-Milne, *The Enigmatic Edwardian, The Life of Reginald, 2nd Viscount Esher*, Sidgwick and Jackson, 1986, p. 338
12. Sean Hignett, *Brett*, Hodder and Stoughton, 1984, p. 42.
13. G. A. Cranfield, *The Press and Society*, Longman, 1978, p. 212.
14. Margaret Fitzherbert, *The Man Who Was Greenmantle*, John Murray, p. 206.
15. J. M. W. Bean (ed.), *The Political Culture of Modern Britain: Studies in Memory of Stephen Koss*, Hamish Hamilton, 1987, p. 155.
16. ibid., pp. 150, 151.
17. John Grigg, *Lloyd George*, Methuen, 1985, p. 84. See also Don M. Creiger, *Bounder from Wales*, University of Missouri Press, 1976.
18. Duff Cooper, *Old Men Forget*, Rupert Hart-Davis, 1954, p. 384.
19. Phillip Ziegler, *Diana Cooper*, Hamish Hamilton, 1981, p. 110.
20. John Charmley, *Duff Cooper*, Weidenfeld and Nicolson, 1986, p. 216.
21. Tom Driberg, *Ruling Passions*, Jonathan Cape, 1977, p. 143.
22. Richard S. Lambert, *The Railway King*, Allen and Unwin, 1934, p. 22.
23. Alan Hyman, *The Rise and Fall of Horatio Bottomley*, Cassell, 1971, p. 132.
24. D. C. M. Platt, 'The Commercial and Industrial Interests of Ministers of the Crown', *Political Studies*, 1961, 1, p. 289.
25. See David Edward (ed.), *Inside Asquith's Cabinet; from the Diaries of Charles Hobhouse*, John Murray, 1977, p. 138.
26. See A. J. P. Taylor, *Beaverbrook*, Hamish Hamilton, 1972.
27. See John Campbell, *F. E. Smith: First Earl of Birkenhead*, Jonathan Cape, 1983.
28. See David Marquand, *Ramsay Macdonald*, Jonathan Cape, 1977, and Tom Cullen, *Maundy Gregory*, The Bodley Head, 1974.

## CHAPTER FOUR: SETTING THE AGENDA FOR TODAY'S SCANDAL

1. Robert Rhodes James, *Anthony Eden*, Weidenfeld and Nicolson, 1986, pp. 332, 347.
2. Donald Johnson, *A Cassandra at Westminster*, Johnson, 1967, p. 136.
3. Iain Crawford, *The Profumo Affair*, White Lodge Books, 1963, p. 58.
4. *Report of the Committee on Intermediaries*, HMSO, 1950, Cmnd. 7904, p. 67.
5. H. H. Wilson, *Pressure Group*, Secker and Warburg, p. 208
6. Graham Turner and John Pearson, *The Persuasion Industry*, Eyre and Spottiswoode, 1965, p. 159.
7. *Pressure Group*, op.cit., p. 95
8. Francis Noel-Baker, 'The Grey Zone: The Problems of Business

Affiliations of Members of Parliament', *Parliamentary Affairs*, 1961–2, vol. 15, p. 91.

9. Anthony Courtney, *Sailor in a Russian Frame*, Johnson, 1968, p. 9.
10. Bernard Levin, *The Pendulum Years*, Jonathan Cape, 1970, p. 68.
11. Randolph Churchill, *The Fight For The Tory Leadership*, Heinemann, 1967, p. 8.
12. Nigel Fisher, *Harold Macmillan*, Weidenfeld and Nicolson, 1982, pp. 364–5.
13. Harold Macmillan, *At the End of the Day Vol. 6*, Macmillan, 1973, p. 437.

## CHAPTER FIVE: MACMILLAN'S MEMBERS

1. Ian Harvey, *To Fall Like Lucifer*, Sidgwick and Jackson, 1971, p. 103.
2. ibid., p. 66.
3. ibid., p. 11
4. Ludovic Kennedy, *The Trial of Stephen Ward*, Victor Gollancz, 1969, p. 23.
5. *Times*, 18.7.1962.
6. Brian Inglis, *Private Conscience: Public Morality*, Four Square Books, 1964, p. 82.
7. Chapman Pincher, *Inside Story*, Sidgwick and Jackson, 1978, p. 95.
8. Rebecca West, *The Vassall Affair*, Sunday Telegraph Publishing, 1962, p. 9.
9. John Vassall, *The Autobiography of a Spy*, Sidgwick and Jackson, 1975, p. 67.
10. ibid., pp. 125, 131.
11. ibid., p. 14.
12. *The End of the Day*, op.cit., p. 424.
13. ibid., p. 431.
14. *The Vassall Affair*, op. cit., p. 71.
15. Quoted in *The End of the Day*, op.cit., p. 430.
16. *The Fight for The Tory Leadership*, op.cit., p. 43.
17. See *Report of the Tribunal Appointed to Inquire into the Vassall Case and Related Matters*, HMSO, Cmnd. 2009, 1963. Earlier reports dealing with aspects of the Vassall case were published in 1962 as Cmnd. 1618 and Cmnd. 1871.
18. *The End of the Day*, op.cit., pp. 435, 436.
19. *The Pendulum Years*, op.cit., p. 62.
20. Warwick Charlton and Gerald Sparrow, *Stephen Ward Speaks/The Profumo Affair*, Today Magazine, 1963, p. 46.
21. Clive Irving, Ron Hall, Jeremy Wallington, *Scandal '63*, Heinemann, 1963, pp. 29, 32.

22. Christine Keeler, *Nothing But . . . Christine Keeler*, NEL, 1983, p. 66.

23. See Anthony Summers and Stephen Dorril, *Honeytrap*, Weidenfeld and Nicolson, 1987.

24. See Phillip Knightley, *The Second Oldest Profession*, André Deutsch, 1986.

25. See Shirley Green, *Rachman*, Hamlyn Paperbacks, 1981.

26. Andrew Roth, *Sir Harold Wilson, Yorkshire Walter Mitty*, Macdonald and Jane, 1977, p. 279.

27. *Lord Denning's Report*, HMSO 1963, Cmnd 2152, p. 39.

28. Iain Crawford, *The Profumo Affair*, White Lodge Books, 1963, p. 12.

29. Nigel West, *A Matter of Trust*, Weidenfeld and Nicolson, 1982, p. 95.

30. See Chapman Pincher, *Too Secret, Too Long*, Sidgwick and Jackson, 1984.

31. Quoted in Alistair Horne, *Macmillan, 1957–1986*, Macmillan, 1989, p. 476.

32. Janet Morgan (ed.), *The Backbench Diaries of Richard Crossman*, Hamish Hamilton and Jonathan Cape, 1981, p. 989.

33. George Wigg, *George Wigg*, Michael Joseph, 1972, p. 267.

34. Hugh L'Etang, *The Pathology of Leadership*, William Heinemann Medical Books, 1969, p. 175.

35. *Scandal '63*, op.cit., p. 108.

36. *The Backbench Diaries of Richard Crossman*, op.cit., p. 994.

37. See Phillip Knightley and Caroline Kennedy, *An Affair of State*, Jonathan Cape, 1987.

38. *The Pendulum Years*, op.cit., p. 61.

39. ibid., pp. 47–8.

40. Wayland Young, *The Profumo Affair: Aspects of Conservatism*, Penguin Books, 1963, p. 55.

41. *The Trial of Stephen Ward*, op.cit., p. 23.

42. *The Profumo Affair: Aspects of Conservatism*, op.cit., p. 111.

43. In Anthony Courtney, *Sailor In A Russian Frame*, Johnson, 1968, p. 9.

CHAPTER SIX: PROFUMO, SCANDAL AND THE MEDIA

1. *At The End Of The Day*, op.cit., p. 451.

2. Ibid., p. 442.

3. *The Backbench Diaries of Richard Crossman*, op.cit., p. 989.

4. *Scandal '63*, op.cit., pp. 217, 219.

5. *At The End Of The Day*, op.cit., p. 451.

6. *The Pendulum Years*, op.cit., p. 78

7. *Sunday Times*, 23.6.1963.

## CHAPTER SEVEN: A DECADE OF . . . PART ONE

1. Peter Tatchell, *The Battle for Bermondsey*, Heretic Books, 1983, p. 55.
2. ibid., p. 63.
3. *Daily Telegraph*, 21.11.1981.
4. *News of the World*, 29.7.1984.
5. *Guardian*, 19.8.1986.
6. *Daily Telegraph*, 12.6.1986.
7. *Observer*, 22.6.1986.
8. Penny Junor, *Margaret Thatcher*, Sidgwick and Jackson, 1983, p. 114
9. Patricia Murray, *Margaret Thatcher*, W. H. Allen, 1980, p. 64.
10. ibid., p. 63.,
11. *Observer*, 5.2.1984.
12. *Mail on Sunday*, 29.1.1984.
13. *Sunday Times*, 4.3.1984.
14. ibid.
15. *Sunday Times*, 12.8.1984.
16. *Observer*, 5.2.1984.
17. *World in Action*, 23.7.1984.
18. *Select Committee on Members Interests*, HMSO, HCP 330, 1983–4.
19. Richard Hall, *My Life with Tiny*, Faber and Faber, 1987, p. 187.

## CHAPTER EIGHT: A DECADE . . . PART TWO

1. Michael Gillard, *In the Name of Charity: The Rossminster Affair*, Chatto and Windus, 1987, p. 170.
2. ibid., p. 272.
3. *New Statesman*, 5.3.198811.
4. Maureen Colquhoun, *A Woman In The House*, Scan Books, 1980, p. 86.
5. Ronald Kessler, *Khashoggi*, Corgi Books, 1986, p. 272.
6. See Alan Doig, *Corruption and Misconduct in Contemporary British Politics*, Penguin Books, 1984, pp. 322–327.

## CHAPTER NINE: FOR THEIR LORDSHIPS' PLEASURE . . .

1. Bert Wickstead, *Gangbuster*, Futura, 1985, p. 104.
2. J. Prior, *A Balance of Power*, Hamish Hamilton, 1986, p. 83.
3. *Gangbuster*, op.cit., p. 106.
4. Chapman Pincher, op.cit., p. 272.
5. *The Times*, 25.5.1973.
6. *A Balance of Power*, op.cit., p. 83

7. *Guardian*, 25.5.1973.
8. John Grant, *Member of Parliament*, Michael Joseph, 1974, p. 158.
9. Geoffrey Marshall, *Constitutional Conventions*, OUP, 1984, p. 103.
10. ibid., p. 105.
11. *Sunday Times*, 27.5.1973.

CHAPTER TEN: THE PROBLEM IS, OF COURSE, ONE OF MONEY . . .

1. Reginald Maudling, *Memoirs*, Sidgwick and Jackson, 1978, p. 143.
2. *Economist*, 22.7.1972.
3. *The Times*, 19.7.1972.
4. *The Times*, 14.2.1979.
5. *Sunday Telegraph*, 14.5.1961.
6. *Report from the Select Committee on Conduct of Members*, HCP 490, 1976–77, para. 467.
7. For a survey of the Seventies' corruption cases see Alan Doig, *Corruption and Misconduct in Contemporary British Politics*, op. cit.
8. Martin Tompkinson and Michael Gillard, *Nothing to Declare*, John Calder, 1980, p. 170.
9. Andrew Roth, *The Business Background of MPs*, Parliamentary Profile Services, 1965, p. xii.
10. See *Guardian*, 21.7.1972 and Michael Gillard, *A Little Pot of Money*, Private Eye/André Deutsch, 1974.
11. House of Commons Debates (5th series), vol. 874, col. 456.
12. See Raymond Fitzwalter and David Taylor, *Web of Corruption*, Granada, 1981.
13. *Memoirs*, op.cit., p. 169.

CHAPTER ELEVEN: NOT EVEN A MINNOW . . .

1. *Nothing to Declare*, op.cit., p. 129.
2. 'The Grey Zone; The Problems of Business Affiliations of Members of Parliament', *Parliamentary Affairs*, op,cit., pp. 91, 92.
3. See *Report of the Select Committee on Members' Interests (Declarations)*, 1969–70, HCP 157.

CHAPTER TWELVE: THE DISAPPEARING MINISTER . . .

1. Richard Crossman, *The Diaries of a Cabinet Minister*, Vol. 3, Hamish Hamilton and Jonathan Cape, 1977, p. 343.

2. John Stonehouse, *Death of an Idealist*, W. H. Allen, 1975, p. 99. See also John Stonehouse, *My Trial*, Star Books, 1976.
3. *DTI Report on London Capital Group Ltd.*, HMSO, 1977, p. 14.
4. *Death of an Idealist*, op.cit., p. 125.
5. *DTI Report on London Capital Group Ltd.*, op.cit., p. 71.
6. *Death of an Idealist*, op.cit., p. 149.
7. *Sunday Times*, 8.12.1974.
8. See the *Reports of the Select Committee on the Right Honourable Member for Walsall North*, HMSO, 1974–5 (First Report; HCP 273. Second Report; HCP 347. Third Report; HCP 373. Fourth Report; HCP 414).
9. *DTI Report on London Capital Group Ltd.*, op.cit., p. 7.
10. ibid., p. 15.
11. *Guardian*, 7.8.1976.
12. Quoted in H. Montgomery Hyde, *A Tangled Web*, Constable, 1986, pp. 322–3.

## CHAPTER THIRTEEN: SLAG HEAPS . . .

1. Richard Crossman, *The Diaries of a Cabinet Minister*, Vol. 2, Hamish Hamilton and Jonathan Cape, 1977, p. 160.
2. Sandy Gall, *Don't Worry About the Money Now*, Hamish Hamilton, 1982, p. 202.
3. Bernard Levin, *The Pendulum Years*, Jonathan Cape, 1970, pp. 244–5.
4. *The Backbench Diaries of Richard Crossman*, op.cit., p. 987.
5. Susan Crosland, *Tony Crosland*, Jonathan Cape, 1982, pp. 169–70.
6. James Margach, *The Abuse of Power*, Star Books, 1978, p. 141.
7. *George Wigg*, op.cit., p. 315.
8. Barbara Castle, *The Castle Diaries, 1964–70*, Weidenfeld and Nicolson, 1984, p. 158.
9. Joe Haines, *The Politics of Power*, Coronet, 1977, pp. 159–60.
10. *Sir Harold Wilson, Yorkshire Walter Mitty*, op.cit., p. 195.
11. George Thomas, *Mr Speaker*, Century Publishing, 1985, op.cit., p. 85.
12. *The Abuse of Power*, op.cit., p. 151.
13. *News of the World*, 20.2.1977.
14. *Sunday Times*, 13.2.1977.
15. Marcia Williams, *Downing Street In Perspective*, Weidenfeld and Nicolson, 1983, pp. 19, 23, 30.
16. *Inside Story*, op.cit., p. 282.
17. *Daily Mail*, 18.2.1977.
18. *Downing Street In Perspective*, op.cit., p. 23.
19. ibid., p. 46.
20. ibid., p. 96.

21. *The Politics of Power*, op.cit., p. 222.
22. Marcia Williams, *Inside Number 10*, NEL, 1972, p. 196.
23. *Inside Story*, op.cit., p. 248.
24. *The Times*, 24.7.1974.
25. *The Politics of Power*, op.cit., p. 218.
26. See *Sunday Times*, 30.5.1976.
27. *Sunday Times*, 14.4.1974.
28. See *Guardian*, 24.3.1976.
29. *Sunday Times*, 14.4.1974.
30. *Inside Story*, op.cit., p. 282.
31. *The Politics of Power*, op.cit., p. 203
32. *House of Commons Debates* (5th series), Vol. 871, col. 1441.
33. *A Woman In The House*, op.cit., p. 28.
34. *Inside Story*, op.cit., p. 286.
35. *Daily Mail*, 8.4.1974.
36. *Sunday Times*, 14.4.1974.
37. Ibid.
38. *House of Commons Debates* (5th series), Vol. 877, col. 32–33.
39. *Downing Street In Perspective*, op.cit., p. 150.
40. *The Politics of Power*, op.cit., pp. 205–6.

## CHAPTER FOURTEEN: TRIALS OF JEREMY THORPE

1. Peter Bessell, *Cover-Up*, Simon Books Inc. (USA), 1980. The book, which covers Bessell's life, was never published in this country.
2. Lewis Chester, Magnus Linklater, David Hay, *Jeremy Thorpe: A Secret Life*, Fontana, 1979, p. 81.
3. *DTI Report on London and County Securities Ltd.*, HMSO, 1976, p. 58.
4. Cyril Smith, *Big Cyril*. Star Books, 1978, p. 187.
5. *A Secret Life*, op.cit., p. 134.
6. *New Statesman*, 13.3.1979.
7. *A Secret Life*, op.cit., pp. 146–7. See also Auberon Waugh, *The Last Word*, Michael Joseph, 1980, pp. 173–4, 189.
8. Gordon Winter, *Inside BOSS*, Penguin, 1981, p. 396.
9. *New Statesman*, 29.6.1979.
10. Barry Penrose and Roger Courtiour, *The Pencourt File*, Secker and Warburg, 1978, p. 155.
11. *A Secret Life*, op.cit., p. 203.
12. *Sunday Times*, 11.7.1976.
13. *Sunday Times*, 14.3.1976.
14. *New Statesman*, 14.9.1979.
15. *Sunday Times*, 4.5.1976.
16. *Guardian*, 15.3.1976.

17. *Mr Speaker*, op.cit., pp. 146–7.
18. *Guardian*, 15.3.1976.
19. *Sunday Telegraph*, 30.10.1977.
20. *The Pencourt File*, op.cit., p. 178.
21. *A Secret Life*, op.cit., pp. 276–7.
22. *Observer*, 23.10.1977.
23. *Sunday Times*, 26.2.1978.
24. *A Secret Life*, op.cit., p. 116.
25. See Peter Chippindale and David Leigh, *The Thorpe Committal*, Arrow Books, 1979.
26. *A Secret Life*, op.cit., p. 300.
27. Sir David Napley, *Not Without Prejudice*, Harrap, 1982, p. 428.
28. *Cover-Up*, op.cit., p. 498.
29. *News of the World*, 31.5.1981.

## CHAPTER FIFTEEN: 1976: HAROLD WILSON'S RESIGNATION

1. See John Walker, *The Queen Has Been Pleased*, Sphere Books, 1986.
2. Harold Wilson, *The New Britain: Labour's Plan*, Penguin, 1964, pp. 13, 59.
3. Interview on ITN *News at Ten*, 15.2.1977.
4. *Downing Street In Perspective*, op.cit., p. 176.
5. *Sir Harold Wilson, Yorkshire Walter Mitty*, op.cit., p. 38.
6. *Sunday Times*, 30.5.1976.
7. ibid.
8. Michael Adams and Christopher Mayhew, *Publish It Not . . .*, Longman, 1975, p. 38.
9. Bernard Donoughue, *The Conduct of Policy under Harold Wilson and James Callaghan*, Jonathan Cape, 1987, p. 87.
10. *Daily Telegraph*, 19.2.1977.
11. *The Politics of Power*, op.cit., p. 212.
12. *Daily Mail*, 26.9.1974.
13. *Sunday Times*, 4.2.1979.
14. *Sunday Times*, 2.10.1977.
15. *Observer*, 4.2.1979.
16. *DTI Report on Peachey Property Corporation Ltd.*, HMSO, 1979.
17. *Sunday Times*, 21.12.1980.
18. *News of the World*, 14.12.1980.
19. *Sunday Times*, 14.7.1981.
20. *Observer*, 17.7.1977.
21. *Inside Story*, op.cit., p. 16.
22. Quoted in *The Pencourt File*, op.cit., p. 233.

23. Peter Wright, *Spycatcher*, Dell (USA), 1988, p. 362–3. See also Phillip Williams, *Hugh Gaitskell*, Jonathan Cape, 1979 and Anatoli Golitsyn, *New Lies for Old*, The Bodley Head, 1984.
24. Barrie Penrose and Simon Freeman, *Conspiracy of Silence*, Grafton Books, 1987, p. 478.
25. Chapman Pincher, *Their Trade Is Treachery*, Sidgwick and Jackson, 1981, p. 248.
26. *Spycatcher*, op.cit., p. 365.
27. ibid., p. 370.
28. David Leigh, *The Wilson Plot*, Heinemann, 1988, p. 252.

## CHAPTER SIXTEEN: PARKINSON

1. *Sunday Times*, 16.10.1983.
2. ibid.
3. ibid.
4. Sara Keays, *A Question of Judgement*, Quintessential Press, 1986, p. 15.
5. *Observer*, 9.10.1983.
6. *A Question of Judgement*, op.cit., p. 14.
7. ibid., p. 25.
8. See Norman Tebbit, *Upwardly Mobile*, Weidenfeld and Nicolson, 1988.
9. *Observer*, 13.10.1985.
10. ibid.
11. Graeme Moodie reviewing *A Question of Judgement* in *Corruption and Reform*, Vol. 1, No. 3, 1986, p. 270.
12. Henry Porter, *Lies, Damned Lies and Some Exclusives*, Chatto and Windus, 1984, pp. 63–4.
13. *Guardian*, 11.6.1985.
14. *Independent*, 31.5.1987.
15. *Observer*, 14.6.1987.
16. Moodie, op.cit., p. 268.
17. *Independent*, 22.10.1988.

## CHAPTER EIGHTEEN: ARCHER

1. *Observer*, 2.11.1986.
2. Harold Wilson, *The Labour Government 1964–70*, Weidenfeld and Nicolson, 1971, pp. 686–7.
3. *Spectator*, 4.3.1972.
4. *Mail on Sunday*, 2.11.1986.
5. See *Sunday Telegraph* magazine, 13.12.1987.

6. See *New Statesman*, 31.7.1987.
7. *Observer*, 2.11.1986.


CHAPTER TWENTY: BEST

1. *Rebecca*, September 1981, p. 20.


CHAPTER TWENTY-ONE: THE PRIVATE LIVES OF POLITICIANS

1. *Independent*, 11.6.1988.
2. Peter Jenkins, *Mrs Thatcher's Revolution*, Jonathan Cape, 1987, p. 204.
3. Quoted in Mark Hollinsworth, *The Press and Political Dissent*, Pluto, 1986, p. 34.
4. *Westminster Man*, op.cit., p. 71.
5. *News of the World*, 20.1.1974.
6. Charles Raw, *Slater Walker*, Coronet Books, 1978, p. 405.
7. Sandra Williams, *Conflict of Interest*, Gower, 1985, p. 130.
8. Andrew Roth, *The Business Background of MPs*, Parliamentary profiles, 1981, p i-ii.
9. *Observer*, 7.6.1987.
10. TV Eye, 'A Word In The Right Ear', *Thames Television*, 26.4.1984.
11. World In Action, 'Plans For Coal', *Granada Television*, 29.10.1984.
12. *A Woman In The House*, op.cit., p. 128.
13. First Report, *Select Committee on Members' Interests*, HMSO 1989-90, HCP 135, pp. xxxii–xxxiii.
14. *The Press and Political Dissent*, op.cit., p. 17.
15. See Peter Carter-Ruck, *Libel And Slander*, Faber and Faber, 1972, and David Hooper, *Public Scandal, Odium and Contempt*, Secker and Warburg, 1984.
16. *Constitutional Conventions*, op.cit., p. 110.
17. *Constitutional Conventions*, op.cit., p. 223.
18. *Independent*, 27.2.1988.
19. Chapman Pincher, *Traitors*, Sidgwick and Jackson, 1987, p. 89.
20. *Independent*, 22.5.1987.

# ADDITIONAL BIBLIOGRAPHY

Bruce Arnold, *Margaret Thatcher: A Study in Power*, Hamish Hamilton, 1984.

Stanley Wade Baron, *The Contact Man*, Secker and Warburg, 1966.

T. V. Beckett, *The Aristocracy in England 1660–1914*, Basil Blackwell, 1986.

Sissela Bok, *Lying: Moral Choice in Public and Private Life*, Pantheon Books (USA), 1978

J. M. Bourne, *Patronage and Society in Nineteenth Century England*, Edward Arnold, 1986.

George Boyce, James Curran, Pauline Wingate (eds), *Newspaper History*, Constable/Sage, 1978.

Andrew Boyle, *The Climate of Treason*, Coronet Books, 1980.

Trevor Burridge, *Clement Attlee*, Jonathan Cape, 1985.

James Champlin, *The Rise of Plutocrats*, Constable, 1978.

Kellow Chesney, *The Victorian Underworld*, Temple Smith, 1970.

Michael Clarke, *Fallen Idols*, Junction Books, 1981.

Michael Cockerell, Peter Hennessy and David Walker, *Sources Close to the Prime Minister*, Macmillan, 1984.

Robert Colls and Phillip Dodd, *Englishness: Politics and Culture 1880–1920*, Croom Helm, 1986.

Richard Deacon, *A History of the British Secret Service*, Frederick Muller, 1969.

Alan Doig, 'Registering Lobbyists', *Parliamentary Affairs*, 1986, Vol. 39.

Alan Doig, 'Access to Parliament and The Rise of the Professional Lobbyist', *Public Money*, March 1986.

Alan Doig, 'You Publish At Your Peril! The Restraints on Investigatory Journalism' in Michael Clark (ed.), *Corruption: Causes, Consequences and Control*, Frances Pinter, 1983.

Frances Donaldson, *The Marconi Scandal*, Rupert Hart-Davis, 1962.

Diana Farr, *Five at 10*, André Deutsch, 1985.

Professor S. E. Finer, 'The Individual Responsibility of Ministers', *Public Administration*, 1956, Vol. 34.

J. L. Garvin, *Life of Joseph Chamberlain*, vol. 3, Macmillan, 1934.

B. B. G. Gilbert, *David Lloyd George: A Political Life*, B. T. Batsford, 1987.

Richard Hamer, *The Vatican Connection*, Penguin Books, 1982.

H. Hanham, 'The Sale of Honours in Late Victorian England', *Victorian Studies*, 1959–60.

James Hemming, 'Morality and Politics', *New Society*, 9.5.1974.

Mike Hepworth, *Blackmail*, Routledge and Kegan Paul, 1975.

Louis Heren, *The Power of the Press*, Orbis, 1985.

E. J. Hobsbawm, *The Age of Empire*, Weidenfeld and Nicolson, 1987.

David Hooper, *Official Secrets*, Secker and Warburg, 1987.

Alastair Horne, *Macmillan 1894–1956*, Macmillan, 1988.

Robert Rhodes James (ed.), *Memoirs of a Conservative*, Weidenfeld and Nicolson, 1969.

Roy Jenkins, *Sir Charles Dilke*, Collins, 1958.

A. G. Jordan and J. J. Richardson, *Government and Pressure Groups in Britain*, OUP, 1987.

George W. Keeton, *Trial by Tribunal*, Museum Press, 1960.

Phillip Knightley, *The First Casualty*, Parnell Book Services/André Deutsch, 1975.

Stephen Koss, *The Rise and Fall of the Political Press in Britain, Vol. 2*, Hamish Hamilton, 1984.

Richard Lamb, *The Failure of the Eden Government*, Sidgwick and Jackson, 1987.

David Leigh, *The Frontiers of Secrecy*, Junction Books, 1980.

Henry Lewin, *The Railway Mania and its Aftermath*, David and Charles, 1968.

T. O. Lloyd, 'The Whip as Paymaster: Herbert Gladstone and Party Organisation', *English Historical Review*, Vol. 89, 1974.

Tom Lupton and C. Shirley Wilson, 'The Social Background and Connections of "Top Decision Makers"', in Richard Rose (ed.), *Policy-Making in Britain*, Macmillan, 1969.

F. S. L. Lyons, *The Fall of Parnell*, Routledge and Kegan Paul, 1960.

Barry Magill, 'Glittering Prizes and Party Funds in Perspective, 1882–1931', *Bulletin of the Institute of Historical Research*, 1982, Vol. 55.

Joyce Marlow, *The Uncrowned Queen of Ireland*, Weidenfeld and Nicolson, 1975.

Donald McCormick, *Pedlar of Death*, MacDonald, 1965.

John McEwen (ed.) *The Riddell Diaries, 1908–1923*, Athlone Press, 1986.

David McKie and Chris Cook (eds), *The Decade of Disillusionment*, Macmillan, 1972.

A. J. M. Milne, 'Reason, Morality and Politics' in B. Parekh and R. N. Berki (ed.) *The Morality of Politics*, George Allen & Unwin, 1972.

C. C. O'Brien, *Parnell and His Party 1880–90*, OUP, 1957.

Frank Owen, *Tempestuous Journey*, Hutchinson, 1954.

Bruce Page, David Leitch, Phillip Knightley, *Philby*, Penguin Books, 1969.

H. Perkin, *The Origins of Modern English Society, 1780–1880*, Routledge & Kegan Paul, 1972.

Ben Pimlott, *Hugh Dalton*, Jonathan Cape, 1985

Edward and Annie G. Porritt, *The Unreformed House of Commons*, CUP, 1903.

Ralph E. Pumphrey, 'The Introduction of Industrialists into The British Peerage', *American Historical Review*, 1959, vol. 65.

Jonathan Raban, *Coasting*, Collins/Harvill, 1986.

Adam Raphael, *My Learned Friends*, W. H. Allen, 1989.

Peter Rawlinson, *A Price Too High*, Weidenfeld and Nicolson, 1989.

J. J. Richardson and A. G. Jordan, *Governing Under Pressure*, Martin Robertson, 1979.

K. G. Robertson, *Public Secrets*, Macmillan, 1982.

Madeline R. Robinton, 'The British Method of Dealing with Political Corruption' in Arnold J. Heidenheimer (ed.), *Political Corruption*, Holt Rinehart & Winston (USA), 1970.

Michael Rosenthal, *The Character Factory*, Collins, 1986.

*Royal Commission on the Press*, HMSO, 1977, Cmnd. 6810.

Anthony Sampson, *Macmillan*, Allen Lane, 1967.

G. R. Searle, *Corruption in British Politics 1895–1930*, OUP, 1987.

Brian Sedgemore, *The Secret Constitution*, Hodder and Stoughton, 1980.

Colin Simpson, Lewis Chester, David Leitch, *The Cleveland Street Affair*, Little, Brown & Co., 1976.

Michael Sissons and Phillip French (eds), *Age of Austerity*, Greenwood Press (USA), 1963.

A. J. P. Taylor, *Essays in English History*, Hamish Hamilton, 1976.

Hugh Thomas (ed.), *The Establishment*, Ace Books, 1962.

Nikoli Tolstoy, *The Minister and the Massacres*, Century Hutchinson, 1986.

R. C. Trebilcock, 'A Special Relationship: Government, Rearmament and the Cordite Firms', *Economic History Review*, 1966, Vol. 2.

E. S. Turner, *Roads to Ruin*, Penguin Books, 1950.

John Turner, *Lloyd George's Secretariat*, CUP, 1980.

John Urry and John Wakeford (eds), *Power in Britain*, Heinemann Education Books, 1973.

Anthony Verner, *Through The Looking Glass*, Jonathan Cape, 1983.

Simon Winchester, *Outposts*, Hodder and Stoughton, 1985.

# Index

Aitken, Jonathan 141
Archer, Jeffrey 15; background, 281–3; contact with Coghlan, 284–5; legal action 285–6; *News of the World* story, 287; *Star* story, 288; libel action, 288–9
Archer, Mary 289
Asquith, H. 34
Atkinson, David 312
Atlee, Clement 49
Avon, Lord 123

Bagier, Gordon 168, 180
Balfour, A. J. 27, 38
Barber, Anthony 123
Bates, Alfred 43
Beaverbrook, Lord 40, 45
Belcher, John 44
Bellingham, Henry 7
Bendelow, Martin 102–3
Benyon, Tom 130, 137
Bermingham, Gerry 146–7
Berry, Antony 127
Bessell, Peter 216, 219, 224–6, 234–5, 237
Best, Keith 295, 296–300
Billing, Pemberton 33
Binstock, Judah 250
Blake, George 63
Bonar Law, A. 40
Boothby, Bob 15, 21, 42, 51, 52
Bordes, Pamella, 4; background 4–5; exposed in press, 8; discovered in Bali, 9; life-stories, 10
Bottomley, Horatio 38

Brayley, Lord Desmond 244, 245–7
Brown, George 69
Brown, Lord Wilfred, 205–243
Brown, Ron 150–2
Brown Nick 311
Browne, Elizabeth, 143
Browne, John 143–6, 312
Brotherton, Michael 126
Buckley, Sheila, 197–8
Burca, Marc 5
Butcher, Herbert 169, 170
Butt, Alfred 43
Byers, Lord 220, 227

Callaghan, James 175, 185, 255
Carr, Robert, 158
Carrington, Lord, 68, 70, 156
Castle, Barbara 82
Cementation International 115
Channon, Henry 'Chips' 36
Channon, Olivia 113
Churchill, Randolph 70
Churchill, Winston (the younger) 126, 142–3, 256
Churchill, Winston 41
Clarke, Kenneth 112
Clarke, Sue 112
Cockeram, Eric 299
Coghlan, Monica 279–81, 284–5, 288
Collinson, Pamela 105–7
Colquhoun, Maureen 135–7, 211, 311
Construction Promotions 169–70, 183

Cooper, Duff 35
Cordle, John 169–70, 175, 179, 182–6
Courtney, Anthony 90–93
Crossman, Dick 16, 20, 82, 84, 188, 203
Cryer, Bob 311
Cudliff, Lord Hugh 305
Cummings, John 132–3
Curzon, Lord George 31

*Daily Express* 3, 9
*Daily Mail*, 4
Dalton, Hugh 44
Davy McKee 144
Deakin, George 233–4, 236, 238
Deeling, Harry 47
Denning, Lord 87, 90; Report 95–6, 139
Dickens, Geoffrey 148–50
Dilke, Charles 30
Dinshaw, Nadir 225, 235
Disraeli, Benjamin 27
Donoughue, Bernard 211, 244
Dover, Den 312
Driberg, Tom 36, 46
Du Cann, Edward 22, 309, 314
Dunn, James 127

Eden, Anthony 47, 48
Edgecombe, Johnny 78
Edwards, Nicholas 110
Emery, Peter 129–130, 312
Esher, Reginald 2nd Viscount 32
Etheridge, Ken 200

Fairburn, Nicholas 137–9
Fallon, Michael 126
Field, Tony 207–210
Field, William 46
Fisher, Lord Samuel 206–243
Fletcher, Sir Alex 310
Fletcher-Cooke, Charles 60–61
Fox, Marcus 276–310
Freud, Clement 128

Galbraith, Thomas 61–71
Galloway, George 147–8
George, David Lloyd 34, 39, 41
Gibson, George 44
Gladstone, William 29
Golding, John 303
Goldsmith, Sir James 242, 245
Goodman, Lord Arnold 142, 206, 210, 225–6, 243
Gordon, 'Lucky' 78, 86
Gowrie, Lord Ian 304
Grant, John 162

Haines, Joe 205, 207, 211, 214, 245
Hampson, Keith 276–8
Harcourt, Lewis 32
Harper, Victor 209
Harvey, Ian 55–7, 91
Hattersley, Roy 314
Healey, Dennis 314
Heath, Edward 17, 308, 314; and Courtney 92; and Lambton 158, 160–1; and Maudlin 186
Heseltine, Michael 276
Hicks, Robert 108
Hoare, Samuel 40
Hogg, Katherine 112
Hollis, Roger 74, 81
Holman, Percy 204
Holmes, David 224, 226, 233–4, 235, 236, 239
Honours, sale of 41
Hooson, Emlyn 220, 227, 228
Horobin, Sir Ian 57–60
Houghton, Harry 62
House of Commons: Research assistants, 6; Select Committee (Commons Services), 7; Financial Rules 37, 40, 42, 118, 174–6, 307–312, 313; Rules and conduct 21, 45, 306–7, 312–3, 316–9; Lobbying 49–51, 167–8, 179–181

Howe, Alex 112
Hudson, George 37

*Independent* 273, 303
Isaacs, Godfrey 39
Ivanov, Eugene 74

Jellicoe, Earl 160–2
Jenkins, Bernard 112
Jenkins, Peter 306
Jones, Gwilym 101
Joseph, Sir Keith 102

Kagan, Lord Joseph 243, 251–55, 257
Kaye, Sir Emmanuel 244
Keays, Sarah 13, and press 262, 67, 271 and Parkinson 262, 264–7, 267, 269
Keeler, Christine 53, 86, 89; and Ward 73; and Ivanov 74 and Profumo 75
Kerby, Henry 81
Key, Charles 44
Khashoggi, Adnan 5, 10, 40, 140–1
Khashoggi, Soraya 140–3
King, Lisa 112
Kinnock, Neil 18, 120, 121, 298
Kissin, Lord 244
Kurtha, Aziz 280–1, 285, 288

Lambton, Lord Anthony 155–164
Lamont, Norman 126
Lawson, Nigel 19
Lawson, Nigella 112
Le Mesurier, John 233–4, 236, 238
Leadbitter, Ted 277
Lee, Erica 8
Leigh, David, 259
Levin, Bernard 87, 97
Levy, Colin 157, 159, 163
Levy, Norma 157–9

Lewis, John 78
Lewis, Ron 311
Lloyd, Nick 304
Longden, Nonna 151–2
Lonsdale, Gordon (aka Molody) 62
Lovell, Terry 304

MacDonald, Ramsey 41, 43
MacInnes, Alasdair 139
MacInnes, Suzanne 139
MacKay, Andrew 311
MacKay, Margaret 167
MacMillan, Harold 52, 60–61, 68, 72, 82, 88, 96
*Mail on Sunday* 116, 285, 286, 305
Makin, Rex 134, 147
Marconi scandal 38–39
Mardy Jones, T. I. 47
Marshall, Geoffrey 163, 315–6
Maudling, Reginald 165, 170–3, 175–7, 184–6, 220, 248
McIlvanney, Hugh 304
McNamara, Kevin 125
Meacher, Michael 16
Members Interests, Select Committees on 120, 181–2, 312
MI5 and Keeler 76, 79, 80, 81, 85; and Lambton 158; and Thorpe 222, 225; and Wilson 255
Milhench, Ronald 209–10
Miller, David 233–4
Miller, Eric 166, 171, 244, 247–251
Milne, Eddie 122
Milne, Pamela 137, 139
Mitchell, Austen 20, 307
Monteagle Marketing 117–8
Montgomery, David 286–7
Moodie, Graeme 269, 270
Moynihan, Colin 7
Murray, Albert 249

Neil, Andrew 5, 269
*News of the World*, 6, 7, 215, 224, 239, 281, 284, 287, 303, 313–4

Newton, Andrew 223, 225, 233–4, 238
Noel-Baker, Francis 50, 180
Nott, John 130

*Observer* 115, 146, 175, 184–5, 290, 297, 303, 305
Oldfield, Maurice 258
Orbach, Maurice 249
Owen, Will 194, 243

Parkinson, Cecil 13, 14, 19, 261, and Sarah Keays 262–3, 267, 269; political life 264, 270–1; financial matters 264, 272–3
Parnell, Charles 30
Peachey Property 171, 173, 247
Penkovsky, Oleg 74
Pincher, Chapman 45, 64, 156, 255, 258, 317
Pollard, Eve 304
Polworth, Lord 308
Porter, Barry 128
Porter, Henry 269
Poulson, John 165, 166, 168, 171, 173, 175, 182, 185
Prescott, John 129
Press Council 136, 163
Price, Bill 108
Price, Joy 108
Prior, James 155, 158, 174
*Private Eye* 172, 236, 261–2, 281
Procter, Harvey 291–4, 318
Profumo, John 52, 75, 89; meets Keeler 75; and letter 79; and colleagues 80, 83, 86; resigns 85

Rachman, Peter 77
Radcliffe Tribunal 64, 71
Raphael, Adam 250, 289
Real Estate Fund of America 165, 170, 172
Rees, Peter 130
Reputation, public 14, 22, 46;

historical development 27; Victorian code 33, 35
Resignation Honours (1976) 242, 244
Rice-Davies, Mandy 77, 89
Ridley, Nicholas 131–2
Roberts, Albert 169–70, 175–6, 184
Roberts, Allan 134–5
Rossminster Group 130
Roth, Andrew 81, 181
Royal Commission on Standards of Conduct in Public Life 175, 184
Ryman, John 122–3

Scandal, 11, 18, 19, 72, 97–8, 268, 290, 306–7, 312–9
Schon, Lord Frank, 243
Scott, Norman 217, 223; personality 218; alleged relationship with Thorpe 218–9, 222; Thorpe trial 237–239
Security Commission 162–4, 319
Sedgemore, Brian 120, 121, 298
Selco Consultants 144, 312
Shaw, David 5, 7
Shenley Trust Services 129
Shore, Peter 120, 247
Short, Ted 174, 185
Smith, Cyril 217, 228, 239
Smith, F. E. 27, 38, 40
Smith, T. Dan 169, 173, 174, 183
Smith, Tim 311
Speed, Keith 310
Stanley, Sidney 43
Stanley, Venetia 34
*Star* 288
Steel, David 13, 185, 305, 314; and Thorpe 220, 225, 236
Steen, Anthony 310
Sternberg, Rudy (Lord Plurenden) 206, 243

Sternberg, Sir Sigmund 242, 244
Stevens, Marten 124
Stevenson, Francis 34
Stockwood, Mervyn 49, 96
Stonehouse, John 187, 200;
    background, 188; companies,
    189–194; and spying
    allegations, 194; disappears,
    195; dealings with Commons,
    195–6; trial, 196–9; DTI Report
    199
Sullivan, David 9
*Sunday Sport* 8, 10
*Sunday Times* 5, 8, 117, 121, 190,
    221, 224, 225, 226, 234, 236,
    244, 254, 268, 269, 305

Tatchell, Peter 103–4
Tebbit, Norman 266, 267, 284, 305
Thatcher, Dennis 108–111
Thatcher, Margaret 112, 116, 119,
    126, 138, 143, 261, 270, 283, 318
Thatcher, Mark 113–122
*The People* 292
Thomas, Daffydd 110
Thomas, George 204, 219, 227
Thomas, J. H. 43
Thomas, Roger, 133–4
Thorpe, Jeremy, Liberal Party
    Leader 215–7; business affairs
    217; Scott's allegations 218;
    dealings with party 220–1,
    227–9; dealings with press 226,
    231–3; trial 221, 236–239;
    resignation 227; party funding
    235
Tomlin, Frank 292–3
Trelford, Donald 5, 307

Vassall, John 65–71
Vickers, Paul 105–7

Wainwright, Richard 227
Walden, Brian 107–8
Walker, Peter 308–9
Ward, Stephen 73, 76, 79, 88
Weidenfeld, Lord George 242,
    243
Wellbeloved, James 142, 162
West, Rebecca 65, 70
Whitelaw, Willie 125
Wickstead, Bert 155, 156, 160
Wigg, George 77, 82, 84, 87, 92,
    203
Williams, Marcia 204, 206, 214,
    217, 248, 252; working for
    Wilson 203–4, 206–7; land
    deals story 208, 212–4;
    ennoblement 214
Wilson, Harold 44; and Profumo
    82, 85, 87; and Lord Lambton
    162; and Lobbying 181; and
    Stonehouse 194; political
    personality 201–4; office fund
    205–6; 243; land deals story
    210–4; and honours 214, 241–2,
    244; and Thorpe 217, 225, 228,
    230; and Miller 248, 250; and
    Kagan 252, 254; resignation
    255–9; and Archer 282
Winter, Gordon 222–3, 230
Wood, Diedre 313
Woods, Terry 291, 293
Woodhams, Wayne 4
World In Action 119, 146
Wright, Peter 63, 255, 258
Wyatt, Woodrow 303

Yeo, Tim 130